Welcome to Detroitland

Great Lakes Books

A complete listing of the books in this series can be found online at wsupress.wayne.edu.

Series Editor

Thomas Klug

Praise for Richard Bak

Welcome to Detroitland: Stories from the Motor City's Captivating Past

"Richard Bak has a gift for telling you things you didn't know about the familiar—Ernie Harwell had a famous brother!—and introducing you to people and places you wish you'd known about all along. Once you cross the border, you'll visit 'Detroitland' again and again."

—Neal Rubin, *Detroit Free Press* columnist

"This is a must-read, full of intriguing pieces of history that will astound Detroiters who think they know their city. Readers will walk away with a newfound appreciation for Detroit and the people who arrived in droves for a taste of a better life and economic opportunity. However, Bak doesn't shy away from tragedies and darker days that left a deep mark on the city. You'll learn about historic moments ranging from the 1967 rebellion to the Detroiters who survived the *Titanic*. Many of the stories detail how strife ultimately led to change for the greater good."

—Stephanie Steinberg, founder and CEO,
The Detroit Writing Room

"Bak takes the time to go a level deeper. Topics that are all too frequently summarized in one sentence are more fully explored, and each chapter—whether an unknown story about a household name, or a headline historical event seen from an unknown perspective—leaves the reader wanting more. A fantastic storyteller."

—Jeremy Dimick, Detroit Historical Society

Detroitland: A Collection of Movers, Shakers, Lost Souls, and History Makers from Detroit's Past

"No one writes Detroit like Richard Bak. For decades, he has probed the back alleys of Detroit history to uncover tales long forgotten. In *Detroitland*, he shares some of his best, taking us on a rollicking journey through time and bringing to life a most astounding parade of dreamers, heroes, and scoundrels."

—Tom Stanton, author of *Ty and the Babe* and *The Final Season*

"If Bak has ever written a dull story, I haven't read it. As you fly through these tales of the beautiful, the grotesque, scoundrels, heroes, old friends, and stone-cold killers, you'll 'hear' the engaging, made-in-Detroit voice of a master storyteller."

—Ric Bohy, veteran Detroit journalist
and owner of Words & Deeds

"Bak's [*Detroitland*] compiles several of his excellent stories into one neat package that's sure to please any die-hard Detroitophile. . . . [T]hese are stories you might have heard traced out for you—heck, even stories you thought you knew. But drawing upon historical records, clippings, and interviews, Bak pens richly evocative histories that bring to life people and events of Detroit during and leading up to 'the American century.' It's all done with the touch of a true storyteller, from the gripping first paragraph down to little kickers at the end that leave you both satisfied and wanting more. *Detroitland* is a wonderful achievement."

—*Detroit Metro Times*

"*Detroitland* is a stunning achievement. Bak's collection of our town's tall tales and true urban legends is the perfect tonic for anyone who has ever loved our city. Or at least their memory of it."

—Harvey Ovshinsky, award-winning producer and
story consultant and president of HKO Media

"*Detroitland* is meant for those who relish the colorful vignettes that abound in Detroit's past and who appreciate the value of popular history. . . . These stories may encourage more people to preserve tales, documents, and records about their local communities. As Neal Rubin says in the foreword, *Detroitland* is, like the city, 'a place of mayhem, magic, and mystery.' Here indeed is a history to cherish."

—*Michigan Historical Review*

WELCOME *to* DETROITLAND

Stories from the Motor City's
Captivating Past

RICHARD BAK

Wayne State University Press
Detroit

ISBN 9780814352564 (paperback)
ISBN 9780814352571 (ebook)

Library of Congress Control Number: 2026932742

On cover (*clockwise from top right*): Henry and Edsel Ford with the 1928 Model A; heavyweight champion Joe Louis; aerial daredevil Clem Sohn, the "Bat-Man"; Hank Ballard, originator of "The Twist"; second baseman Herman "Germany" Schaefer; and Hazel Beach and Violet Nash posing for a real-photo postcard. (Ford image courtesy of Collections of The Henry Ford. Hank Ballard promotional photo, Ace Records UK.) Cover design by Ashley Muehlbauer.

Wayne State University Press rests on Waawiyaataanong, also referred to as Detroit, the ancestral and contemporary homeland of the Three Fires Confederacy. These sovereign lands were granted by the Ojibwe, Odawa, Potawatomi, and Wyandot Nations, in 1807, through the Treaty of Detroit. Wayne State University Press affirms Indigenous sovereignty and honors all tribes with a connection to Detroit. With our Native neighbors, the press works to advance educational equity and promote a better future for the earth and all people.

Wayne State University Press
Leonard N. Simons Building
4809 Woodward Avenue
Detroit, Michigan 48201-1309

Visit us online at wsupress.wayne.edu.

To big brother Bob

Once upon a time there was what there was, and if nothing had happened there would be nothing to tell.

—Charles de Lint, *Dreams Underfoot*

CONTENTS

PREFACE

It's been observed that the past is an enormous place. With that in mind, consider this second compilation of Detroit-centric stories my latest effort at pruning the vast sweep of history into more manageable size by emphasizing the parochial. As with a previous assemblage of local history pieces put out by the good folks at Wayne State University Press—*Detroitland: A Collection of Movers, Shakers, Lost Souls, and History Makers from Detroit's Past* (Painted Turtle, 2011)—the stories in *Welcome to Detroitland* originally appeared in various regional periodicals, in this case *Hour Detroit*, the *Detroit Free Press, Detroit Monthly, Friends,* and *Michigan Historical Review*. All have been reworked to some degree for this collection, many of them quite significantly. I updated and corrected information, rewrote and rearranged passages, and added fresh material and illustrations. Now and then I blended a couple of features into a single story. As before, there is no chronological or thematic pattern to how they are presented. Each chapter is meant to stand on its own, a self-contained narrative to be appreciated for what it is—so-called popular history. Throughout my many years of exploring and writing about the past, I've never apologized for emphasizing the "story" in history. As chroniclers from Rudyard Kipling to David McCullough have pointed out, no harm is done to history by making it something a person would want to read.

Prophet Jones sits in splendor in this photograph from 1952. The canopied throne was modeled after that of Solomon, the wisest and richest king of Israel, though the gold-plated telephone in a niche was a modern touch. (Tony Spina/Walter P. Reuther Library)

1

The Messiah Wore Mink

Celebrity preacher Prophet Jones had God's ear, a loyal following, and a mansion in Detroit until a scandal caused heaven to come crashing down on him.

A catheter, intravenous drips, and a flickering television screen. For the Universal Dominion Ruler, this was no way to celebrate Philamathyu.

For years, Prophet Jones had presided over the eight days of festivities that commenced on his November 24 birthday. During Philamathyu, which by his decree had replaced Christmas on his sect's calendar, the self-styled messiah was presented with a ten-foot cake, mounds of cash, and a pile of expensive gifts, some of them bought on credit by devout followers who would struggle for years to make the payments. For Dominionites, such sacrifices were a small price to pay to be part of Prophet's fantastic religious kingdom.

"All is well," Jones would assure them.

"All is well," they would respond.

Proclaiming himself "God's sole representative on earth," with the power to mend the sick and foresee the future, Prophet Jones displayed an ostentatiousness that enthralled worshippers and drew the attention of the press. At the height of his fame in the 1950s, until a sex scandal brought heaven crashing down on him, Jones lived in a magnificently appointed mansion in one of Detroit's finest neighborhoods. He was attended to by a dozen uniformed servants, ate off gold plates, and was chauffeured around in a fleet of luxury automobiles. With hundreds of finely tailored suits to choose from, he favored wearing green because, as an aide once noted, "It's the color of money."

Jones was an early advocate of what has come to be known as the "prosperity gospel," which *Christianity Today* magazine has criticized as an "aberrant theology that teaches God rewards faith—and hefty tithing—with financial blessings." The Prophet's "blessings for sale" approach to redemption—"An open mind, a clean heart, and one dollar, please"—won over cash-strapped congregants and was an inspiration to future televangelists like Jimmy Swaggart, Jim and Tammy Baker, and Reverend Ike. The latter explained his own transparent money-grubbing by saying, "The best thing you can do for the poor is not to be one of them."

The Prophet's wardrobe included flowing silk robes (some of which took his full-time seamstress months to create), a velvet-lined white mink coat, a gold-handled cane, and a jewel-encrusted turban. His willowy, six-foot frame glistened with tens of thousands of dollars' worth of jewelry, including a topaz earring, diamond and ruby rings, diamond bracelets, and heavy gold chains. He wore his bling exclusively on his left side, he explained, because God always approached him from the right. Even his gold fillings were limited to the left side of his jaw.

Now, though, in the closing weeks of 1970, with the right side of his body crippled by a stroke, his valuables seized by relatives, and his ministry adrift, Prophet Jones spent his last Philamathyu on earth confined to a bed at Henry Ford Hospital. Unable to walk or speak, he passed most of his time watching television, including reruns of one of his favorite shows, *It Takes a Thief.*

* * *

James Francis Marion "Prophet" Jones was born into a poor Birmingham, Alabama family in 1907. An only child, he earned his nickname as a two-year-old when one day he said, "Poppa tum home buddy." His mother translated the words as "Papa come home bloody," which is exactly what Jones's father, a railroad brakeman, did, having gotten into a fight at work. Convinced of his mystical powers, the Prophet dropped out of school at eleven to evangelize full-time for a southern-based Pentecostal sect known as Triumph the Church and Kingdom of God in Christ.

After several years of moralizing in the South as an ordained Triumph missionary and rising through the church's ranks, "Prince" Jones was sent to Detroit in June 1938. He was accompanied by his mother and a dapper aide, James Walton, who the *Detroit Tribune* identified as "the young man who carried the money bag." Jones quickly grew a congregation. His followers were principally poorly educated southern Black people who had moved north to find factory work. They felt alienated in the big city, cut off from the comforting rhythms and sense of community that characterized the rural life they'd left behind. Women were a slight majority. About 10 percent of the congregation was White.

The first mention of Jones in the city appeared in the January 6, 1940, edition of the Black weekly *Detroit Tribune,* about eighteen months after his arrival. Under the heading "Rev. J. F. Jones Performs Great Works," Dorothy Folmar described the pastor's "impressive services."

> The crowd was tense and motionless as the Holy prophet, the Rev. Jas. F. Jones expounded the eternal truth and stood swaying by the rhythm of the voice of God. God Almighty's gospel is now being revealed through a clean and chosen vessel. His words sounding like peals of thunder, shaking the shackles of death from the minds of the people. He made a vivid description of his divine purpose, particularly outlining God's progressive steps against wickedness and showing the final overthrow of the devil and all of his wicked institutions. . . . Prophet Jones made a prophecy stating that our winter this year would be much better than the one last year, and we would have many days of sunshine. I am proud to state that the sun shone practically every day in November and December. He also prophesied for the death of a government official. Several hours later the shocking news of the death of [US Supreme Court]

Judge Pierce Butler was smeared across the headlines.
God's word has never failed and never shall.

Followers supplemented Jones's meager salary with cash and gifts, convinced of his ability to foretell the future or mend an ailment. Rugs, furniture, clothes, an automobile—Triumph Church's leaders considered all such offerings as the church's property, not that of any individual minister. Jones disagreed. He started his own sect, a decision prompted by a direct call from God, he said. At precisely 1 a.m. on September 28, 1944, the Almighty fanned a breeze in his right ear, telling him to stand under a streetlamp. There he was told that he was being granted special powers.

As the freshly minted Dominion Ruler of the Church of the Universal Triumph, the Dominion of God, which he incorporated in 1945, Jones issued a set of fifty decrees. Only by strictly following them, he instructed, could Dominionites—whom he called "citizens"—hope to stay alive until the Year 2000, when all beings would become immortal as heaven came to earth. Tobacco, alcohol, coffee, and tea were banned. Dominionites were prohibited from playing checkers, poker, and other games, and from socializing with non-Dominionites. In addition, nobody could have a baby out of wedlock or marry until the Prophet first approved it. The decrees also mandated girdle wearing, proper nail polish application, and weekly laxative use. "Everyone must be 100-percent with the Dominion Ruler," stated Decree No. 50. "All disobedience to God is a sin. . . . The wages of sin is death."

Saving Detroit's sinners was never going to be easy. Temptation lurked around every corner as the city, which struggled to absorb hundreds of thousands of newcomers during the 1940s, grew more wicked and impersonal by the day. Healers, prophets, and self-anointed saviors were in greater demand than ever. There was, for example, "Bishop" Wallace Robinson, a Mississippi native who came to Detroit when he was thirteen. Robinson established the Alpha & Omega Spiritualist Church and in January 1940 became the first Black minister to air Sunday services on Detroit radio. Robinson knew many of his followers played the illegal but wildly popular daily lottery known as "the numbers," and he never discouraged the notion that whatever biblical citation he stressed in either a sermon or a private consultation might pay off.

Once the Bishop cited Corinthians 7:11 during his sermon, which caused half the congregation to bet the numbers 711. The digits hit, and the payout almost broke several numbers operators. The following day, people lined up outside the Bishop's church on Holbrook Avenue. One was an undercover cop. "What's troubling you, son? No luck with the evil numbers?" asked the Bishop, who haggled a five-dollar fee before police arrested him for fortune-telling. Police impounded an accounting book listing other negotiated blessings and cures: "Want husband back—ten dollars down, thirty-seven owed" and "magic oil—five dollars." Robinson spent a day in jail, paid a small fine, and resumed dispensing blessings, some on easy credit terms.

Another prominent preacher was J. Frank Norris, an ornery Texan who between 1935 and 1949 commuted between his church in Fort Worth and Temple Baptist Church in Detroit. Norris, "a hellfire-and-brimstone evangelist of the old school," had a congregation composed principally of transplanted southern Whites. They listened to the fundamentalist pastor rail against labor unions, the New Deal, liquor, Catholics, Communists, and women who bobbed their hair. Worshippers tread lightly around Norris, who in Texas had once shot a man dead during an argument inside his church office.

Also operating during this period was Ethel Ruby Willetts. The young, semiliterate preacher and healer settled in Detroit in 1939 after conducting tent meetings for years around the Midwest. The self-described "Famous Bible Preacher" held "old-fashioned gospel meetings" at Everybody's Tabernacle on Conner near Mack. The racially integrated gatherings, which typically featured a large choir and a full orchestra, concentrated more on entertainment than religion. Robinson and Norris both died in 1952, by which time Willetts had moved her base of operations to Miami, where her flock accused her of absconding with "satchels of love offerings" for personal use.

It was in this environment of remunerative moralizing that Prophet Jones flourished. Among his most generous followers were two spinster sisters from Chicago, who bought him a $13,500 mink coat and a $10,000 Cadillac despite each living on a schoolteacher's salary. These gifts were in gratitude for the Prophet curing their widowed mother of "swelling ankles" and "blood hemorrhages." Jones admitted the sisters into the inner circle of family members and sycophantic aides, giving them such royal titles as "Prince," "Princess," "Lord," and "Lady." Jones reserved the title "Queen" for his mother, to whom he was devoted. When Queen Catherine Jones passed away in 1951, he estimated that during their entire lives they had spent exactly two months and twenty-eight days apart.

The Prophet and his coterie resided in "The Castle"—a magnificent French chateau-style mansion at 75 Arden Park in the Boston-Edison neighborhood. Congregants purchased the home, which once belonged to gambler Danny Sullivan and stood opposite the Kresge mansion, for $35,000 in 1944. Its fifty-four finely furnished rooms included a barber shop, ballroom, and perfume room. "The Prophet proudly showed us around the house, which he personally decorated, with his followers footing the bills," Herbert Brean reported that year in *Life*. "Its furnishings were an ingenious blend of modern decor and Louis XV. Prophet Jones was able to recite from memory the price of virtually every object in the room."

Living a couple of blocks away was Rev. C. L. Franklin, a leading Baptist pastor. Franklin considered the Prophet's ministry a cult (though his young daughter, the future "Queen of Soul" Aretha, secretly admired Jones's flamboyance). Another critic was Rev. Horace White, pastor of Plymouth Congregational Church and a state legislator. In an editorial published in the *Michigan Chronicle* shortly after the Prophet's ostentatious splash on the pages of *Life*, White deplored the city's "spiritual charlatans" and "religious racketeers" who were exploiting their insecure and unschooled followers.

> Our "Prophet" Jones knows how frightened and superstitious the Negro people are. He knows how deeply they feel about religion, and how uncritical the humble people, who

> are the majority, are about things done in the name of religion. He senses with an uncanny sense how truly easy it is to be representative of their fears and confusions by his rhetorical and physical antics.
>
> The "Prophet" asks them to deposit their hopes, desires and their ambitions in his keeping, and he will make all things right. . . . Many people are surprised at the adoration and homage intelligent people give to the fact that "Prophet" Jones has a radio costing so much, a rug from this store, two hundred suits of clothes, and so forth. This should not be surprising. . . . We have been a starved people. Things for us have represented equality. Things represent an effort at throwing off the bonds and chains of race discrimination and denial of opportunity. Therefore, when one has them, we like to say to the White world, "See here what one of our race has—we are just as smart as you." The poor will give of their earnings far beyond reason and prudence to help a "Prophet" give off a show of affluence. They will do this because there are certain vicarious experiences of grandeur the poor have as their "Prophet" lives in luxury.

The Dominion Ruler shrugged off such criticism. When not sermonizing to local Dominionites, he continued to hit the road to help charter thankful centers as far away as Colorado and California, with each satellite required to send a set percentage of offerings back to Detroit. Thanks to a compliant Dominion Council, whose members he could appoint and discharge at will, Jones had control over the sect's finances. In 1952, the council authorized the purchase of the 2,000-seat Oriole Theater at the corner of Linwood and Philadelphia. This was to replace his original thankful center, a nondescript frame dwelling at 1169 Hague on the lower east side. Jones had craftsmen build a giant, plushly upholstered canopied throne modeled after King Solomon's. It was crimson red, trimmed in canary yellow. He also installed a $35,000 organ and state-of-the-art sound system. In all, renovations cost $200,000.

The Prophet's original "Thankful Center" was a frame building on Detroit's near east side. In late 1952 services shifted to the former Oriole Theater at the corner of Linwood and Philadelphia. (Author's collection)

With Joe Louis's former publicist, Ulysses Boykin, working hard behind the scenes, the Prophet's activities—from prophecies and parties to patriotic pronouncements and shopping trips for groceries or jewelry—appeared regularly in the Negro press. Boosted by his weekly radio sermons on CKLW, the powerful 50,000-watt station in Windsor, the Prophet's profile grew beyond Detroit until he was one of the most recognizable Black celebrity preachers of midcentury America. He was invited to President Eisenhower's inauguration, gave the invocation at the opening session of the Michigan state legislature, and hosted jazz great Lionel Hampton at his mansion. Local politicians cozied up to him. He became one of the few prominent Black figures to appear in mainstream White publications. *Saturday Evening Post* dubbed him "The Messiah in Mink."

By 1955, Jones was boasting of 425 thankful centers in the US, the West Indies, and Africa, with a combined membership of 6 million. In reality, he lorded over a loose-knit consortium of about fifty self-governing churches, most with no more than a few hundred members. Thankful Center No. 1 in Detroit, with perhaps 2,500 adherents, was the largest. The only other sizable charters were in New York (where he kept a second residence), Chicago, and Philadelphia. That year, Jones began buying time on WXYZ, the local ABC affiliate, making him the first Black minister to host a television program in Detroit. WXYZ broadcast the hour-long show live from the Oriole Theater each Monday starting at 1 a.m., just as the Sunday midnight worship service was really getting started and there was nothing else on the air except test patterns.

Ron David, the stage manager for these holy-rolling spectacles, describes them as "wild and fun to watch." As the organ played, housewives and maids garbed in long flowing formals and workingmen sporting suits and tuxedos danced their way down the aisles. Jones himself was "quite a dancer," recalled one member, "and would go into a sort of tap-dance routine as the members would promenade up front during his services."

The Prophet's sermon would go on for hours, with parts of it delivered "in a chanting, rhythmic 'unknown tongue' peppered with phrases like 'cosmic illuminability' and 'the lubritorium of lubrimentality,'" said an attendee. "It has the same electrifying effect on his listeners as red-hot jazz." Sometimes during the service the Prophet would nod off for half an hour or so, and congregants would patiently wait for him to wake up.

Jones was never too tired to solicit donations. David recalls the Prophet's approach to squeezing every last dollar out of his followers.

> He'd say, "I really need your help to keep spreading the word of God. I want you to give $20 and I'll give each of you a blessing." A tarp would be spread out in front of his throne and some people would line up and drop their $20 on it. Then he'd tell them to go out in the lobby, have a drink of water, and wait and he'd come out and give them his blessing. He'd have his assistants close the doors between the lobby and the auditorium.
>
> Then Prophet would say, "I understand that not everybody can afford $20, but certainly you can afford $10." So some more people would come up and drop a $10 bill, then go out and join the others in the lobby. He'd repeat his pitch, this time for $5. By now the pile of green is growing and people are packed like sardines in the lobby. All that's left are the pikers. They're standing there, looking around at each other, and Prophet would say, "Now, I know the rest of you can at least afford $3. I'm asking for $3—one for the Father, one for the Son, and one for the Holy Ghost."

When the shakedown fell short, Jones had ushers lock the theater's exit doors until the faithful coughed up a satisfactory amount. Only then could the penned-in congregants, drained of energy and cash after a rousing five- or six-hour service, stumble out into the night. David laughs at the memory. "He'd do that every week and get away with it."

Even at the peak of his fame, the Prophet ranked a notch below a couple of older and more prominent national figures: Sweet Daddy Grace and Father Divine. Grace, a native of the Cape Verde Islands, was a bulky figure with a Portuguese accent, shoulder-length locks, and inch-long fingernails painted red, white, and blue. He headed the United House of Prayer for All People, which claimed 3 million followers in some 350 churches in 60 cities. Father Divine (whom FBI files identified as "George Baker alias God") oversaw International Peace Mission "heavens" in several states, principally New York and Pennsylvania. A short, dapper son of slaves, Divine advertised himself as Jesus Christ reborn. The Prophet's more famous contemporaries had larger followings and died multimillionaires. (Grace's estate was worth $26 million, more than a quarter-billion in today's dollars.) However, Jones's ministry was characterized by

Wearing his $12,000 mink coat and carried aloft by four uniformed guards Prophet Jones is about to make a grand entrance on his portable throne, circa 1953. (Author's collection)

the same kind of charismatic synergy, with leader and flock feeding off each other. And like them, the Prophet was always keenly mindful of his public image. When he went east to visit Father Divine to discuss a possible merger, his entourage included four valets, four bodyguards, three secretaries, his housekeeper, a hairdresser, three musicians, sixty singers, a personal cook, and a dietician.

Supporting such a lifestyle required various revenue streams, with grifting supplementing congregants' outright gifting. Jones bought miniature salt and pepper shakers for pennies apiece and sold the "blessed" versions for several dollars each. He offered pictures of Christ on the cross. "These are lucky pictures," he explained. "On the back of each one are some numbers. They have nothin' to do with any kind of gamblin', but people who have sent in a donation and got a picture say these numbers have been lucky for them." Now and then one of those combinations would hit in that day's lottery, earning some bettor a week's pay on a nickel bet and enhancing the Prophet's reputation for divining the future.

* * *

Despite the Prophet's regularly stated vow of celibacy, it was a poorly kept secret that the unmarried, self-described "savior of the dark boy" was a sexually active gay man. Indeed, his theatricality, over-the-top opulence, and overall swishiness were remindful of entertainer Liberace, the exemplar of 1950s "fruit-flavored" showmanship. One bedroom in Jones's mansion was set aside as a shrine to the late James Walton, the aide with whom he said he had enjoyed a "holy union" for many years. At a time when homosexuality was considered a crime and an indelible social stain, Jones's "perversions" troubled pastors, publishers, and other prominent Black figures. However, they never directly tackled the subject in print or from the pulpit, instead hinting at "sinister facts" not told to the public.

In 1953, one of the Prophet's live-in valets was convicted of accosting an undercover cop inside a downtown men's room. The judge put him on probation and ordered him to move out of Jones's castle. Two years later, a handsome young army veteran named

John Henry began visiting the Prophet, seeking "spiritual solace" for his ailing back. "He took three leaves from a rose," Henry would later testify, "and told me to put them under the sheets of my bed and they would cure my sore back." During one visit when they were alone inside the library, Jones suggested Henry disrobe, at which point he made an indecent proposal.

To Jones's eternal dismay, Henry turned out to be a member of the vice bureau. When police came to arrest the Prophet several weeks later, they found him clad in pajamas, on his bed with two teenage boys he had just met that morning. He was giving them singing lessons, he said. Later, as the humiliated preacher sat in a cell awaiting arraignment, his face buried in his hat, others in lock-up mocked him. "The Lord can't help you now!" they yelled. "All is not well!"

Jones was charged with gross indecency. He stood trial in July 1956, ailing and looking gaunt. He faced five years in prison and a $2,500 fine. After a week of testimony, during which the defense accused the police department of entrapment, the jury of seven men and five women retired to deliberate. Ninety-five minutes later, they returned with a verdict: not guilty. "All is well!" Dominionites shouted as they followed the teary-eyed defendant out of Recorder's Court and to a nearby flagpole, where they sang "The Star-Spangled Banner."

The Prophet was legally exonerated, but his image and purse took big hits. The stations had yanked his radio and television programs, which cost about $1,200 weekly to air. If followers wished them to resume, they needed to "get in some more green," he said.

But large amounts of green were not forthcoming. In the run-up to trial, Jones sold the Arden Park mansion and theater-cum-church to Sweet Daddy Grace for $50,000 cash. "Detroit needs help," Grace said from his palatial home in Washington, DC, where he oversaw the many properties he owned around the country. "The place is loaded with sinners. I must get there soon."

Upon his arrival, Sweet Daddy threw some shade at the Prophet ("Somebody around here has been making God look bad") before setting about changing things to his liking. Grace painted the gray stone mansion on Arden Park a gaudy red, white, and blue, and lit it up at night with giant floodlights. The changeover was more raucous in the Philadelphia-Linwood neighborhood, where sound trucks cruised the streets, blaring "Hurrah for Daddy Grace! Come to my church and worship!" A mass baptism involving fire hoses and bugle blasts snarled traffic for blocks around and prompted 137 exasperated neighbors to sign a formal complaint, stating Grace "has bombarded the residents night after night, day after day, with the beating of drums and tambourines, the clapping of hands and dancing outside the building." Sweet Daddy was stubbornly unrepentant about the commotion and ill will he was creating. "That idiot said if we didn't like it, we could buy the house for a million dollars," one resident grumbled.

While the Prophet's former neighbors dealt with the newest messiah in the neighborhood, Jones embarked on a national "soul-saving" tour. He was eager to escape pesky creditors—including one who entered his home firing a pistol—and looking to replenish his coffers. "The Scriptures tell me that if a prophet is in a city and he is not wanted, then he must wipe the dust off his feet and go to another place," he said.

The road proved just as unwelcoming. At one point Jones and his retinue were stranded in St. Louis, too broke to continue to California until followers wired them $200. In Maryland, authorities accused the Prophet of "bewitching" a janitor into turning over his keys. Someone used one of the keys, which were to be blessed in order to cure the man's hand rash, to break into a loan office. The man sentenced to prison in the break-in implicated Jones, who managed to avoid prosecution. Later, Jones stood trial in New Jersey, accused by a local medical society of "selling destinies" to a woman who, upon his advice, canceled a vital breast cancer operation. He was acquitted.

Jones spent his last dozen or so years commuting between thankful centers in Chicago, Philadelphia, and Detroit. It undoubtedly stung when Rev. Franklin, a longtime critic, bought the old Oriole Theater after Sweet Daddy Grace died in 1960 and converted it into the New Bethel Baptist Church. The remodeled

Sweet Daddy Grace bought the Prophet's mansion and church after Jones was charged with gross indecency for soliciting an undercover cop. (Author's collection)

church became the center of the local Civil Rights Movement and continues to serve the community today. While Franklin hosted Rev. Martin Luther King Jr. and other national figures, the Prophet ministered to his depleted flock in a second-story hall above an adult movie house on Woodward. During one service in 1970, he called for "fifty people to run up here and leave one dollar on the table so we can pay the light bills," then cryptically instructed donors to mail a postcard with the word "sleep" on it to an address in Pontiac "and everything will be all right."

Jones's most loyal supporters stuck with him up to the very end, unwavering in their belief in his powers and refusing to countenance slights, even from family members. John and Curtis Abbott were among five brothers who, during their teens, worked as valets and bodyguards for "His Holiness," as they called him. "His Holiness was the only father Curtis and I ever knew," said John, who remembered Curtis, a seventh-grade dropout, chafing under the Prophet's rigid rules. The boys needed Jones's permission to eat or bathe and had to sleep in the basement.

After four years of serving the Prophet and accompanying him on extended train trips, Curtis grew rebellious. One day in Chicago, the eighteen-year-old sat in the Prophet's portable throne—off-limits to everyone—and mimicked him delivering a sermon. When Jones heard about this blasphemy, he told the boy's mother that God had cursed Curtis and that he was going to have a short and wretched life.

Years passed. Then one winter day in Detroit, Curtis, by now a middle-aged drifter suffering from mental illness, was found frozen to death outside the abandoned car he'd called home. Jones's prophecy had come true. "You didn't mock His Holiness," said John Abbott. "That was just like mocking God."

* * *

In September 1970, Jones suffered a crippling stroke. His throne was covered in plastic. As he lay in a private hospital room, out-of-town relatives swooped in and took jewelry and other valuables out of his house for "safekeeping." Jones was recuperating at the home of top aide Claude Haley, his court-appointed guardian, when he suffered a fatal heart attack on the afternoon of August 12, 1971. He was sixty-three years old.

Morticians laid out the Prophet in a hot-pink embroidered robe. His white mink was draped over the casket. The press described a "free-for-all dance arena" as the choir belted out "Oh Mighty God" before 2,500 hand-clapping devotees, many of whom had traveled great distances to see the Prophet off. Jones was interred at Woodlawn Cemetery. Eighteen months after his death, bank officials opened three large lock boxes inside a Chicago bank. The boxes belonged to "Dr. Sterling," the Prophet's favorite alias. They were stuffed with cash.

The sect survived the passing of its charismatic founder. Today, local Dominionites assemble in an unassuming one-story building on Ferry Park. The affluence and controversy once associated with Prophet Jones are gone, but the refrain inside Thankful Center Universal Missionary Church remains unchanged. All is well, congregants rejoice, even when it isn't.

A view of Springwells in the 1870s. (Author's collection)

2

The Springwells Horror

The unsolved massacre of a Detroit-area farm family in 1885 remains part of a larger mystery. Why did members of the Knoch clan always seem to die under unusual and violent circumstances?

And much of Madness, and more of Sin,
And Horror the soul of the plot.

—Edgar Allan Poe, "The Conqueror Worm"

In the bleak and frigid predawn hours of December 16, 1885, several men on Fort Street noticed a reddish-amber glow pulsating in the distance. Alarmed, they hurried on foot and by carriage, past the entrance to Woodmere Cemetery and up a bordering dirt road, before finally arriving at the orderly nine-acre garden farm of Frank Knoch and his young family. The property fronted on the north bank of Baby Creek, which flowed along the heavily wooded back end of the adjacent graveyard. The entire area was part of Springwells, a township later incorporated into Detroit and Dearborn.

The men came upon a hellish scene. The Knochs's farmhouse was ablaze, turning the inky rural night into garish day. A stiff wind whipped the flames and spread the mingled odor of roasted turnips and burning flesh. Would-be rescuers futilely tossed snow and helplessly watched two figures framed by a window melt away like wax. Late-arriving neighbors formed a strung-out bucket line, hauling water from the creek a quarter-mile away, but it was too late. Gone were Frank Knoch, his wife Susan, and their sons, two-year-old George and baby Frank—all evidently done in by a faulty chimney or exploded oil lamp.

The following day, however, as the funeral cortege filed past the smoldering ruins on its way from St. Paul's Lutheran Church to Woodmere Cemetery, authorities discovered that the family had not perished by accident. Rather, they had been the victims of an incomprehensible atrocity. Over the next several weeks, the Knoch massacre dominated local news and conversation, with the *Detroit Free Press* calling it "the most pitiable and horrible tragedy that has been recorded against Wayne County in years." Even the *New York Times* covered its twisted storyline. Then, like most tragedies, it faded away.

Several generations later, the so-called Springwells Horror fails to ring a bell with most local historians and cemetery buffs. The oversight becomes more understandable when trying to locate the family plot one recent winter day. After some fruitless wandering in the snow, a couple of cemetery workers fetched a section map and interment card from the cemetery's office. The slaughtered family was buried without a stone, one of them explained. Using nearby tombstones as a guide, the workers determined the rough

Woodcuts of Frank and Susan Knoch, who along with their two infant children were murdered one night inside their Springwells farmhouse. (*Detroit Free Press*)

coordinates and vigorously boot scuffed the slate-like turf. It was on a raw day like this that a single coffin, containing what little was left of the four victims, was blessed by a priest and then lowered into the ground as mourners remained huddled inside their carriages.

Standing on the same frozen patch well over a century later induces dark visions. Underfoot is a row of four deteriorating wooden coffins. Besides the one containing the victims, three others hold the remains of Frank Knoch's parents and his oldest brother. All died separately under violent or suspicious circumstances. Their intertwining fates comprise one of the most baffling mysteries of old Detroit, a saga of familial madness that, like the grave that holds them, has been swallowed by time.

* * *

Wayne County physician Dr. F. W. Owen, who conducted the autopsies, quickly dismissed the possibility that Frank Knoch's family had perished as a result of an accidental fire. Probing the charred remains, he found two .22-caliber bullets that had been fired from the warped, rusted revolver dug out of the wreckage. The weapon, discovered near the sewing machine, had been fired twice. "Bullets In Their Brains," the *Free Press* announced, and with that the tragedy turned into a quadruple murder investigation.

Frank Knoch, twenty-six, and his twenty-three-year-old wife had been married three years. They were known to be hard-working and prudent, and their homestead reflected those virtues. The larders were full, the firewood was stacked, and everything "told of a hearty, healthy, happy pair, contented with their lot, good to themselves, their children and their cattle." But then, in a flash, it was all snatched away. An intruder fired a round from a .22-caliber revolver into Frank's left temple, shot Susan in the right temple, and then disposed of the children while turning the snug, comfortable home into an inferno. More horrifying details soon emerged. Investigators found a hatchet blade in the cooling coals, and a second postmortem examination revealed that the perpetrator had used it to chop the oldest boy's head into pieces. There was too little left of the baby to determine whether it had been similarly butchered. Veteran detectives speculated that the murderer-arsonist, in a hurry to flee the scene, had probably left the infant in his cradle to roast alive.

George Stellwagen, the Wayne County sheriff, quickly took charge of the case. A capable man preparing to celebrate Christmas with his wife and four children, the forty-six-year-old German immigrant and Civil War veteran was deeply affected by the massacre. He announced that he would "leave nothing undone in searching for the guilty parties."

Stellwagen's first call was to Frank's mother, Elizabeth Knoch, who lived on Dix Road and just a couple of miles from Frank's place. Mrs. Knoch shared the family farm with four grown children, including sons Gustave and Herman. Gustave, twenty-two, managed the property, assisted by Herman, a powerfully built "half-wit" who had spent some time in an asylum.

Mrs. Knoch, who dressed in black and spoke little English, had previously buried her husband and oldest son. Now she was being asked what she knew about the deaths of four more family members. As Stellwagen conversed with her in German, it developed that she didn't know much. Neither did Gustave and Herman, who spoke reluctantly. A thorough search of the property turned up no incriminating items, though Gustave admitted that a pair of .22-caliber revolvers and box of cartridges—not of the type used in the murders—were his. He had a third pistol, though he didn't know where it was. "There is something very strange about this family," Stellwagen said as he left the premises.

At the same time, the sheriff was anxious to speak to a Polish immigrant known only as "Aleck." The itinerant farmhand had become angry after Frank let him go a week earlier. Aleck, who boarded with the Knochs, presumably knew that Frank kept his money inside a drawer of Susan's sewing machine. Aleck was last seen driving a manure wagon from Springwells to Detroit, after which he disappeared.

A coroner's inquest was convened two days after the murders, with the large number of spectators causing the daily sessions to be moved from Judge Kurth's courthouse to a large hall above a Fort Street saloon. Seventy-five witnesses were subpoenaed over the course of a month, including members of the Knoch family. Frank Knoch's prosperity was no secret, as he often talked about how much his seeds, plants, and vegetables brought at market.

Money was the focus of a recent argument Frank had with Gustave. Frank had made roughly $1,500 in 1885 and had about $800 in savings—impressive numbers at a time when most Americans earned only a few hundred dollars a year. Two years earlier, he had taken out a $2,889 loan from his mother, and an annual installment payment was soon due. However, he intended to pay less than what was expected. The disagreement didn't help the poor relations Frank already had with his family, who considered Susan and her relatives a pretentious bunch. Gustave once fired his revolver over Susan and her brother's heads as they were crossing a field—just for fun, he later explained.

On the day before the murders, Frank went to the bank, then stopped for a beer at a nearby saloon. He planned to pay his taxes and had as much as $400 on his person. Someone may have followed Frank home, Stellwagen reasoned, then waited until nightfall to enter the house. Or perhaps it was a random break-in. Tramps were a menace in the countryside, accounting for numerous thefts and the occasional rape or murder. Frank, not known to own a gun, had on at least one occasion mentioned getting one to deal with them.

The revolver pulled from the rubble was too damaged to trace to its owner. If it was Frank's, it would lend credence to an alternative theory offered by Dr. Felix Fettig, the Knochs's family physician. He firmly believed the massacre was the result of the couple's ongoing differences over religion, an issue other witnesses mentioned. Frank was a Lutheran but Susan insisted on raising the boys as Catholics. Fettig theorized that, following an argument, Frank had impulsively killed his family, set the house on fire, and then shot himself. Many dismissed the murder-suicide scenario as an unlikely act of madness—but, as the *Free Press* noted, "it is quite well-established that insanity is hereditary in the family."

Frank's grandfather, Fred Knoch, a German immigrant who worked as a butcher, was insane. Two of Fred's children (Frank's aunt and uncle) also were institutionalized. In fact, in the immediate aftermath of the murders, it was feared that the uncle had escaped and committed the deed. Frank's father, Christian, was the third of Fred's offspring to suffer from dementia, though his condition apparently was milder. At the time, there was no sophisticated treatment of the mentally ill. People suffering from conditions now recognized as schizophrenia, manic depression, and other psychiatric and behavioral disorders were lumped together in the broad category of "lunatics." Most were tolerated, ignored, or ridiculed until they became too troublesome to society, at which point they were shipped off to the hell of an asylum.

* * *

Christian and Elizabeth Knoch raised eight children on their Springwells farm. Charles was the oldest of their four sons, followed by Frank, Gustave, and Herman. One day in August 1879, Christian was working in the barn when, according to Elizabeth, he was kicked in the head by a horse—twice.

Despite the two pulverizing blows, the fifty-four-year-old farmer was able to crawl into the house and tell Elizabeth what had happened. He died the following day without uttering another word. There was blood on the barn floor, but the story didn't sound right to everyone. "My father's injuries were on the top of his head," Herman said. "I should think one would have to get down to be kicked in that place."

Christian's death was ruled an accident, and he was buried at Woodmere. Charles, now in charge of the farm, paid thirty-six dollars for the twelve-by-twelve-foot family plot in Section D, situated halfway between the cemetery's main entrance and Baby Creek. (The creek was dredged in 1967 and is now Riverside Drive.)

On the morning of November 11, 1882, Charles vanished. Neighbors would later remark that the family seemed largely unconcerned by his absence.

The following spring, Charles's body was found in the Detroit River. Someone had shot him in the right temple and weighed down his body. A coroner's inquest determined that the pump chain wrapped around his neck and the copper wire attached to his coat came from the Knoch farm. Gustave testified that he had gone to the markets in Detroit on the day his brother disappeared, returning home at midnight to find the rest of the family in bed. The next day, he produced $100 that he said Charles had left behind in a tin box in the greenhouse.

Years later, Gustave would say that he always believed Charles had killed their father in an argument and that their mother had covered up the crime. According to Gustave, Charles lived with his guilt for three years until one day, he wrapped himself with a chain and weight, stood on the edge of a dock, and shot himself before toppling into the river.

This seemed a rather elaborate suicide. A more plausible scenario had the twenty-four-year-old bachelor, his pocket stuffed with money, being waylaid en route to enjoying a Saturday in Detroit. A farmhand said that the day before Charles went missing, he had noticed two strangers sitting on a nearby fence, speaking in a language he couldn't understand. He called Charles's attention to the men, but by the time he and Charles went to investigate, the strangers were gone. Authorities ultimately judged the death a homicide, though nobody was ever arrested.

The deaths of Christian and Charles were revisited as the inquest into the Springwells massacre continued through the 1885 holiday season. The demeanor of the Knochs on and off the witness stand aroused suspicion. They seemed cold, indifferent, though some in Springwells said that was their natural mien. Herman Knoch admitted that when he heard frantic shouts that Frank's house was ablaze, he went back to bed. One witness described how Gustave had visited the site of the tragedy the following day and flippantly remarked, "Well, they're gone." Mrs. Knoch, who testified that her sons were home the night of the fire, laughed at inappropriate times, drawing a rebuke from the prosecutor.

However, the ordeal exacted a toll from the family matriarch. When saloonkeeper and family friend Eli Unruh visited Elizabeth the day after Christmas, he observed that she was visibly distraught. "I have nothing to say now, when I try to say a word they tell me to shut my mouth," she said, referring to her children.

She took to her bed, complaining of stomach and head pains. On the afternoon of December 31, Stellwagen heard rumors that the ailing woman wanted to make a statement, possibly a confession. The sheriff and prosecuting attorney went to her home the next day, only to be told that they were too late. Elizabeth Knoch had slipped into a coma on New Year's Eve and died in the wee hours of 1886.

Authorities suspected the sixty-one-year-old woman was poisoned. As was the custom then, the family laid out the deceased in her coffin at home. On the evening of January 2, the county physician conducted an autopsy by lamplight in the living room. When Dr. Owen pulled back the scalp, he was surprised to discover a skull fracture that extended from one temple to the other. There was no bruising or other external signs of trauma, which might indicate a recent accidental fall. He theorized that Mrs. Knoch had been struck in the side of the head with a heavy bag of sand, a blow designed to kill while leaving no visible mark.

"The Mother Murdered!" one newspaper declared. "The Seventh Tragic Death in the Knoch Family." Authorities put the inquest into the Springwells massacre on hold to deal with this jolting turn. Prosecutors ordered a new autopsy, this time with three other doctors joining Owen, including Mrs. Knoch's physician. Meanwhile, Herman and Gustave were arrested and locked up inside separate five-by-seven-foot cells at the county jail on Clinton Street.

Feelings were running high. D. J. Campau, a well-fixed landowner who had conducted business with the Knochs for years, came to the family's defense, paying for all legal and medical representation. "I have known these boys for a long time as honest, industrious and frugal," he explained. "In the excited condition of the public mind they were liable to be unfairly dealt with and having the utmost confidence in them I propose to stand by them to the last."

Doctors performed the second autopsy on January 4 at Woodmere and produced an entirely different verdict. The new team of examiners decided that Mrs. Knoch had not been poisoned or murdered, but had most likely died of inflammation of the brain brought on by pneumonia. Owen stood by his belief of foul play, bristling when it was suggested that he had inadvertently created a post-mortem fracture while chiseling off the skullcap during the original autopsy. Afterward, the deceased was interred without her head, which was kept at a doctor's office in case further examination was required.

Having been whipped into a state of near-hysteria by rampant rumor peddling and dueling press reports, not everyone readily accepted the revised finding. Stellwagen, worried about a possible lynching, kept the Knoch brothers locked up until the day after the funeral. Upon their release, Campau expressed his fear that Herman, sporting a strange, fixed smile and a piercing look in his eyes, had been "affected by the excitement" and "might sustain another attack." Gustave said he would watch after him.

Dr. Owen's theory that Mrs. Knoch had not died a natural death found support with the boys' uncle, John Knoch, who was Christian's brother. Most evenings John frequented saloons, freely voicing his opinions. Gustave and Herman had killed Frank, their mother, the whole family, he said. Gustave warned him to watch his tongue, or he'd report him to authorities.

A short while later, John nearly met his own untimely end when he steered his wagon straight into the path of an oncoming train. The wagon exploded into splinters and John was hurled like a rag doll into the night. He survived, but the incident underscored how a strange or violent death always seemed to be just around the corner for members of the Knoch clan.

* * *

On January 21, 1886, the coroner's jury investigating the deadly inferno at the Knoch farm a month earlier released its verdict. Frank Knoch and his family had been murdered "by persons unknown."

Those persons remained unknown as rumors continued to fly. In early February a laborer discovered a bloodstained vest and trousers near the destroyed farm, prompting newspapers and gossipers to rush a new round of speculation into circulation. Investigators found no link between the clothing and the murders. Meanwhile, law enforcement agencies far and wide continued to keep a lookout for the Knochs's missing hired hand. Since the murders a dozen different "Alecks" had been detained and released.

On March 7, a Detroiter named Govinski approached Sheriff Stellwagen and told him he knew of the real Aleck's whereabouts. The suspect had drifted through several jobs since leaving the Knochs and was now working at a foundry in Hamtramck. Aleck was arrested at a boardinghouse on St. Antoine and interrogated. Described as "a big lump of humanity," the man struggled to comprehend the brutality conveyed to him through a translator. "All dead?" he asked in disbelief. Stellwagen ended the interview. "He is an ignorant Polander," the *New York Times* concluded, "and evidently knew nothing of the murder."

With nobody in custody, the public was jumpy. When an elderly couple in Ohio perished in a suspicious house fire in April, there were unfounded fears that the fiend had journeyed south to strike again. A few weeks later, the body of twenty-three-year-old Frank Henry was found "cut to pieces" on the Wabash railroad tracks near the Fort Street crossing. Although it was determined that Henry had been hit and torn apart by a train, the jitters remained.

Stellwagen was obsessed with the case, spending long hours and a chunk of his own money to solve it. Recognizing the limitations of his understaffed department and his own ordinary investigative skills, he personally retained the services of a private detective. Citizens were not optimistic, despite the posting of a $1000 reward. The general opinion in Springwells, observed one Detroit daily, "is that the present generation will not see the mystery solved and that further investigation will be fruitless."

In July 1886, Stellwagen received word that two crooks serving time at the state prison in Jackson had incriminating information about a man named William Horrigan. Con Kane, recently sentenced to ten years for safe blowing, and Charles "Kid" Smith, a "gentleman thief" who had just gotten six years for stealing a batch of suspenders, were willing to testify that, in September 1885, they had been approached by Horrigan to "do up" a local farmer who was known to keep a lot of cash at home. It would be an easy

George Stellwagen, the sheriff of Wayne County, was obsessed with finding the perpetrator of the massacre. (Wayne Historical Society)

job, Horrigan allegedly told them, but they declined. Now, seven months after the quadruple murder, they decided to come forward with what they knew.

Although Stellwagen hinted at circumstantial evidence tying Horrigan to the crime—evidence that prosecutors apparently never produced—any case brought to trial clearly would hinge on the credible testimony of Kane and Smith. The sheriff had misgivings about their story. There were always convicts willing to perjure themselves for ulterior motives.

Nonetheless, authorities located Horrigan, arrested him, and took him to the county jail to await a pretrial examination. Two weeks later, Kane and Smith were delivered in handcuffs. Early on August 7, just prior to the start of the hearing, Stellwagen brought the pair into his office separately to identify the suspect. Kane was first. "All right then," Stellwagen said, "is Horrigan the man or not?"

Kane eyed the suspect, then asked to hear him speak.

"He looks just like the man," Kane said, "but he is an inch shorter than the one who spoke to us."

Smith was ushered in next. He barely looked at Horrigan before saying he did not recognize him. Stellwagen was frustrated but not surprised. Upon his recommendation, the prosecutor immediately asked the court to release Horrigan—a decision that disappointed the large number of people who had made the six-mile trip from Springwells on a Saturday morning to catch a glimpse of the Knochs's purported executioner.

Stellwagen's suspicions about the accusers soon proved correct. Two days later, a prison turnkey was returning Kane and Smith to Jackson when they made a break for it at the Michigan Central Depot, with Kane brandishing a revolver that an outside accomplice had slipped to him. Their carefully planned escape was thwarted by the actions of a quick-thinking porter, who "knocked the pistol out of Kane's hand and caught him by the throat, choking him until his tongue protruded from his mouth," the *Free Press* reported.

Few doubted that Horrigan was capable of breaking into an isolated farmhouse at night, especially after he was sentenced in October to five years in prison for the after-hours burglary of a Detroit shoe store. But could a practiced thief, whose self-composure during weeks in custody had been favorably noted by the press, mutate into the kind of monster capable of the atrocities committed upon the Knochs?

"You never hear of a professional thief or burglar committing murder unless he is 'pinched,' and then they only kill enough to save themselves," ex-detective James McGuire told the press. McGuire's theory was that Frank or Susan Knoch had detected an amateurish "bungler," at which point the startled intruder "committed murder, and to cover up the first murder he killed three more people."

The Horrigan fiasco was the last significant event of the Knoch family murder investigation, though Stellwagen doggedly kept at it. "I may not meet with success," he said, "but when I retire from office I will have the consciousness of knowing that I did what the people expected of me."

Despite the sheriff's best efforts, the case was at a standstill when his term expired in 1887.

The widespread fear engendered by the murders gradually dissipated. In August 1892, seven years after the massacre, authorities arrested Herman Knoch for assaulting a Springwells resident named William Roeser. Under the headline, "A Raving Maniac," the *Free Press* described the "desperate resistance" Knoch put up before deputies finally overpowered him inside a barn and took him to jail: "While being registered he became very violent, and it required the combined efforts of five deputies to place him in a cell. When Deputy Sheriff Hayes brought him some bread Knoch hurled the dishes against the sides of the cell."

The probate court sentenced Herman to the state asylum in Pontiac. He spent the rest of his life there, dying in 1911 from what the coroner described as "exhaustion from insanity."

Meanwhile, Gustave Knoch married a sixteen-year-old Detroit girl named Minnie, and together they raised eight children to adulthood. For many years Gustave operated a successful flower shop on Fort Street, near the cemetery's entrance. One winter day in 1917, the fifty-three-year-old florist went into the boiler room behind the greenhouse and hanged himself. Like Herman, Gustave was buried in a separate plot at Woodmere, taking with him whatever secrets he may have held about the family deaths that had preceded his.

Stellwagen moved on to other endeavors after leaving office. He helped organize a bank, became the president of a carriage factory, and made a good deal of money. Upon his death on August 13, 1904, mourners eulogized him as "successful in all his work" and one of Wayne's leading citizens.

A general view of the unmarked Knoch family plot at Woodmere. (Ted Fines)

But open questions pestered the erstwhile sheriff to the end. Who was responsible for the Springwells massacre—a tramp, a thief, a lunatic, or even Frank Knoch himself? Were Gustave and Herman, either individually or jointly, complicit in the murders, or in any of the other family deaths? Could the deaths of the parents, Christian and Elizabeth, really have been homicides? Could the murders of the brothers, Charles and Frank, actually have been suicides? Or was the string of tangled tragedies the work of outside forces, a cruel cosmic joke played on an unhinged and unfathomably luckless family? The multitude of theories kept tongues wagging in Springwells for years.

There was a grim postscript to Stellwagen's passing, as if the dementia associated with the Knochs had somehow infected his own bloodline. On Thanksgiving morning in 1905, his nephew and namesake walked into a parlor and, in front of family members, ran a razor across his throat. There was no satisfactory explanation for young George Stellwagen's suicide. Perhaps none could be expected. As a forsaken plot in Woodmere suggests, what is life but madness?

3

Going Out a Winner

As the foil to television attorney Perry Mason, Detroit actor William Talman compiled "the longest losing streak in history." But at life's end he redeemed himself with a remarkable anti-smoking commercial.

The commercial that first aired in the fall of 1968 featured a face familiar to millions of television viewers. As fictional prosecutor Hamilton Burger, Detroit-born actor William Talman had lost case after case to defense attorney Raymond Burr during nine seasons of *Perry Mason*. Now Talman reached out from beyond the grave to issue a startling firsthand warning about the lethal effects of smoking.

Donald Hillman produced the landmark commercial, the first anti-smoking spot to feature a celebrity—and a dead one at that. The American Cancer Society "decided to do this film," he explained at the time, "because it presented a unique opportunity for the society to dramatically and realistically portray to the American television audience the beliefs and feelings of a man soon to be a victim of his own smoking habits." Besides, Hillman continued, William Talman was "all the more effective because he had previously been established as a loser."

Loser? Jim Caldwell considers Talman a savior. Stuck at home that fall because of a lingering illness, the ten-year-old schoolboy was jolted by the black-and-white images he saw flickering across the screen of the family's RCA television.

"Hamilton Burger looked terrible," remembers Caldwell, today a teacher in New York. "Sickly. Horrible. At death's door. That sat me right up, let me tell you. He looked like he had one foot in the grave. I can still see his face. But it was his pleading that deeply, deeply impressed me." Aside from "a cigarette or two in college," Caldwell kept away from tobacco, "thanks in no small way to Hamilton Burger."

Whether cast as serial loser Hamilton Burger, as the ruthless killer Emmett Myers in the film noir classic *The Hitch-Hiker* (1953), or as a phantasmal spokesman for the American Cancer Society, William Talman had a penchant for memorable performances. "We're just that way," says Tim Talman, one of the late actor's seven children and himself a veteran of various stage, film, and television productions. "We don't do anything unless there's an effect. What my dad was telling the world was, 'When you see this, I'll be gone.' It doesn't get any more dramatic than that."

* * *

William Whitney Talman Jr. was a third-generation Detroiter whose ancestral line included a member of George Washington's staff during the American Revolution. Talman's father and namesake was born in 1878 in the family home at Congress and St. Antoine, then attended the University of Michigan before embarking on a career in industrial electronics. On February 4, 1915, the second anniversary of William Sr.'s marriage to a New Jersey girl named Ada, William Jr. came into the world. He had blue eyes and curly blonde hair.

The future actor and his two younger brothers, Jim and Tom, grew up in a privileged household that during the Depression numbered more servants than children. The imposing century-old house, erected on a half-acre lot on Seminole Street in Indian Village, still stands. Every day, Talman rolled up to school in a chauffeured limousine. "Public school," he later said. "That meant I had to fight my way in and out." In self-defense, he joined the boxing program sponsored by the local Episcopalian church. He developed a lifelong passion for baseball, golf, sailing—and cigarettes.

Talman was exposed to theater at an early age. His father was involved with the all-male Players Club of Detroit, which by 1925 was staging its one-act "frolics" from a newly built clubhouse on East Jefferson. Talman and his brothers attended the Cranbrook academy in Bloomfield Hills. All performed in the drama club. Although Tom would go on to teach at Rutgers and Jim would become an aeronautical engineer, "Bill had the most brilliant mind in the family," insists Jim Talman, who today lives in Pennsylvania. "He could read a page once, turn it over, and recite every word by heart."

Talman entered Dartmouth College in 1932. Tragedy struck during his sophomore year. Talman, who had borrowed another student's car to take a girl from Smith College out on a double date, was forced off the road by a bus. The car crashed into a tree. Talman and two girls survived the accident, but a young man was killed. To make matters worse, it turned out that the loaned auto was actually stolen. "He was encouraged to resign," Jim Talman says. "Dartmouth invited him back a year later, but he didn't go. He played some roles at the Players Club before leaving for New York."

The young actor was just starting his Broadway career when World War II broke out. He was performing in the comedy *Spring Again* at Henry Miller's Theatre when he was drafted into the army. He went into the Signal Corps as a private and came out three years later a major, having spent his time in the Pacific arranging shows and training service teams that won championships in baseball and boxing. After his discharge he returned to Broadway, landing roles in the postwar productions of *Dear Ruth* and *A Young Man's Fancy*. He moved to Hollywood in 1949, looking to break into films.

He first appeared on the big screen as gangster Bunny Harris in *Red, Hot and Blue*, a 1949 musical comedy starring Betty Hutton and Victor Mature. He went on to perform in nearly twenty features, including such stylish crime dramas as *I Married a Communist* (1949), *Armored Car Robbery* (1950), *The Racket* (1951), *Big House, USA.* (1955), and *Two-Gun Lady* (1956). His cynical and hard-boiled characters rarely made it to the end of the movie alive. His

This 1950s studio handout shows actor Bill Talman with an ever-present cigarette in hand—an addiction he came to regret and publicly campaigned against in an unusual postmortem commercial. (Author's collection)

most memorable role was in the 1953 film *The Hitch-Hiker.* Cast as the murderous kidnapper Emmett Myers, Talman "makes the most of one of the year's juiciest assignments," wrote a reviewer in the *New York Times.* "He is a braggart who taunts his captives, mocks their softness and proclaims that 'you can get anything at the end of the gun.'"

Talman's performance inspired an unusually affective response from one moviegoer. Shortly after the film came out, Talman was stopped at a traffic light in Los Angeles when he noticed the driver of the car idling alongside his glaring at him. "You're the hitchhiker, right?" the stranger asked. When Talman acknowledged that he was, the man got out of his car, walked over to Talman's convertible, and slapped him hard across the face. The stunned actor watched his assailant calmly return to his car and drive off. "You know," Talman said later, "I never won an Academy Award, but I guess that was about as close as I ever will come to one."

* * *

In 1956, CBS announced it was creating a television show based on fictional Los Angeles defense attorney Perry Mason, a character found in the crime novels of Erle Stanley Gardner. Talman originally auditioned for the role of Mason, but lost out to a heavyset veteran character actor named Raymond Burr. Producers then offered him the part of district attorney Hamilton Burger. "Bill Talman is really a wonder," Gardner later said. "He actually looks like he expects to win a case."

Perry Mason debuted on the evening of September 21, 1957. It was the first of 271 hour-long episodes, all but one filmed in black and white. A pattern quickly emerged. "Burger would always present a seemingly airtight case against Mason's hapless client," observed an Associated Press writer. "But Burger never won a case because the script was loaded against him. . . . More often than not, one of Burger's star witnesses went to pieces and confessed on the stand that it was he, and not Mason's client, who really committed the murder."

Perry Mason was a success from the start, turning cast members into pop-culture figures that remain vivid today thanks to perpetual reruns and the internet. In 2009, the US Post Office issued a commemorative first-class stamp featuring Burr and Talman. By the early 1960s, Burr had won two Emmy Awards and was commanding an annual salary of $1 million. Talman earned $65,000, just a fraction of the show's star but still a healthy figure for the time.

Talman was an affable man with a wry sense of humor and a live-and-let-live attitude that instantly put strangers at ease. But trouble seemed to follow him around as much off screen as on. Heavy drinking contributed to domestic discord. He had married actress Lynne Carter prior to going into the army. They divorced in 1952, with his ex-wife claiming extreme cruelty. The court awarded her custody of their daughter, Lynda, and 24 percent of his income. The following year Talman married actress Barbara Read, with whom he had two children, Barbie and Billy. This marriage also unraveled, the result of Talman's chronic overindulgence.

On March 12, 1960, *Perry Mason* fans watched Hamilton Burger lose yet again in an episode called "The Case of the Singing Skirt." The following day, Talman was one of eight people arrested during a sensational raid in Hollywood. Police claimed to have found four men and four women smoking marijuana inside a private home. All were naked. Talman maintained he had just dropped by a friend's house for a drink. While tabloids had a field day describing Perry Mason's foil "gamboling without clothes," the network quickly fired Talman for violating the morals clause in his contract. In June, a judge dismissed the charges of lewd and indecent conduct, saying, "I don't approve of their conduct, but there has been no violation of the law established." The network refused to hire Talman back.

As the blacklisted actor scrounged around for work in Hollywood, the members of *Perry Mason*'s remarkably close-knit cast worked hard to have CBS reinstate him. A small but potent symbol of protest was their refusal to remove Talman's coffee cup from the crew's famous rack of personalized mugs. In December, due largely to a letter-writing campaign orchestrated by Burr, CBS brought Talman back to the show.

By then Talman and his second wife had divorced. In 1963, Barbara Read closed up her California home and turned on the gas stove. She left a suicide note blaming her poor health. That year, Talman married Peggy Flanigan, a fun-loving divorcee he had met at a friend's poker party. Talman adopted her two children from a previous marriage. The couple went on to have two children of their own, Susan and Tim.

Meanwhile, Perry Mason continued to outwit Hamilton Burger. Fans of the legal drama begged for the hapless prosecutor to win just one case, with a professional gambler once approaching Talman about the possibility of springing a surprise courtroom victory. "He wanted me to say the wrong thing, cross 'em up and win the case," Talman said. "He was going to cut me in. Said he could get 30-to-1 on it." When Talman made his first and only appearance on the cover of *TV Guide* in 1963, the weekly programming magazine carried the headline: "Biography of a Loser—Bill Talman." As the defeats stacked up, week after week, season after season, Talman wryly touted the distinction of having "the longest losing streak in history."

Perry Mason concluded its nine-year run of original episodes on May 22, 1966, with Hamilton Burger outdoing himself by losing two cases in the final show. "Once again good old Hamilton Burger picks the wrong man to prosecute in both cases," Talman told the press. "Mason gets one of them off on a trick and I get sore about it.

Courtroom rivals Perry Mason (Raymond Burr) and Hamilton Burger (Bill Talman) in a still from a 1964 episode of *Perry Mason*. The popular television drama aired for nine seasons on CBS, with prosecutor Burger never winning a single case in 271 episodes. (CBS)

I wouldn't want to hit Ray Burr, but I think Hamilton Burger would like to hit Perry Mason."

As reruns of the show immediately went into syndication, Talman cashed residual checks and tried to keep busy. He spent six weeks in Vietnam entertaining the troops and worked with Doris Day in *The Ballad of Josie* (1967), a comedy western. His role wasn't much of a stretch: he played a district attorney who fails to convict a young woman of murder. It turned out to be his last film.

In September 1967, Talman visited his doctor to treat a cough he couldn't seem to shake. X-rays showed a mass in his left lung. He underwent surgery, and the biopsy result was chilling. His cancer had spread and was inoperable. He underwent radiotherapy treatments, but the cancer soon moved into his other lung and his brain. By the following summer he was taking increasingly larger doses of morphine to fight the pain, which left him dazed and weakened. Then, one Friday afternoon in July 1968, Talman called the American Cancer Society in New York. "He spoke to me very directly," recalls Irving Rimer, then head of public relations for the organization. "He said, 'I want to do a TV spot. I'm not going to be around very long so you better get a crew out here right away.' "

The dying actor had unwittingly prepared for what would become the role of a lifetime by smoking up to three packs of unfiltered Camels a day for more than forty years—somewhere between 750,000 and 1 million cigarettes in all. When he was a youngster, his father had offered him $1,000 and a gold watch if he could reach the age of twenty-one without smoking. As Talman ruefully noted, "I lost that case before I was twelve."

Talman was hardly alone in his nicotine addiction. "Smoking was the thing to do," says Rimer, now retired and living in North Carolina. "In the army you got free packages of cigarettes, and that's where many picked up the habit. In Hollywood movies, a cigarette was the perfect prop. Everywhere you looked—magazines, billboards, TV—you had famous athletes and entertainers and even doctors encouraging people to smoke."

Celebrity pitchmen included John Wayne, Gary Cooper, and Steve McQueen, all of whom subsequently died of cancer. Actors often stayed in character, making their endorsements more persuasive. For example, in one of the spots for Winstons that ran each week during *The Beverly Hillbillies,* Granny Moses (actress Irene Ryan) put a cigarette from Jed Clampett into the bowl of her corncob pipe, took a puff, and exclaimed, "My thunder, Jed! That *is* good smoking!" Even popular cartoon characters Fred and Wilma Flintstone fired up cigarettes in primetime commercials.

In June 1967, the Federal Communications Commission ruled that all stations airing cigarette commercials also had to broadcast anti-smoking ads as part of the agency's "fairness doctrine," a policy designed to assure a variety of viewpoints.

"Anti-smoking ads were just starting to hit the airwaves," Tim Talman recalls. "My father had read somewhere that actors were unwilling to make them because they were getting paid pretty well to endorse cigarettes. He said, 'Okay, that's it.' "

The filming took place at Talman's home in Encino, California. Burr was on hand to lend support. It was an ordeal, with Talman undergoing cobalt treatments at the hospital the morning of the shoot. "Dad barely fit into his suit, he'd lost so much weight, and he was slurring his words," Tim Talman says. "Mom was shooting morphine into him every twenty minutes just so he could make it through the spot."

Filmmakers created a three-minute film from the day's shooting for limited circulation, showing it to American Cancer Society volunteers for fundraising purposes. A sixty-second public service announcement was carved out of the footage. That was the message most of the country would see.

The commercial began with Talman's smiling children being introduced one by one as they frolicked outdoors, followed by a shot of his wife Peggy, "who looks after all of us," Talman said in the voice-over. From there the view shifted to an interior shot of Talman seated on a chair in the living room, next to an oversize photo of him and Burr that had once appeared on the cover of *TV Guide.* "And that's me, Bill Talman, with a friend of mine you might recognize," he said.

"You know," he continued, "I didn't really mind losing those courtroom battles, but I'm in a battle now I don't want to lose at all. Because if I lose it, it means losing my wife and those kids you just met."

The camera then moved in on Talman's anguished face. "I've got lung cancer," he said. "So take some advice about smoking and losing from someone who has been doing both for years. If you don't smoke, don't start. If you do smoke, quit!"

With that Talman gave a quick wink and said, "Don't be a loser."

Everybody present marveled at Talman's courage, stamina, and concentration. He was groggy and in obvious pain throughout. "Later, I asked the writer about the script," Rimer recalls. "He said, 'I didn't write a word.' He did it all off the cuff. It was just a remarkable performance." Adds Tim Talman: "People who saw the ad were blown away. Everything he said came straight from the heart."

On August 30, 1968, six weeks after filming the commercial, the fifty-three-year-old actor died at West Valley Community Hospital in Encino. He was buried at Forest Lawn Hollywood Hills. "He was the consummate joker, right up to the end," Tim Talman says. "He was still paying alimony to his first wife. The day before he died, the whole family is gathered around his bed, there's all this gloom and tension, as you can imagine, and he says, 'Well, at least I won't have to pay her another red cent.' "

Talman's groundbreaking advocacy encouraged other celebrities to take up the cause. Soon John Wayne was warning of the perils of tobacco and Brooke Shields was posing with cigarettes stuffed in her ears. In 1985, Yul Brynner, a five-pack-a-day smoker dying of lung cancer, echoed Talman's performance by recording a commercial for posthumous release. "Now that I'm gone," the actor said, "I tell you: don't smoke."

Despite sophisticated public awareness campaigns, a better understanding of the physiological nature of nicotine addiction, an array of options to treat the craving for "cancer sticks," and a societal crackdown on smoking in public spaces, anti-smoking advocates know there is much work still to be done. According to the Centers for Disease Control and Prevention, cigarettes continue to account for one of every five deaths in the United States. That's roughly 443,000 victims annually, including more than 49,000 from exposure to secondhand smoke.

Peggy Talman, also a chain smoker, quit briefly after her husband's death and later died of lung cancer. Jim Talman, now ninety-five, never touched tobacco and stopped playing competitive tennis only because he'd outlived everybody else in his age bracket. Jim Caldwell, scared straight as a youngster, figures that if William Talman's final role saved just a single life—his own—then the eternal loser went out with a winning performance.

"I still watch the old *Perry Mason* reruns with my wife," Caldwell says. "Great show. Raymond Burr was a class act all the way and William Talman was a great, great man."

One of the many postcards published in the aftermath of the *Titanic* disaster. (Author's collection)

4

A Night That's Still Remembered

More than a century after the Titanic *famously went to the bottom of the Atlantic, fascination with the ill-starred liner and its passengers is as strong as ever.*

The drifting slab of ice rose as high as the fourth floor of Henry Ford's Model T plant, an iconic symbol of American promise that few of the passengers bound for Michigan would live to see. The liner steaming towards the iceberg carried a small city within its hull—restaurants, a hospital, Turkish baths, a heated pool, a gymnasium, a post office, a wireless station, and an estimated 2,224 passengers and crew members, double the population of Royal Oak, Michigan, at the time. It was late in the evening of April 14, 1912, a moonless, chillsome Sunday night, and the RMS *Titanic* was on the cusp of fulfilling a terrible destiny.

Among those on board was twelve-year-old Ruth Becker, who was traveling in second class with her mother, Nellie, and two younger siblings. They were headed for Benton Harbor, Michigan, having spent the last several years in India, where Ruth's father was a Lutheran missionary.

"We've had a little accident," a steward told Nellie, shortly after the ship unexpectedly stopped dead in the water. "They're going to fix it, and then we'll be on our way."

Today, that remark is thick with irony. However, at the time nobody aboard the *Titanic* could have imagined that the mighty ship's first voyage would be its last, that boasts of "unsinkable" would devolve into the unthinkable: one of the greatest maritime catastrophes ever and the symbolic beginning to the end of the unbridled confidence of the Edwardian Age.

The Beckers managed to make it safely off the doomed vessel, but 1,514 others did not. The *Titanic,* lights blazing and band playing almost to the very end, disappeared at 2:20 a.m.

"It was bitter cold, a curious, deadening, bitter cold," Ruth would later say of her experience in a lifeboat filled with trembling, half-dressed passengers. She described watching the dying ship's final moments, its upright stern standing like a large building before sliding into the sea, followed by "the most terrible noises that human beings ever listened to, the cries of hundreds of people struggling in the icy cold water, crying for help with a cry that we knew could not be answered."

For more than a century, the *Titanic* has served as shorthand for epic disaster. That most people today have at least a cursory knowledge of history's most famous shipwreck is due in no small part to James Cameron's 1997 film. *Titanic* was an international blockbuster and pop-culture phenomenon that, with nearly $2.2 billion in ticket sales worldwide, remains one of the highest-grossing movies of all time. The fictionalized love affair of Jack (Leonardo DiCaprio) and Rose (Kate Winslet) aside, the film is commendably faithful to historical facts. "Cameron liked to joke that he made a 'chick flick' with no possibility of a sequel," says maritime historian Cris Kohl of Windsor, Ontario. "Still, he went all out in re-creating the ship and the sinking. There is meticulous attention to detail."

Merchandisers' favorite disaster received even more exposure with the centenary of the *Titanic*'s sinking in 2012, with books, documentaries, recordings, games, exhibitions, auctions, and tributes appearing on both sides of the Atlantic. The outpouring included a worldwide 3D theatrical reissue of Cameron's film and a joint US-British television miniseries.

Why this continuing fascination with the *Titanic*? According to Kohl, beyond the "supreme irony" of the world's greatest ship plunging to the ocean floor on its maiden voyage, "much of the interest lies with the large number of rich people on board and how they acted."

Ruth Becker in 1912. The twelve-year-old girl, bound for Benton Harbor, survived the sinking, but 1,514 others did not. (Author's collection)

Millionaires were the rock stars of their day, their lives followed with a mix of aspiration and curiosity. Among the "money kings" who went down with the ship were John Jacob Astor IV, whose wealth today would be measured in the billions of dollars; George Widener, heir to the largest fortune in Philadelphia; and John B. Thayer, vice president of the Pennsylvania Railroad and a shipping magnate who two years earlier had launched the freighter *Allegheny* on the Detroit River. Other notables included millionaire playboy Benjamin Guggenheim; Macy's co-owner Isidor Straus and his wife, Ida; artist Francis Davis Millet (whose 1883 painting, *Reading the Story of Oenone*, is in the collection of the Detroit Institute of Arts); Grand Trunk Railway president Charles M. Hays, whose oversight included the Detroit, Grand Haven & Milwaukee line; and Major Archibald Butt, the influential advisor to US presidents Roosevelt and Taft. There were others. Never before in American history had a single calamity claimed so many members of the social elite.

To Kathleen Marcaccio of Royal Oak, the tales of the more ordinary people aboard the *Titanic* are the most enthralling. "I was surprised at how many steerage passengers there were on a luxury liner," says the history-minded information services technician, who saw the movie twenty times in the theater and owns thousands of pieces of memorabilia associated with the film. "When you start looking at the people involved, you find this wide range of human-interest stories."

There are surprisingly strong Michigan ties to the *Titanic*. Sixty-nine passengers, most of them immigrants, were headed for destinations around the state. Thirty-one were bound for Detroit or Pontiac, with most of the rest traveling to the mining regions of the Upper Peninsula. The very first person put into a lifeboat was Helen Bishop, a newlywed from Sturgis. The only rescued passengers to subsequently have their ashes spread over the actual site of the sinking—Frank Goldsmith Jr. in 1982 and Ruth Becker Blanchard in 1994—were both Michigan-bound. (The only other person whose ashes were scattered over the ship's final resting place was a deck officer, not a passenger.)

Moreover, the US senator who chaired the high-profile investigation into the tragedy was William Alden Smith. The white-haired

Republican from Grand Rapids used the proceedings to hammer home maritime reforms and to scold the world about its excesses. "What this nation needs is a severe lesson that will strengthen the pillars of its faith," he said. "We are running mad with the lures of wealth, of power, and of business. We are setting society into castes, with the forces of wealth and power on one side and destitution and poverty on the other."

* * *

The *Titanic* was all about wealth and power. The White Star Line spent three years building the "ship of dreams," and everything about the British luxury liner was gargantuan. It was as long as three football fields. The anchor weighed more than 15 tons. Each of its outside propellers measured almost 24 feet across and weighed 38 tons. At a time when a new Model T roadster cost $680 and gas was 7 cents a gallon, the price of a first-class parlor suite was $4,350. Second-class accommodations on the *Titanic*, geared to society's growing and newly affluent middle class, were equal to first-class on other liners. Those in third class (also known as "steerage") paid as little as forty dollars for a one-way ticket in the bowels of the ship. That amount still represented several weeks' pay for the typical laborer in 1912.

The *Titanic* left Southampton, England, on April 10, 1912, stopping at ports in Cherbourg, France, and Queenstown, Ireland, to take on additional passengers before heading for New York. Traveling in second class were Jane Quick, thirty-three, and her daughters, eight-year-old Winifred and two-year-old Phyllis. "My grandmother, Jane, was taking the family to Detroit, where her husband worked with a contractor," says Troy resident Jeanette Happel. "They were originally supposed to leave England on another ship, but a coal strike forced them to change their tickets to the *Titanic*. My grandmother didn't want to go. She said, 'I don't want to go on any ship that hasn't been tried.' But she didn't have any choice."

Another reluctant passenger was Frank Goldsmith. His wife's relatives had lived in Detroit for several years and regularly encouraged the family to emigrate from their home in Kent, England.

Goldsmith, a thirty-three-year-old toolmaker who was terrified of the sea, finally gave in, his fears offset by the prospect of making a much better living in booming Detroit. He packed up his tools and booked third-class passage for him, his wife Emily, and their nine-year-old son, Frank Jr., persuaded that the *Titanic* was the safest vessel afloat.

The storyline from that point on is all too familiar. On April 14, its fourth night out at sea, the *Titanic*—moving too fast for the conditions—narrowly averted a head-on collision with an iceberg. The resulting scrape along the starboard side initially seemed innocuous. The ship was designed to stay afloat even if five of its bulkhead compartments were breached. But on this starlit evening some four hundred miles southeast of St. John's, Newfoundland, rivets popped, plates buckled, and suddenly six forward compartments were taking on water. The *Titanic*, carrying lifeboats for only half of its passengers and crew, slowly began to sink bow-first into the Atlantic. In less than two and a half hours, it would be completely gone.

The collision occurred at 11:40 p.m., as most passengers readied for bed. Shortly after midnight, Captain Edward Smith ordered all lifeboats prepared for launch.

Dickinson and Helen Bishop—a young, wealthy couple who were the only Michigan-bound passengers in first class—joined the growing crowd of officers ordered to the boat deck. There appeared to be nothing wrong, and for the next hour or so deck officers had a difficult time convincing people to leave the warmth and perceived security of a luxury liner for an uncomfortable seat in an open lifeboat.

"It was then almost impossible to get people to venture into them," Dickinson Bishop, a twenty-five-year-old native of Dowagiac, Michigan, later told the press. "The officers implored people to get aboard, but they seemed to fear hanging out over the water at a height of 75 feet, and the officers ordered the boat away with only a small portion of what it could carry."

Helen Bishop, nineteen and pregnant, was the first person seated in Lifeboat No. 7, which at 12:45 a.m. was the first boat lowered down the side. She had reluctantly left behind a toy poodle named Freu Freu, acquired while on honeymoon in Europe. "When I started to leave her she tore my dress to bits, tugging at it," she said later. "I realized, however, that there would be little sympathy for a woman carrying a dog in her arms when there were lives of women and children to be saved." There were a dozen dogs on the *Titanic*, of which three remarkably survived. Two were smuggled onto lifeboats and the third was pulled from the water. However, the frantic Freu Freu, locked inside her owner's stateroom, went down with the ship.

Although there were isolated episodes of cowardice and some panic toward the end, calm and the tradition of "women and children first" generally prevailed as the gravity of the situation gradually became apparent. Overall, four of every five men on the *Titanic* would die while three-quarters of the women were rescued.

Frank Goldsmith Jr. recalled being placed in a lifeboat with his mother while his father stood back. "My dad reached down and patted me on the shoulder and said, 'So long, Frankie, I'll see you later.' He didn't and he may have known he wouldn't."

Alfred Rush, who was traveling with the Goldsmiths to Detroit, had turned sixteen on April 14, proudly exchanging his knickers for a pair of pants. When a crew member tried to put the undersize lad in a boat, he jerked his arm free and declared, "No! I'm staying here with the men." Goldsmith later wrote: "At age sixteen, he died a hero."

By 2 a.m., the last of the *Titanic*'s distress rockets had been fired into the sky and all sixteen wooden lifeboats had shoved off, most of them only partially filled. Left behind were more than fifteen hundred people, whose final minutes those rowing away viewed with a mixture of pity and helplessness. The escapees were desperate to flee the expected suction when the ship went under.

"The water was like glass," Helen Bishop remembered. "By the time we had pulled 100 yards the lower row of portholes had disappeared. When we were a mile away the second row had gone, but there was still no confusion. Indeed everything seemed to be quiet on the ship until her stern was raised out of the water by the list forward. Then a veritable wave of humanity surged up out of the steerage and shut the lights from our view. We were too far away to see the passengers individually, but we could see the black masses of human forms and hear their death cries and groans."

Frank Goldsmith's destination was Detroit. The English toolmaker saw his family off in lifeboats before going down with the *Titanic*. (Author's collection)

Hundreds of people were entombed in the ship as it broke in half and plunged nearly two and a half miles to the ocean floor. Others either leaped or spilled into the icy sea. "They jumped and they screamed and they yelled for help, and of course nobody came to help," an aging Ruth Becker Blanchard told a documentary producer near the end of her life. "I can still hear them."

Those in lifeboats guiltily kept their distance, lest the overwhelming numbers of desperate human beings swamp those already saved. All those struggling in the twenty-eight-degree water had only a short while to live. Few actually drowned. Most succumbed to hypothermia. Children and the elderly were dead within a few minutes; the more physically fit lasted perhaps half an hour before their internal organs permanently shut down. The anguished cries and desperate flailing petered out. Soon all was quiet. Hundreds of frozen corpses, held upright in life belts, bobbed macabrely on the lightly rippling surface.

The Cunard liner *Carpathia,* which raced at full speed for four hours through ice fields to answer the *Titanic*'s distress signals, reached the scene ninety minutes after it sank and began plucking the 706 half-frozen and badly shaken survivors out of lifeboats. Throughout Monday, the outside world received conflicting reports of what had happened. The *Detroit News,* for example, splashed the headline "Titanic's 1,470 Passengers Taken Off in Mid-Ocean Without Loss of a Life" across its front page. It wasn't until Monday evening, as the overcrowded *Carpathia* headed for New York, that officials confirmed the sinking. For concerned Detroiters, the local White Star Line unintentionally added to the confusion. The Great Lakes' most successful passenger steamship company (its fleet included the famous side-wheel excursion boat *Tashmoo*) was unrelated to the British saltwater firm of the same name, but for days its office on Griswold received a steady stream of phone calls and telegrams inquiring about passengers on the *Titanic.*

Roughly one-third of all those on board the *Titanic* survived. Over the next three days, word of who had been rescued and who was missing arrived in slow and piecemeal fashion. Anxiety and sorrow recognized no class distinctions, as an illustration by political cartoonist Burt Thomas in the *Detroit News* made clear. Under the title, "Waiting," a society lady and an immigrant woman unaccustomedly clung to each other, united in grief.

Gertrude Judd, whose stately home on Iroquois was the scene of "many elaborate social affairs," fretted over the fate of her mother, Emma Bucknell, a regular visitor to Detroit. She was relieved to find that the fifty-nine-year-old widow of the founder of Bucknell University had made it safely into a lifeboat, taking her turn at the oars until her soft hands were blistered. Meanwhile, inside a modest apartment on East Columbia, seventy-year-old George Eitemiller was described as being "in a state of utter collapse." The old man's worst fears had been realized. His twenty-three-year-old son and namesake, an auto engineer returning from a trip to London, was lost. His body, if recovered, was never identified.

On Thursday evening, April 18, the survivors disembarked at a floodlit New York pier as thirty thousand people jostled in the rain and called out names. Fred Quick, anxious to find his wife, "gave the old whistle just like I used to whistle when we were sweethearts back in England." Soon Jane Quick and daughters came running, and "I grabbed all three of them," he said.

The next day, most survivors boarded trains to their final destinations. A group arrived in Detroit "hysterical, sobbing and nerve-shattered, often too excited to talk coherently, and still shuddering from the horror of their memories," observed the *Detroit Free Press*. Their number included "three Belgians, who left the old country to seek fortune in Detroit and almost lost their lives on the way [and] were sorrowing because of the 17 friends who went down into the depths." The only unaffected one was an immigrant's infant son, "whose one year of life prevents him, happily enough, from a knowledge of the meaning of it all."

What *was* the meaning of it all? Many thought the world was getting too big for its britches, that there was a misplaced trust in technology. "It would seem that we have too much confidence in the ingenuity of man," Detroit Mayor William B. Thompson said, "and too little faith in Providence." On Sunday every church held its own memorial service. The sermons carried such titles as

"Lessons from the Loss of the *Titanic*" and "The *Titanic* and Its Message for Us."

Amid the admonishments, the grim chore of recovering the dead continued. Passing steamers and specially chartered "death ships" found 337 drifting bodies in all, the last corpse pulled out of the sea almost two months after the sinking. Bodies in good enough shape to be preserved were embalmed on board and brought to Halifax, Nova Scotia, the center of the recovery effort. Social proprieties were observed to the end. First-class passengers were placed in coffins; others were put in canvas bags. The majority of those buried at sea were steerage passengers and crew members.

Thirty-seven people traveling to Michigan perished, but crews recovered and identified the bodies of only seven of them. Of those seven, three were buried at sea, one rests in an English graveyard, and the remaining three lay at Fairview Lawn, the Halifax cemetery where many of the 150 unclaimed or unidentified victims were interred.

One of the block granite stones in the cemetery's *Titanic* section bears the name of steerage passenger Achille Waelens, a twenty-two-year-old unmarried farm hand from Ruiselede, Belgium. "My father settled in Ithaca [Michigan] in 1903, when he was about fourteen," says Waelens's nephew, Bernie Waelens of Warren. "The story is that my dad sent his brother Achille twenty-five dollars to join him in Michigan." A bank draft for that amount, along with a watch, pipe, and knife, was found in the pockets of Achille's new suit when his body was pulled out of the Atlantic.

Several years ago, Waelens made the long drive to Nova Scotia, curious about the lost young man his father rarely spoke about. He was moved by the calm and apple-pie order of the cemetery, so much at odds with what he imagines his ancestor's desperate last moments were like. "I never met my Uncle Achille," he says. "My father had no picture of him. But he was my dad's twin brother, so I guess I know what he looked like."

In New York, a Congressional inquiry began the morning after the *Carpathia* docked. Senator William Alden Smith grilled White Star Line managing director Bruce Ismay, whom the

American press vilified for leaving the sinking liner in a half-filled lifeboat. The British press ridiculed the US senator from Michigan, an erstwhile farm boy with little knowledge of nautical matters, as "Watertight Smith" for his insistence that witnesses discuss technical points in layman's terms. But the simplified testimony had the desired effect of educating the public about overdue maritime reforms. Congress quickly enacted laws requiring every ocean-going passenger vessel to carry enough lifeboats for every person aboard, maintain a twenty-four-hour radio watch, and conduct regular lifesaving drills. An ice patrol service, the forerunner to the US Coast Guard, was established.

Survivors had no choice but to try and put the tragedy behind them. The official British investigation was a whitewash, absolving the White Star Line of blame and thus limiting their liability. By and large, passengers were dependent on the kindness of friends, relatives, and private charities to help rebuild their lives.

Some took to the stage in Detroit, Grand Rapids, and elsewhere, capitalizing on their fleeting celebrity to earn a few dollars. Jane Quick was one. "My grandmother would go on stage and tell her story," Happel says. "She'd bring out her kids. It became too much, reliving the experience over and over. She told me she did it long enough to pay for her furniture, and then she quit."

As their lives played out over the coming years, many survivors suffered emotionally from what today would be recognized as post-traumatic stress disorder. Haunted by nightmares and flashbacks, some refused to ever set foot on a boat or go swimming again. Frank Goldsmith Jr., whose family settled in Detroit's Corktown neighborhood, never attended a ballgame at Navin Field. The cheering from the nearby ballpark, which had opened just five days before the sinking, reminded him too much of the din aboard the doomed ship.

Few spoke openly of their experiences. Nellie Becker screamed and cried whenever someone brought up the tragedy in her presence, leading her to become permanently estranged from her youngest daughter. Two Detroiters who had been youngsters on the *Titanic* committed suicide. Just before Christmas in 1951, forty-eight-year-old John Davies—an English immigrant who had moved from Calumet to Detroit during World War II—poisoned himself at his home on Kendall. In March 1954, Happel's aunt—now Phyllis Quick Murphy and the forty-five-year-old mother of four—shot herself in the head inside her house on Marlborough. Both victims were having marital problems. The degree to which trauma or depression associated with the *Titanic* contributed to their troubled state of mind is impossible to determine.

Even the wealthy and well-connected Bishops couldn't escape post-*Titanic* contretemps. The child Helen Bishop was carrying died two days after delivery; then a near-fatal car accident near Kalamazoo left her with a plate in her head and a radically changed personality. Dickinson Bishop divorced her and remarried on March 14, 1916; the following day, twenty-three-year-old Helen died during emergency brain surgery. Until his own death in 1961, Dickinson was hounded by rumors that he had disguised himself as a woman in order to flee the liner.

In 1985, an expedition led by Robert Ballard discovered the broken liner on the ocean floor, making front-page news around the

The epic final moments of the "unsinkable" liner as depicted by illustrator Willy Stöwer for the weekly German magazine *Die Gartenlaube.* (Willie Stöwer)

world. By then, decomposition and marine life had taken care of any human remains, including bones, while iron-consuming microbes were steadily eating away the hull. The ship's discovery, and the controversial retrieval of thousands of artifacts that followed, focused renewed attention on the handful of survivors still alive at the time, including a retired Vernor's delivery driver named Michael Joseph.

In 1912, Joseph was returning to Detroit from Lebanon with his mother and two-year-old sister. In the confusion surrounding the launching of the last few lifeboats, the four-year-old boy lost his grip on his mother's skirt and became separated. With the ship just minutes from sinking, a man grabbed the youngster's hand and led him to a lifeboat. He was reunited with his family on the *Carpathia*. Back in Detroit, he was nicknamed "Ty"—but not after the Tigers' famous centerfielder, Ty Cobb, as other boys of the era were. Joseph, who always referred to his unknown savior as "my guardian angel," married and raised a family before dying in 1991. At Resurrection Cemetery in Clinton Township, he is commemorated with one of the most impressive monuments of any survivor: a seven-foot-high black granite slab dominated by a detailed etching of the *Titanic*.

The last Michigan survivor of the *Titanic* was Happel's mother. Winifred Quick van Tongerloo died July 4, 2002, in East Lansing. She was ninety-eight and had outlived all but three others from that awful night. (The final survivor, ninety-seven-year-old Millvina Dean, who as a three-month-old had been the youngest person aboard the liner, died in England in 2009.) According to Happel, her mother never could fathom the world's fascination with a distant event that had caused so much heartache. "She used to say, 'I don't understand it. There have been so many other disasters since then. Why doesn't it just go away?' "

For Happel, at least, there has been no evading the subject. The retired accounting clerk recalls the job interview she had with her last employer, a funeral home director in Warren. In the course of their conversation, the man mentioned how much he admired his recently deceased grandfather, who had come to Detroit as a boy in the early 1900s and persevered through an unfathomable series of tragedies. The nuns who educated the orphaned youngster called him a "miracle child" because prior to losing his little sister to a house fire in 1914, his mother to tuberculosis in 1915, and his father in 1920, Michael "Ty" Joseph had barely made it off the *Titanic.*

A chill ran through Happel. "My God," she blurted out. "My mother was on the *Titanic.*"

"Then I did something that you're never supposed to do in a job interview," she says, sheepishly. "I went over and put my hand on his shoulder." Happel was hired on the spot. "I was just so overwhelmed with emotion," she explains. "The *Titanic* can bring out those feelings."

A Grim Accounting: Michigan's *Titanic* Death Toll

Thirty-seven passengers bound for Michigan died on the *Titanic*: thirty males and seven females. Most were immigrants from England, Belgium, and Sweden. The victims' average age was twenty-six. The oldest was John Lingane, a sixty-one-year-old Chelsea farmer returning home from a visit to his native Ireland; the youngest was two-year-old Margit Skoog, a Swedish toddler whose entire family perished in the sinking.

The bodies of seven of the thirty-seven were recovered: William Carbines, who was subsequently buried in England; Joseph Nicholls, Philip Stokes, and Thomas Theobald, who were buried at sea; and Jenny Henriksson, Frederick Sawyer, and Achille Waelens, who were laid to rest in Halifax. It's possible that the bodies of some of the others listed here were recovered but could not be identified, causing them to be buried as "unknown" either at sea or in Halifax.

Name, Age, Occupation	Home	Destination
Second-Class Passengers		
Frank Andrew, 25, miner	England	Houghton
Frederick Banfield, 28, miner	England	Houghton
William Berriman, 23, farmer	England	Calumet
William Carbines, 19, miner	England	Calumet
George Eitemiller, 23	England	Detroit

Name, Age, Occupation	Home	Destination
Charles Fillbrook, 18, painter	England	Houghton
Marta Hiltunen, 18	Finland	Detroit
John Lingane, 61, farmer	Chelsea	Chelsea
Joseph Nicholls, 19, miner	England	Houghton
Samuel Sobey, 25, quarryman	England	Houghton
Philip Stokes, 25, bricklayer	England	Detroit
Third-Class Passengers		
Ida Andersson, 38, housekeeper	Sweden	Manistee
Petar Calic, 17, farmhand	Croatia	Sault St. Marie
Alfred Davies, 24, caster	England	Pontiac
John Davies, 22, ironworker	England	Pontiac
Joseph Davies, 17, ironworker	England	Pontiac
Alfons De Pelsmaeker, 16, farmhand	Belgium	Gladstone
Frank Goldsmith, 33, toolmaker	England	Detroit
Leo Hampe, 19, painter	Belgium	Detroit
Jenny Henriksson, 28, servant	Sweden	Iron Mountain
Stephen Jenkin, 32, miner	England	Houghton
James Lester, 39, ironworker	England	Pontiac
René Lievens, 24, farmer	Belgium	Detroit
Ellen Pettersson, 18	Sweden	Iron Mountain
Alfred Rush, 16, porter	England	Detroit
Frederick Sawyer, 33, gardener	England	Halley
Anna Skoog, 43	Sweden	Iron Mountain
Harald Skoog, 5	Sweden	Iron Mountain
Karl Skoog, 11	Sweden	Iron Mountain
Mabel Skoog, 9	Sweden	Iron Mountain
Margit Skoog, 2	Sweden	Iron Mountain
Wilhelm Skoog, 40, laborer	Sweden	Iron Mountain
Thomas Theobald, 34, groom	England	Detroit
Philemon Van Melkebeke, 23	Belgium	Detroit
Victor Vandercruyssen, 46, farmer	Belgium	Detroit
Achille Waelens, 22, farmhand	Belgium	Ithaca
Camille Wittevrongel, 36, farmer	Belgium	Detroit

5

Those Amazing Harwell Brothers

One was an exuberant man of the people, the other quietly prospered out of the limelight. Both siblings enjoyed great success in their respective fields.

That Harwell boy from Georgia really made something out of himself, didn't he?

He grew up in Atlanta loving baseball, graduated from Emory University, served his country in the Pacific during World War II, and returned from overseas to become a standout in his profession. He wrote books, treasured music, and amassed an impressive trove of collectibles. He's long gone now, but people who knew him recall a man of intelligence, curiosity, generosity, and impeccable Southern manners.

Yes, Rick Harwell really was something.

That's right, Richard Barksdale Harwell. You know, Ernie's brother.

Well, you probably don't know. But that's to be expected, said Steve Davis, a marketing executive and self-described armchair historian in Atlanta, Georgia. "In Civil War circles, we all know Rick," he said. "We would have blanked on Ernie."

In Detroit, of course, such amnesia is unpardonable. Ernie spent forty-two of his fifty-five big-league seasons broadcasting the Tigers, his distinctive Southern-inflected voice the soundtrack of summer for generations of fans. Many remember that the iconic broadcaster had interests beyond baseball, particularly music. (Ernie had sixty-six compositions recorded by various artists.) There are several ways to measure his illustriousness, but this is as good as any: In 1981, even though his career still had another two decades to run, Ernie became the first active announcer inducted into the broadcasters' wing of the Baseball Hall of Fame.

If Ernie were around today, he would be the first to express regret that there isn't a hall of fame for Civil War bibliographers, *Gone with the Wind* experts, mint julep aficionados, or all-around nice guys, because his brother surely would be worthy of induction in any of them. No less a luminary than James I. "Bud" Robertson Jr., formerly one of the country's eminent Civil War scholars, considered Rick "my guru."

Robertson, retired today after a forty-four-year teaching career at Virginia Tech, was completing his doctorate at Emory when he sought Rick's help in shaping his thesis into a publishable manuscript.

"You know how a thesis can be cold and dry," Robertson said from his home on Virginia's Potomac River. "Rick helped me to rewrite the manuscript and showed me how to inject drama into it."

Robertson's book on General "Stonewall" Jackson's brigade was the first of his many well-received works. Rick also persuaded the reluctant Robertson to accept an offer to become executive director of the Civil War Centennial Commission in 1961. Robertson successfully melded competing factions into a cohesive national commemoration and went on to become a consultant to presidents (he helped plan President Kennedy's funeral) and filmmakers, a career trajectory that might have taken a different course without Rick's guidance. "He was my mentor in every way," Robertson said.

Rick was born in 1915 in the small town of Washington, Georgia, and Ernie came along two-and-a-half years later. After a boll weevil infestation ruined the local economy, their father, who ran a furniture store, moved the family one hundred miles to Atlanta. There, Gray Harwell's tough luck continued as surgery to remove a brain tumor left him confined to a wheelchair for the rest of his life. Unable to work, his wife and sons became the breadwinners, with Helen Harwell making sandwiches and baked goods and Ernie and Rick delivering them via bicycle and streetcar.

The boys grew up working a variety of odd jobs that kept them busy outside of school, but not so busy that they didn't have time

Rick Harwell—librarian, Civil War historian, and mint julep expert—was most comfortable in the stacks. (Emory University Archives)

for baseball. Along the way, their personalities developed. Ernie, undersized and perpetually upbeat, was an instantly likable sort and a natural salesman. Rick, quiet and sardonic, loved few things better than cozying up with a book.

Ernie was a student at Emory when he began his broadcasting career at Atlanta's WSB in 1940. By then Rick had already earned a BA in English and a graduate degree in library science at the same school. After starting his professional career with a two-year stint at

Duke University's library, Rick was returning to Emory to begin a sixteen-year career in the stacks at his alma mater.

Both siblings had their aspirations put on hold by World War II. Ernie served as a correspondent with the Marines, his assignments taking him from the White House to a Chinese brothel, while Rick reportedly became the navy's youngest minesweeper commander. After the war, each resumed his career in earnest. Ernie started doing big-league play-by-play for the Brooklyn Dodgers in 1948, moving on to the New York Giants and Baltimore Orioles before settling into the Tigers' broadcast booth in 1960.

As Ernie became a familiar presence in the lives of millions, his brother quietly became a widely respected historian and bibliographer. In 1949, Rick helped found the Civil War Round Table of Atlanta, an organization devoted to the serious study and discussion of the Civil War. The chapter issued him membership certificate No. 1 and elected him its first president. In 1956, he left Emory for the Virginia State Library. This was followed by stays at Bowdoin College, Smith College, Georgia Southern College, and the University of Georgia. He retired in 1980. Throughout, he published dozens of books, most of them dealing with some aspect of the Civil War, particularly as it pertained to the Confederacy. He also wrote pamphlets, articles, and reviews, and was active in various professional societies. A man of wide interests, he even wrote a booklet about the treatment of stuttering in adolescence, a topic he knew intimately. Growing up, he had watched Ernie overcome the speech disorder after much effort.

Ernie received praise for his own books, all of which were chatty accounts of his life in baseball, but he always deferred to his scholarly brother. "He's the real writer in the family," he'd say. Ernie's personal favorite was a little volume about the history and proper making of the mint julep, a drink Rick was acknowledged as an expert at making. "It's a fun read," said Philip Racine. "Rick was a man who knew his whiskey."

Racine, today a retired history professor in Spartanburg, South Carolina, wrote his thesis at Bowdoin College, in Brunswick, Maine, under Rick's direction.

"Rick was very Southern," he remembers. "Not in his attitudes, but in his demeanor. He spoke very softly and was very courtly. He was a gentleman and really nice guy." James Robertson recalls a colleague who "listened more than he talked. I never heard him laugh, just smile. He never argued. He just wouldn't respond if he didn't agree with you."

Racine was among a group of friends Rick once took to Boston to meet Ernie, who was in town to broadcast a series at Fenway Park. "Rick was very proud of Ernie," Racine said. "They looked a lot alike. When you saw them together it was just so obvious they were brothers. They were two interesting guys to be around."

Ernie, who loved trivia, always enjoyed bringing up the nugget that he had once been Margaret Mitchell's paper boy. But that was before the Atlanta author had gained worldwide fame for writing *Gone with the Wind,* a fame so suffocating that she never wrote another book.

Rick, active in the same literary and historical circles as Mitchell, knew the writer intimately. In fact, she inscribed the very first copy of her bestseller to him. On August 11, 1949, Rick was supposed to meet Mitchell and her husband for dinner. She canceled in favor of seeing a movie, and that evening was struck by a taxi while walking to the theater. Her tragic death caused Rick to start collecting materials associated with Mitchell, her book, and the film. Eventually he assembled the second largest *Gone with the Wind* collection in the world, a treasure trove that fetched a six-figure sum after his death. He published four *GWTW*-related books, including an annotated volume of the author's correspondence that fanatical "Windies" consider the closest thing they'll ever get to Mitchell's autobiography.

Ernie assembled an impressive memorabilia collection of his own. His centered on vintage guidebooks, photographs, scrapbooks, programs, scorecards, and other sports-related ephemera. Soon the hoard of materials outgrew Ernie's home. In the 1960s he donated it to the Detroit Public Library, where it exists as the Ernie Harwell Collection.

When it came to money, one might reasonably assume that a Hall of Fame broadcaster made a lot of it, certainly more than

Ernie Harwell (*right*) in the broadcast booth with George Kell, 1960. (Author's collection)

a librarian. But it was Rick who was more comfortably situated. Ernie, who had a wife and four children to provide for, was chronically underpaid during the first half of his career, and it took a long time to catch up. Meanwhile, his brother was living the single life and using his discretionary dollars to become an early investor in Xerox. As a librarian, Rick had recognized the potential for the new copying machines the company brought out in the late 1950s. He was also a shrewd dealer of rare books and manuscripts. His professional knowledge allowed him to buy low, sell high, and use the gains to enjoy the opera, foreign travel, and other good things in life.

Robertson remembers the house Rick owned in Washington, Georgia. "The place was impeccable. Rick was not a messy man. You could spend the night, get up, then go back into the room a few minutes later and it was as if nobody had ever slept there."

Rick never married. According to a niece, he once was engaged to a girl who died in a car accident. Former colleagues in Maine and Georgia, knowing his orientation, smile about this old chestnut trotted out by families in denial. It was difficult being "different" in the Baptist South, especially when your famous born-again brother was helping to establish the Baseball Chapel in big-league locker rooms. "Even though I love baseball," said Ernie, who repented at a Billy Graham Easter service during spring training in 1961, "I love my Lord Jesus Christ much more." However, Ernie was not one to force his beliefs, religious or otherwise, on anyone, least of all his brother, whose lifestyle choices were his own affair.

Rick Harwell died on March 9, 1988. He was seventy-two and had spent his final months wasting away from what doctors described as a stubborn respiratory illness. His body was cremated. Ernie, with the Tigers in spring training, missed broadcasting a game for the first time in his career to attend his brother's funeral. Robertson, a deacon, presided over the service. "That's the one time I met Ernie," he said. "An absolutely lovely man. He was very emotional at his brother's passing."

The funeral featured none of the blandishments that accompanied Ernie's death from cancer on May 4, 2010, when more than 11,000 people filed past the ninety-two-year-old announcer's open casket at Comerica Park. Crowds always energized Ernie, who even in death remains a man of the people. There's a life-sized statue in the main concourse at Comerica Park to help keep his memory alive. In addition, Wayne State University's (WSU) athletic department named its renovated baseball facility Harwell Field.

"Ernie touched millions of people's lives," said WSU athletic director Rob Fournier. "Just by listening to him on the radio, summer after summer, you got the feeling that you knew him and he knew you. When a ball would go into the stands and Ernie would say, 'A man from Hamtramck caught that one,' or from Bay City or wherever, you'd think, 'How does he know?' Then you'd say to yourself, 'Well, Ernie probably does know everybody in the park.'"

Rick Harwell's legacy is commemorated in a more subdued fashion, something appropriate for a man most at ease in the quietude of the stacks. Every year since 1989, the Civil War Round Table of Atlanta has presented the Richard Barksdale Harwell Award to the author judged to have written the year's best book on the Civil War. Though it took a while, the organization finally got around to publishing a short biography to accompany the award for the benefit of younger members.

"We'd been giving out this award for years," said chapter president Art Carey, "and a lot of us didn't really know who the guy was."

Which was precisely the way Richard Harwell preferred it.

6

The Missing Marine of Mount Suribachi

After surviving the battle of Iwo Jima, Harold Schultz was content to spend his postwar years quietly sorting mail while someone else took his place in history.

It's the most iconic photograph of World War II: six faceless figures straining in harness to plant the Stars and Stripes on windswept Mount Suribachi, high above the volcanic killing grounds of Iwo Jima. The powerful image, taken by Associated Press photographer Joe Rosenthal in the early afternoon of February 23, 1945, immediately won acclaim as an artistic masterpiece and gained wide dissemination as a symbol of American resolve and triumph. The composition was so perfect that some insisted the Pulitzer Prize–winning photo was staged.

It wasn't. The tragic reality is that three of the flag raisers—Sergeant Michael Strank, Corporal Harlon Block, and Private First Class (PFC) Franklin Sousley—later died during the five-week campaign to seize the Japanese-held island. Sergeant Bill Genaust, the cameraman who filmed the flag raising—more proof of its authenticity—also was killed.

President Franklin D. Roosevelt, preparing to once again ask a weary nation to sacrifice part of their paychecks to help finance the war, quickly sized up the photo's public relations value. The survivors—officially determined at the time to be PFC Ira Hayes, PFC Rene Gagnon, and Navy corpsman John Bradley—received orders to return to the states to headline the 7th War Loan Drive. The

Joe Rosenthal's iconic image is thought to be the most reproduced photo in American history. The identities of the six figures lifting the flag were revised after investigations in 1947, 2016, and 2019. Their names appear here in bold with the names of the men originally thought to be in the photo, and the period of the misidentification, in italics. (Joe Rosenthal/National Archives)

fifty-eight-city bond tour included a two-day stop in Detroit in May 1945. One thousand schoolchildren greeted the heroes at Michigan Central Station. The bond drive, coupling artwork of the flag-raising with the slogan "Now . . . All Together," was a great success, raising $26.5 billion, nearly half a trillion in today's dollars. The flag raising has since become embedded in American culture, an instantly recognizable image believed to be the most reproduced photo in US history.

But over the last few years, comprehensive investigations authorized by the Marine Corps have revealed that officials erroneously identified two of the long-feted flag raisers, Bradley and Gagnon, as being in Rosenthal's photo. Bradley's removal from the famous tableaux was especially surprising. He'd been the focus of a best-selling book coauthored by his son, James Bradley, *Flags of Our Fathers*, which later was turned into a critically acclaimed film by Clint Eastwood.

As a result of the findings, an obscure Detroit native was elevated to his rightful place in history: Harold Schultz, an amiable if solitary individual who had died years earlier. Schultz would have been embarrassed by the attention the revelation brought. According to his stepdaughter, Dezreen MacDowell, the former Marine "never sought fame or glory."

Harold Henry Schultz was born January 28, 1926, and grew up on Boyd Street in southwest Detroit, in the old Springwells neighborhood. His father toiled in the foundry at the Ford Rouge plant while his mother was a machine operator at a screw products factory. His older sister and only sibling, Emma, worked the counter at a candy store.

Schultz graduated from Southwestern High School before enlisting in the Marines on December 23, 1943. He was a month shy of his eighteenth birthday. He was 5 feet 6 inches, 150 pounds, with blue eyes, brown hair, and a ruddy complexion. Perhaps Harold's decision to enlist was influenced by his Uncle Julius—his mom's troubled younger brother—who had lived with the family. One morning four years earlier, just before Christmas, Julius was found dead near the Michigan Central railroad tracks. The unemployed factory worker, who police suspected had spent the night drinking radiator alcohol, was a lifelong bachelor who'd served in the Marines during World War I. One can imagine former PFC Julius Abromoski sharing a few stories over the years with his young and impressionable nephew.

Upon completing boot camp in early 1944, Schultz trained as a gunner on a mortar crew and was assigned to Easy (E) Company, 2nd Battalion, 28th Regiment of the newly formed 5th Marine

Division. In September 1944, the division moved from Camp Pendleton, California, to Camp Tarawa in Hawaii, where they prepared for the invasion of Iwo Jima. The island, located about 650 nautical miles south of Tokyo, had airfields that the United States wanted for the expected invasion of mainland Japan.

Harold Schultz of Detroit posed for this identification photo on January 28, 1944, his eighteenth birthday. The photo and serial number were part of his personnel file. (US Marine Corps)

On February 19, 1945, three weeks after turning nineteen, the stocky Detroiter was among the 30,000 men who came ashore at Iwo. The eight square miles of cold lava smelled like rotten eggs. The stench was due to the sulfuric mists emanating from Mount Suribachi, the extinct 546-foot-high volcano that dominated the southwest tip of the island. Opposing the invasion force were 21,000 Japanese soldiers, who had fortified themselves inside a complex web of bunkers, caves, and tunnels. The defenders, well-armed, well-trained, and well-concealed, waited until the Marines got on the beach before cutting loose. The invaders plodded through the terraces of loose ankle-deep volcanic ash, leaning into a hailstorm of machine-gun and artillery fire. As night fell, the Marines burrowed in and sweated out the giant mortar shells that came crashing down on them. Japanese infiltrators moved among the foxholes with grenades and bayonets. Navy destroyers fired a steady stream of illumination shells, casting an eerie light over the beachhead. "That was rough," Chuck Lindberg says of that first night on Iwo. "You didn't sleep at all."

Iwo Jima was Corporal Lindberg's third island campaign. Knitting his large hands in his lap, the retired electrician sits inside the study of his Richfield, Minnesota, home and remembers how daylight brought a fresh view of hell. The Marines moved inland, beginning the slow, arduous process of flushing out the enemy with grenades, dynamite, and jellied gas. Lindberg's and Schultz's regiment was assigned the task of capturing Suribachi, which was being continually pounded by naval guns, airstrikes, tanks, and field artillery. By the evening of the fourth day, men of the 28th Regiment had reached the foot of the embattled bastion. "That night we were told that we were going to be the first combat patrol up the mountain," Lindberg says. "I didn't like it when I heard that."

On the morning of Friday, February 23, the 2nd Battalion commander, Lieutenant Colonel Chandler Johnson, sent over forty men up the mountain with orders to secure the summit and set up an observation post. Sergeant Lou Lowery, a photographer for *Leatherneck* magazine, and Navy corpsman John Bradley were part of the group. Lieutenant Harold Schrier led the patrol, and Johnson handed him a 54-by-28-inch flag. "If you get to the top of the mountain," Johnson instructed, "put it up."

"That 'if' word kind of got to me," Lindberg says. "I still think about that."

A Marine Corps maxim is that every Marine, no matter what his specialty, is first and foremost a rifleman. Thus, with casualties piling up, mortar man Schultz joined the E Company grunts trudging up Suribachi, his M1 Garand in hand. Although there really was nothing that set Schultz apart from his fellow Marines, small details in the photos Sergeant Lowery and others took that day would make him conspicuous to investigators many decades later. For some reason, the sling on Schultz's rifle was improperly attached to the uppermost swivel (the stacking swivel) instead of the swivel on the upper hand guard, causing the rifle to hang lower on his shoulder. Also, a thin leather strap, designed to keep his helmet attached to the liner underneath, was broken and dangled off the left side of his helmet.

The patrol worked its way up Suribachi, encountering surprisingly little resistance. By mid-morning the men found themselves in a crater at the top. Lieutenant Schrier, as instructed, brought out the flag while others scrounged around for something to attach it to. Someone found a twenty-foot length of broken metal pipe. Schultz and other Marines fanned out to provide security. As Private Phil Ward held one end of the pipe horizontal and steady, Schrier, Lindberg, and Sergeant Henry "Hank" Hansen tied the flag to the other end, threading rope through a convenient bullet hole. Then, together with Sergeant Ernie Thomas, they carried the makeshift flagstaff to the highest spot on the crater's rim. Lindberg remembers trying to stomp the ground flat before he and the others set it in place. "We just wanted to get the flag up and get the hell out of there," he says.

With high winds buffeting the summit, Bradley grasped the leaning pole while Ward piled rocks at its base to help stabilize it. Sergeant Lowery captured much of the activity in and around the crater with his camera. However, compared to the dynamic flag raising soon to follow, the photos documenting this initial planting of the Stars and Stripes on Mount Suribachi were not particularly stirring. In fact, no images of the actual raising in progress exist because at that moment Lowery was reloading his camera.

It was about 10:20 a.m. For a minute the war halted. Cries of "The flag's up!" swept across the beach below. Thousands of weary and unshaved Marines whistled and shouted. Cheers poured from the decks of vessels in the harbor. Foghorns sounded. "I can't tell you the feeling we had up there," says Lindberg, still visibly moved by the memory. "All the troops down below were cheering and the ship whistles were tooting." After more than three years of war, it marked the first time the American flag had flown over Japanese home territory.

The men had little time to admire their handiwork. The enemy quickly moved out of their caves. The Marines took fire and returned it, and Lindberg put his flamethrower to good use. Lowery slid fifty feet down the side of Suribachi to avoid a grenade. The fall destroyed his camera, but the film survived. Although there still was some mopping up of Japanese emplacements, Suribachi was declared secure. The Americans now controlled the high ground on "sulfur island," a crucial operational victory and a significant boost to morale.

As Lindberg went back down to replenish his fuel tanks and find some chow, a small patrol made its way to the summit. It was composed of members of the same rifle squad: Sergeant Michael Strank, Corporal Harlon Block, PFC Franklin Sousley, and PFC Ira Hayes, all from Easy Company. Their orders were to deliver some supplies to the observation post, then raise a second flag to replace the first. This new flag measured a much larger 96 by 56 inches, double the size of the original. PFC Rene Gagnon, a slightly built teenager from New Hampshire who was the company's runner (messenger), delivered it.

Why exchange flags? The chief reason was that the original was considered too small to be seen by men fighting on the far side of the island. But there also was word that Secretary of the Navy James Forrestal, who had just arrived on the beachhead, wanted the historic banner as a souvenir. "To hell with that!" responded

One of several photos of the first, smaller flag planted on Mount Suribachi on the morning of February 23, 1945, shows corpsman John Bradley with a hand on the improvised flagstaff and Corporal Chuck Lindberg—who along with Bradley and several others who had just put the flag in place—looking on. Among those on guard is PFC Harold Schultz, at bottom left. (Sgt. Lou Lowery/US Marine Corps)

Lieutenant Colonel Johnson, who ordered Gagnon to retrieve the first flag so it could be locked up in the battalion safe.

Upon reaching the rim of the crater, Hayes and Sousley fashioned a flagstaff out of a long section of steel water pipe. They took it over to Strank and Block, near the spot where the first flag was standing, and together they lashed the replacement flag to it. Lieutenant Schrier, the only officer on the summit, oversaw the second flag raising, just as he did the first. He instructed that the lowering of the original flag should coincide exactly with the raising of its replacement. This orchestration would ensure that the national colors would fly over Iwo without a moment's interruption.

The pipe weighed a hundred pounds or more, and the large flag, whipped by high winds, would make it an even more difficult lift. As Sergeant Strank and his three squad mates held the pipe at waist level, preparing to push it upright, he yelled out to a couple nearby members of Schrier's patrol to come over and help. One of the Marines milling around was PFC Schultz, who shouldered his weapon and grabbed an upper part of the pipe.

By this time Joe Rosenthal and a couple of Marine photographers, tipped off by a departing Sergeant Lowery about a new flag going up, had already arrived on the mountaintop and were setting up their shots. The thirty-three-year-old Rosenthal, the son of Russian Jewish immigrants, had grown up in Washington, DC, before joining the staff of the *San Francisco News*. Rejected for military service because of poor eyesight, he wound up covering the war in the Pacific for the Associated Press. Rosenthal and Sergeant Bill Genaust, a former newspaperman now handling a 16-millimeter Bell and Howell movie camera, stood nearly shoulder to shoulder just a few feet away from Sergeant Strank's little group. As the two veteran correspondents were politely jockeying for position, Rosenthal—who at five-foot-five needed to hurriedly pile rocks and a sandbag to give himself a better angle—spotted movement out of the corner of his eye. He reflexively swung his 4×5 Speed Graphic camera around and, without using his viewfinder, snapped the unfolding scene. It was all over in 1/400th of a second, the time it took the shutter to blink. "When you take a picture like that," he later said, "you don't come away saying you got a great shot. You don't know."

As was routine, Rosenthal sent the film to a lab in Guam for development. What emerged from the tray was an almost too-good-to-be-true image that would soon have some art experts comparing it to the finest neoclassical paintings. Rosenthal ascribed his masterpiece to fortuitous timing, not artistic intent, though all the elements were in place. "The sky was overcast, but just enough sunlight fell from almost directly overhead" to give the figures a sculptural depth, he said. The heavy pipe forced the men to strain, "imparting that feeling of action. The wind just whipped the flag over the heads of the group, and at their feet the disrupted terrain and the broken stalks of shrubbery exemplified the turbulence of war."

Genaust's footage shows Schultz wandering off moments after the raising, then returning with some rocks to help shore up the flagpole. Marines strung guy-lines to stabilize it. Those present considered replacing the original flag so unremarkable that nobody bothered to officially note when it happened. Estimates range from about 12:30 p.m. to 2 p.m. Rosenthal himself thought it was closer to noon. When Lindberg came back up later that afternoon, he didn't even notice that the flag he had helped put in place a few hours earlier had been swapped out. He and the first band of flag lifters had more important things to worry about. Within a week two of them, sergeants Hansen and Thomas, would be killed, with Hansen shot through the head as he stood only a few feet from Lindberg.

The taking of Suribachi was just the beginning of the struggle to capture Iwo Jima. The fighting raged across the central and northern parts of the island through the end of March, by which time combatants had earned an astonishing twenty-seven Medals of Honor. Many were awarded posthumously—no surprise, given that the battle accounted for more than one-quarter of all Marine deaths in World War II. On March 13, Schultz became one of the nearly 29,000 casualties American forces took on Iwo. He suffered severe shrapnel wounds to his stomach and thigh and was evacuated from the island. He was discharged as a corporal in October 1945, a month after the war ended. With the bloodletting behind him, he looked to get on with his life.

* * *

The flag raisings on Mount Suribachi, spaced as little as a couple of hours apart, caused considerable confusion after Rosenthal's photo began appearing in print on February 25, less than forty-eight hours after it was taken. That Sunday it appeared on the front page of the *New York Times*, just one of countless periodicals across the nation, from small weekly newspapers to large-circulation magazines, to publish the image over the coming days and weeks. Chuck Lindberg caught his first glimpse of the photo at a hospital on Saipan, where he'd been evacuated after being shot through the forearm on March 1. "I thought, 'Gee, that's not the way I remember it,'" he says. "Then I got transferred to a hospital in Pearl Harbor where I saw a magazine with pictures of both flag raisings. Then I knew what had happened."

What had happened was that a fleeting, inconsequential moment had swiftly and unexpectedly gained epic proportions—so much so that officials decided to basically quash news or photos of the first flag raising. *Life* and *Time* magazines tried to sort things out with stories of what had happened that day on Mount Suribachi, but by then neither the public nor the government was concerned with the details. With Washington clamoring for the men in Rosenthal's photo to be brought home, the rush was on to identify the country's newest heroes. However, the lifters' obscured faces, and Rosenthal's failure at the time to get their names, hindered positive identification, as did the deaths of several of the men involved. Sergeant Michael Strank and Corporal Harlon Block were killed on March 1, possibly by the same shell blast, and three weeks later a sniper shot PFC Franklin Sousley dead. A mortar round blew apart Lieutenant Colonel Johnson, who had ordered both flag raisings. Surviving Marines who were interviewed by public affairs officers weren't always sure, in the rush of events, which flag raising they had either seen or participated in, nor were they certain who else may have been involved. Some men, including Ira Hayes, were intentionally vague, not wanting to have anything to do with the business of being a so-called Hollywood Marine.

John Bradley and Rene Gagnon, interviewed separately, identified themselves and some others, including Hayes, as being part of the second flag raising. The reluctant Hayes knew that the roster of names soon released to the public wasn't correct, but a colonel told him to keep quiet. At some point Bradley and Gagnon began to privately doubt their own presence in Rosenthal's photo. However, with "events spiraling out of control," it was too late to set the record straight, military affairs journalist Bill Ivory says today. Bradley and Gagnon "went along for the ride" as the photo became the centerpiece of the 7th War Loan Drive, with more than 3.5 million copies of the poster appearing in practically every store, school, train depot, and subway station in the country. The photo also became the basis for a postage stamp and the model for the massive Marine Corps Memorial in Arlington, Virginia.

Hollywood did its part, as Sergeant Genaust's color footage of Old Glory going up over Iwo appeared in documentaries and newsreels shown in every theater, reinforcing public perception that there had been only one flag raising. It also provided the dramatic climax to the 1949 film, *Sands of Iwo Jima,* in which John Wayne starred as hard-ass Sergeant John Stryker and Bradley, Gagnon, and Hayes appeared in cameos. Countless Americans would glean what little they knew of the battle and its most famous moment from the Oscar-nominated film, which wholly ignored the first flag raising, fabricated a story about the second, and reduced the horrors experienced on Iwo to sanitized sentimentality. At one point, a character who has just been shot melodramatically clutches his unblemished shirtfront and mumbles, "I'll get a good night's sleep tonight," before pitching forward.

"I go nuts when I see that movie," Lindberg says. "It gives the public a good deal, I suppose. But it makes you a little disgusted." Unlike cinematic Marines, those on Iwo were not given to speechifying at the drop of a grenade. No stirring orchestral music accompanied their departure. On Iwo, when you were dead, you simply were dead.

As a corpsman and an undertaker, Bradley was intimately acquainted with death. He worked as a funeral director in his hometown of Antigo, Wisconsin until his own passing in 1994. He "spent his life fudging around" his presumed presence in Rosenthal's photo, Ivory says. As the years went by, the discomfited ex-corpsman continued to dodge interviews. By the time the thirty-fifth anniversary rolled around in 1980, he was the last of the six purported flag raisers, having outlived Hayes and Gagnon, who died in 1955 and 1979, respectively.

From left: Rene Gagnon, John Bradley, and Ira Hayes during the 1945 war loan drive. Only Hayes had actually been in Rosenthal's photo. (National Archives)

Hayes's death was especially tragic. An Akimel O'odham Indigenous American from Arizona (and invariably nicknamed "Chief" by his fellow Marines), he had encountered prejudice even on the bond tour, with hotels sometimes turning him away. His struggles with alcoholism ultimately led to his death, which eerily mirrored that of Harold Schultz's Uncle Julius. One winter morning, Hayes was found dead of alcohol poisoning and exposure. He was thirty-two and had endured years of strangers seeking him out on the reservation to ask, "Are you the Indian who raised the flag on Iwo Jima?"

There was more to Bradley's reluctance to talk than guilt over his mistaken status. There are indications that he, like Hayes and countless other returning combat veterans, suffered from what we now know as post-traumatic stress disorder (PTSD). Bradley's condition was not helped by pestering reporters or well-meaning admirers continually dredging up the past. One memory from Iwo Jima was especially haunting. Japanese soldiers pulled a young Marine Bradley had buddied up with into a tunnel and methodically tortured him; Marines later found his horribly mutilated body. Bradley shared the story only once, with his son, who included it in *Flags of*

Our Fathers. It wouldn't be until after Bradley died that his family learned that, two days before the flag raisings, he had saved a fallen Marine's life under withering enemy fire, an action that earned him the Navy Cross. While on Iwo he suffered serious shrapnel wounds to both legs, causing him to use crutches when he embarked on the war loan tour. Bradley was indisputably a hero, Ivory says, just not one of the acclaimed figures in Rosenthal's photo.

Ivory, a native Detroiter who served with the 1st Marine Division in Vietnam, has long been active in veterans affairs. From his Maryland home, where he's working on a book about the battle, he shares the few biographical scraps he's been able to collect about the man Bradley substituted for all those years, Harold Schultz.

"Schultz settled in Los Angeles after the war," he says. "He'd met a girl from Glendale, named Mary, who he corresponded with while overseas. But she died young of a brain tumor." Mary, an Armenian girl, referred to Harold as "her handsome blonde."

Schultz landed a job with the US Postal Service in Los Angeles, where he spent thirty-five years processing mail before retiring in 1981. He worked the night shift at the main post office downtown the entire time. Despite the warm, sunny clime, he was no shorts-and-sandals kind of guy. He dressed "like a factory rat," Ivory says. "It's like he never left Detroit."

But he had, and aside from a brief period following his discharge, he evidently never returned. Over the years, the infrequent phone calls to family in Detroit "would start off cordial, then grow angry and end abruptly."

Ivory speculates that Schultz probably suffered some undiagnosed psychological damage, the kind of intense emotional torment that members of his generation felt uncomfortable sharing with family or therapists. On Iwo, Schultz saw his best friend "blown to bits just a few feet away." After the trauma of combat and anguish over his fiancée's untimely death, he was content to spend the balance of his life quietly sorting mail and fostering stray cats.

Schultz lived in the Pico-Union district in central Los Angeles, a struggling neighborhood heavily populated by Latinos and immigrants fleeing the wars in Central America. He never had a driver's license, preferring to take public transportation wherever he went. He didn't drink, smoke, or swear. He had a weakness for Glenn Miller records, Hedy Lamarr movies, and the two-dollar window at local racetracks. He once took the bus to attend a 5th Division reunion in San Francisco. There he met Rosenthal but made no claims to fame.

As Schultz and his contemporaries from the Great Depression and World War II aged and began to die off, there was a surging interest in what the media was now calling the "Greatest Generation." Schultz, whose favorite subjects in school were history and English, might have produced a bestselling memoir that would have rewritten one of the storied chapters of the war, had he been so inclined. He was not.

In 1989, when he was sixty-three, Schultz married a longtime neighbor, Rita Reyes. According to Dezreen MacDowell, her stepfather was "a progressive in his beliefs. He was pro-animals, pro-civil rights, pro-Native American rights, and pro-gay rights." He "had a Midwestern way about him, where he never talked too much and never complained about anything." He only mentioned the flag lifting once, a passing remark made during dinner.

"My God, Harold, you were a hero," Dezreen said.

"No, not really," he said. "I was a Marine."

"And then he didn't want to speak any more of it. He just felt like he was doing his duty to his country."

* * *

On May 16, 1995, Harold Schultz was found dead in his bed, the victim of a heart attack. He was sixty-nine. The self-effacing ex-Marine wasn't buried at a veterans cemetery. Instead he was interred at Hollywood Memorial Park, now known as Hollywood Forever Cemetery, its grounds populated with entertainment types who had spent their lives in the spotlight. The small marble memorial bench in the rose garden indicates Schultz's service and Purple Heart, but not his brush with history.

Schultz's role didn't come to light until twenty years after his death. There had always been questions regarding the identities of some in

Rosenthal's photo, particularly Bradley. Amateur sleuths pointed out obvious discrepancies, arguing that a corpsman would not be wearing a cartridge belt and have wire cutters hanging out of his pocket. Moreover, the figure in question also was wearing a fatigue cap under his helmet and had uncuffed trousers; as other images taken that day showed, Bradley wore his pants cuffed, didn't have a cap, and had bags of medical supplies strapped across his chest.

There were several military and civilian press photographers on Mount Suribachi the day the flags went up, and over the course of several hours they collectively shot hundreds of photos and a small amount of movie footage. These offered a wide variety of views, though the majority never saw the light of day. Higher-ups ignored or suppressed some images in 1945 because they conflicted with the official narrative. Army and Coast Guard photographers filed away other photos that could have assisted in proper identifications, and these would remain unseen until the Marine Corps launched a pair of probes seven decades later.

The Marine Corps had previously acknowledged one misnamed figure. This was in 1947, after an investigation supported Ira Hayes's assertion that the crouching figure at the base of the flag raising actually was Harlon Block, not Henry Hansen. After making that public correction, the Marines remained adamant for the next sixty-nine years that they now had the correct lineup. From right to left in the photo, they were identified as Block, Gagnon, Bradley, Strank, Sousley, and Hayes. Any subsequent challenges to the official roster of flag raisers were routinely swatted away by the branch's history division.

There the matter stood until 2016, when the Smithsonian Institute turned over compelling evidence it had gathered from amateur historians, journalists, and photo analysts in the process of producing an upcoming television documentary. The material was persuasive enough to cause the commandant of the Marine Corps to establish a nine-person panel, chaired by retired three-star general Jan Huly, to take a deep dive into the controversy.

The panel combined scientific investigation with historical research, reviewing documents, witness statements, and photographs.

Archival forensic experts used the latest digital enhancement technology to scrutinize all still photos and motion picture footage taken on February 23, 1945. An intriguing part of the detective work involved examining the camouflaged cloth coverings the Marines wore on their helmets. Due to the camouflage pattern and fabric creases, each covering is nearly as unique as a fingerprint. It was possible for analysts to match the blown-up speck of a camouflaged helmet from Rosenthal's photo with that from another image, then trace some other small detail—say a wedding band or an untucked shirt—to another photo, moving along from image to image and detail to detail until a visible face and positive identification could finally be made.

On June 23, 2016, the Marine Corps officially announced the Huly Commission's conclusions. The commission found Bradley to have been a hands-on participant in the first flag raising but not the second, though he was on the scene at both events. The figure investigators believed to be Bradley in Rosenthal's photo actually was Sousley, and the figure long thought to be Sousley was the previously unknown Schultz.

Tell-tale clues to Schultz's identity included his broken helmet liner strap and the unusual rifle sling attachment, a combination unique among all the Marines on Mount Suribachi that day. Another distinctive feature was the bulging right pocket of his field jacket. Photographs documented Schultz's presence at both flag events, leading investigators to wonder how he had been overlooked in the first place and to muse over his reasons for never speaking up.

"A low-key, deliberate man, Schultz may have thought he had simply done what was expected of him and recognized the event for what it was: putting a flag up, not some courageous action," concluded panel member Mary H. Reinwald, a retired Marine colonel. "In a war in which so many acts of courage, bravery, and self-sacrifice were common, he may have believed that his participation in raising the flag that day was not worthy of adulation or recognition, let alone fame."

It also was possible, Reinwald continued, that Schultz had "heard the gripes" regarding the separate flag raisings and didn't care to get involved.

In these stills taken from film footage of the second flag raising, PFC Harold Schultz (X) lends a hand getting the heavy pipe upright, then moments later, after the flag is in place, walks away to find some rocks to help shore up the makeshift flagpole. He is readily identifiable by a broken helmet strap and the uncommon way in which his rifle is slung. (Sgt. William Genaust/National Archives)

> During the passing years, the Marines who raised the first flag on Iwo Jima felt resentment and jealousy about the subsequent fame that the Marines of the second flag raising experienced. While countless Americans know of the second flag raising, most assume that it was the only one. Some of the first flag raisers felt ignored, one stating that "we did the dirty work and they got the credit." Another plausible reason might be that Schultz did not appreciate the fame in the immediate aftermath of the battle, and when he finally did, proving his presence would be too problematic given the distance, time passed, and death of so many others who were there. He also may have wanted no further reminder of that day, that battle, or that war nor did he want to constantly relive it either on a war bond tour or during interviews or whenever he met other Marines. His refusal to acknowledge his participation could have been a coping mechanism. Or it could be that he was not interested in fame.

The Huly panel also confirmed the identities of the other four men in Rosenthal's photo: Block, Gagnon, Strank, and Hayes. In announcing its findings, the Marine Corps was careful to emphasize that, no matter who actually was in the photograph, the flag raising was meant to symbolize the collective effort and sacrifice of all Marines, especially the thousands who fell taking Iwo Jima.

* * *

Remarkably, three years later, in 2019, a follow-up investigation revealed that Schultz was not the only missing Marine of Mount Suribachi. The Marine Corps, utilizing the FBI's digital evidence lab and facial recognition software, determined that the figure identified since 1945 as Rene Gagnon actually was Corporal Harold "Pie" Keller, a twenty-three-year-old native of Brooklyn, Iowa. Gagnon may have delivered the second flag and retrieved the first (after helping to lower it), but analysts concluded he had raised neither one. Today both flags are preserved at the National Museum of the Marine Corps in Quantico, Virginia.

Whereas Gagnon had grown increasingly coy about his seeming presence in Rosenthal's photo—his family enjoyed the attention more than he did—Keller was aware all along of his own participation in the flag raising. He had first mentioned it in a battlefield letter to his wife. Several months later, when the Marines stationed him stateside, he wrote his base commander in an attempt to correct the record. But after being chastised by the general for "unproved and malicious gossip," Keller decided not to make a fuss. He never mentioned the mix-up publicly nor even privately to his children.

Coincidentally, the two close-mouthed Harolds—Schultz and Keller—are pictured alongside each other, giving a rousing cheer, in another well-known Rosenthal image known as the "gung-ho photo." Rosenthal took it shortly after the second flag raising and it shows a group of about twenty Marines and corpsmen gathered under the just-planted banner, hoisting their helmets and weapons in triumph. "I went around and said, 'Come on, fellows, I want to get a bunch of you. Wave your helmets and give it the old gung-ho,'" Rosenthal recalled in a 1975 interview. "They said, 'Nah. We don't want—.' I said, 'Come on. It's a historic picture.' I was just kidding, of course. I had no idea that any picture that I was taking had any lasting value."

Decades later, the gung-ho photo was an invaluable piece of evidence in helping analysts track the movements of individuals associated with both flag raisings. Schultz's stepdaughter found a copy of the photo in his desk drawer after his death. On the back he had written his name and those of other Easy Company Marines, several of whom were subsequently killed in the fighting.

Keller returned to his hometown after the war, eager to put it all behind him. He had survived three years of island-hopping across the Pacific, a sniper's bullet to the shoulder, and several months of hospitalization. When he died in 1979, he was chief of Brooklyn's volunteer fire department. Bill Ivory was present in June 2022 when, three years after Keller was officially given his proper place in Marine Corps lore, the community held a ceremony honoring its celebrated native son.

A pair of high-tech investigations identified these six Marines as the men in Rosenthal's photograph. All were members of Easy Company, 2nd Battalion, 28th Regiment, 5th Marine Division. Three of the flag-raisers—Block, Sousley, and Strank—were later killed on Iwo and never knew the impact of their fleeting shared moment in time. (US Marine Corps)

"It's just amazing that two men could be in the most famous photo in Marine Corps history and keep it a secret their entire lives," Ivory says. In today's fame-obsessed, look-at-me world, where people readily share their lives with millions of strangers online, "that probably says more about us than it does about them."

Herman "Germany" Schaefer at Detroit's Bennett Park, circa 1905. (Author's collection)

7

Playing for Laughs

In the early days of baseball, Herman "Germany" Schaefer was the game's consummate prankster and one of its top drawing cards.

At the ballpark or away, Germany Schaefer was always putting on a show. On this winter evening in 1908, the zany ruddy-faced second baseman of the Detroit Tigers was appearing at a burlesque house in Chicago with his lifelong pal and double-play partner, shortstop Charlie O'Leary. The pair, dressed as leprechauns and dancing a jig, were making their vaudeville debut in front of a rowdy, liquored-up crowd on amateur night.

The skit had already incited several minutes of groans and catcalls when Schaefer invoked the name of his brilliant but insufferable teammate, Ty Cobb.

"Why," Schaefer asked, "does Tyrus tire us?"

The audience erupted over the stale pun. Vegetables and cries of "Give 'em the hook!" filled the air. Amid the barrage of eggs, turnips, and tomatoes, two great shepherd's crooks reached out from the wings and dragged the failed act off the stage. "For years after," remembered a sportswriter in attendance, "Schaef used to dwell on how the career of a great thespian was ruined by such frivolous first-night criticism."

Few figures in the long history of baseball have ever craved the spotlight as much as Herman "Germany" Schaefer, for whom no gag was too outrageous or primitive and no audience too small or unfriendly. To protest an umpire's decision to keep a game going in fading light, he once trotted out to his position holding a lit lantern in his hand. On rainy days, he might carry an umbrella onto the field, wear a raincoat and boots to home plate, or take off his spikes and splash barefoot in the puddles. On other occasions he would tip-toe along the foul line like a tightrope walker, wrestle an imaginary adversary, or pantomime rowing across the outfield grass using two bats as oars. Most famously, he occasionally stole first base.

According to Davy Jones, a Tigers outfielder from 1906 to 1912, Schaefer first pulled off his signature stunt in a game against Cleveland, most likely in 1908. (The exact date is unclear.) "They say it can't be done," Jones told author Larry Ritter many years later, "but I saw him do it."

In Jones's recollection, he was perched on third base in the late stages of a tied ballgame. Schaefer was on first base. Hoping to draw a throw that would allow Jones to race home with the go-ahead run, Schaefer stole second. However, the catcher, wise to the strategy, held onto the ball.

"So now we had men on second and third," Jones recalled. "Well, on the next pitch Schaefer yelled, 'Let's try it again!' And with a blood-curdling shout he took off . . . back to first base, and dove in headfirst in a cloud of dust. He figured the catcher might throw to first—since he evidently wouldn't throw to second—and then I would come home same as before. But nothing happened. Nothing at all. Everybody just stood there and watched Schaefer, with their mouths open, not knowing what the devil was going on."

Even if the catcher had thrown to first, Jones said, he was too flabbergasted to move off third. "The umpires were just as confused as everybody else. However, it turned out that at that time there wasn't any rule against a guy going from second back to first, if that's the way he wanted to play baseball, so they had to let it stand. So there we were, back where we started, with Schaefer on first and me on third. And on the next pitch darned if he didn't let out another war whoop and take off again for second base. By this time the Cleveland catcher evidently had enough, because he finally threw to second to get Schaefer, and when he did I took off for home and both of us were safe."

Over the years, fans have enjoyed the intermittent appearances of crowd-pleasing jokesters and genuine flakes—gangly, mop-haired pitcher Mark "The Bird" Fidrych, for example, who gave a pep talk to the ball before each pitch and got on his hands and knees to pat dirt whenever the mound needed grooming. For the mythic Schaefer, one has to reach even deeper into the past, back to an era when players wore pancake gloves, slept two to a bed, and traveled to games in horse-drawn buses known as tally-hos. Baseball was still a pastime of absurdity, melodrama, comedy, and improvisation, a far cry from the self-conscious and over-engineered industry it is today.

Nobody embodied the free-minded spirit of the times better than the uninhibited Schaefer. He was a natural showman. He had a quick wit, a strong baritone voice, and was a master of mimicry, making him a favorite of the writers who delighted in recounting his antics. "Everybody loved the jovial, droll, pock-marked Chicago Dutchman," said New York sportswriter Fred Lieb. Damon Runyon, whose distinctive journalism and short stories embraced such eccentrics as Schaefer, observed that Germany "managed to inject his humor into baseball in a manner that made him one of the most popular men who ever appeared on the diamond, and one of the greatest drawing cards. It was always good, clean fun, and wholly extemporaneous. Millions of people have roared with laughter . . . and have gone home from a ball game feeling they had been mighty well entertained, regardless of the result of the game."

The *Detroit Free Press'* Malcolm Bingay knew Schaefer from covering the Tigers in the early 1900s. In the 1930s, having adopted the persona of "Iffy the Dopester" to comment on a fresh crop of pennant-chasing Detroit stars, Bingay introduced Schaefer to a new generation of fans. Germany was "the soul of baseball itself, with all its sorrows and joys, the born troubadour of the game," he declared. However, Schaefer also was "a strange, moody guy," he admitted, "a comedian with the soul of a tragedian."

* * *

A man who steals bases in the opposite direction should be accustomed to reverses, and Herman William Schaefer certainly experienced his share during a condensed lifetime. He was born in Chicago on February 4, 1876, to immigrant German parents, Charles and Sophia Schaefer. He and his seven siblings grew up in the poor and vice-ridden Levee District on the city's South Side. At some point, young Herman fell victim to one of the deadly smallpox epidemics that regularly swept through the tenements.

As part of the disease's usual progression, blisters cover a victim's body before turning to scabs and falling off. Smallpox killed 30 percent of all those it afflicted and blinded many others. The disease marked survivors for life, some more severely than others. Smallpox left Schaefer's large and pleasant face, habitually split by a wide smile, pitted from hairline to neck. Several pebble-like protuberances clustered around the tip and bridge of his nose. When Schaefer stripped off his uniform in the clubhouse after a game, teammates couldn't help but notice the scars that ran along his arms and legs and sprinkled his torso.

Schaefer was understandably sensitive about his looks, but dermal fillers, chemical peels, microdermabrasion, and other cosmetic procedures were unknown then. Charlie O'Leary remembered a streetcar conductor calling the disfigured youngster a "sauerkraut-faced boob," one of the gentler insults people regularly tossed Schaefer's way. To survive in the hard-boiled world of sandlots and saloons where Schaefer came of age, one had to respond forcefully to taunts—sometimes with an exaggerated insouciance, sometimes with biting wit, and now and then with balled-up fists.

Schaefer, who filled out to be a solid 5-foot-9 with muscular legs and a broad set of shoulders, took on all tormenters. A correspondent in Sioux City, Iowa, where Schaefer played semipro ball in 1898, described the young player regularly "climbing into the grandstand to whip a rooter because of remarks about his pock-marked face. . . . Sometimes it took the combined efforts of his teammates and a couple of policemen to pry him loose from the rooter."

A right-handed batter and thrower, Schaefer was quick, agile, and versatile. He eventually played every position except catcher. Moved around like "a human checker board," Schaefer's value as a utility player would help extend his big-league career by several seasons.

Detroit fans first became acquainted with Schaefer in the summer of 1900, when he came to town as an infielder with the Kansas City Blues of the American League, which is what Ban Johnson's old Western League (of which the Tigers were a charter member) was now calling itself. Schaefer's most notable moment was rushing into the Bennett Park stands to assault a heckler, an action that earned him a five-day suspension from commissioner Johnson.

After a stint in the minors, Schaefer signed with his hometown Chicago Cubs (then known as the Orphans). There he was a footnote to an historic event. On September 13, 1902, he was the third baseman as the legendary double-play combination of "Tinker-to-Evers-to-Chance" (shortstop Joe Tinker, second baseman Johnny Evers, and first baseman Frank Chance) first took the field together. The trio, whom Franklin P. Adams immortalized in verse, ultimately made it into the Baseball Hall of Fame. Meanwhile, the odd man out in the storied infield moved around for a couple of summers. Schaefer was playing for a minor-league team in Milwaukee when he attracted the eye of Frank Navin, then the business manager of the Tigers and soon to be part-owner.

Navin wasn't sure he wanted to sign the mercurial shortstop, who during his baseball travels had already acquired a reputation as a "jakey," slang for a hardcore alcoholic. "I have heard so many conflicting stories about Schaefer that I am somewhat dubious regarding him," he admitted.

Nonetheless, in November 1904, Navin sent popular infielder Clyde "Rabbit" Robinson and $2,500 to Milwaukee for Schaefer. The newcomer's feistiness accounted for the Tigers' unexpected third-place finish in 1905, claimed White Sox owner Charles Comiskey. "The Detroit teams of recent years have been in the habit of losing heart as soon as their opponents got a few runs ahead. With old Schaefer in there, fighting all the while, there has been a marked difference in their playing."

It was against the White Sox that Schaefer pulled off one of his most memorable stunts. On June 24, 1906, the visiting Tigers were losing, 2–1, and down to their last out. O'Leary was on first base when Schaefer stepped up to the plate to pinch-hit for Francis "Red" Donahue. Schaefer, who was nursing a sliced thumb from prying the cap off a beer bottle, had spent the day in the coaching box, where fans had razzed him mercilessly.

Now he was facing "Doc" White, one of the toughest pitchers in the game. Just as he was about to step into the batter's box, Germany turned around, took off his cap, and addressed the large Sunday crowd.

"Ladies and gentlemen," he announced, "you are now looking at Herman Schaefer, better known as Herman the Great, acknowledged by one and all to be the greatest pinch hitter in the world. I am now going to hit the ball into the left-field bleachers. Thank you."

Lost in the folklore surrounding this incident is the fact that Schaefer, who claimed to be "psychic," often entertained the crowd by telling them what was going to happen on the field. Fans either hooted or cheered; it was all part of the usual give-and-take between the babblative ballplayer and the public. Nobody kept track of the number of empty boasts or failed predictions Schaefer made.

This time, however, Schaefer delivered. With a mighty swing, he sent White's first pitch into the bleachers, just as advertised.

Germany, a .258 career hitter with a paltry total of nine home runs in fifteen big-league seasons, may have been the most surprised person in the park. He jumped with glee as the ball cleared the fence. Seizing the moment, he bolted like a racehorse toward first base—then dove headfirst into the bag. He got up and shouted, "At the quarter, Schaefer leads by a head!" A few moments later he slid into second, yelling, "At the half, Schaefer leads by a length!" He then slid into third, announcing, "Schaefer leads by a mile!" He concluded his gallop around the bases with a fancy hook slide into home plate and a cry of "Schaefer wins by a nose!" He dusted himself off, doffed his cap, and bowed. "Ladies and gentlemen, this concludes this afternoon's performance. I thank you for your kind attention." The Tigers won, 3–2, and another chapter in the legend of Germany Schaefer, the "clown prince of baseball," was written.

Detroit was a much smaller place then, and big leaguers were very approachable public figures. Schaefer, always impeccably dressed and invariably accompanied by his best friend since childhood days, O'Leary, was a familiar presence at local saloons, racetracks, theaters, and restaurants. He was always good for a laugh and a beer or three—"a regular fellow," as he was often described. Once, when he was laid up at Grace Hospital, he was inundated with gifts and well-wishers. "Fruit and flowers were piled about the room, covering the table and littering the floor," a visitor said. "In the middle of it sat the German smoking an excellent cigar—a box of perfectos, sent by an admiring fan, was at his elbow—and telling stories as only he can reel them off."

Schaefer seemingly was pals with everybody he met. He took the field against Black players in offseason exhibitions in such places as Harlem and Cuba, happily exploring the local culture in post-game revelries, and back-slapped stern-looking dignitaries as if they were old friends.

A few years ago, an album of century-old snapshots by Tigers outfielder Matty McIntyre came up for auction, creating a minor stir among collectors. It was a rare peek into the everyday world of baseball, circa 1905. Unsurprisingly, Schaefer was the center of attention in many of the candid "Kodaks." In them he approaches a washwoman on the sidewalk of an unidentified Southern city during spring training, talks animatedly with a bearded Jewish peddler in downtown Detroit, and mugs with some barefoot Black kids in Georgia. One could get the impression that Schaefer was having fun at someone else's expense while McIntyre snapped away with his one-dollar Brownie camera, but contemporary accounts of Schaefer's shenanigans insisted his humor was never cruel, belittling, or patronizing. "With all his 'kidding' and fun-making Schaefer is never offensive," the *Cleveland Plain Dealer* observed in 1908. "He never gets off anything that hurts and he is a gentleman at all times."

The outgoing Schaefer strikes up a conversation with a laundress in an unidentified location—most likely Augusta, Georgia, where the Tigers held spring training between 1905 and 1907. (Author's collection)

The silver-tongued Schaefer was relentless. Cobb recalled how Schaefer would position himself on the back step of the tally-ho taking players to the ballpark, and hold running conversations with strangers.

"My, what a pretty infant!" he'd call out to some lady pushing a baby carriage on the sidewalk. "What's his name?"

"Augustus!" the startled mother would shout.

"And how old is the little darling?" Schaefer would bellow as the clopping horses continued to put distance between them.

"Ten months!"

"Is he an only child . . . ?"

"By now," Cobb marveled, "all street traffic would have stopped to listen open-mouthed to the dialogue and Germany never considered the stunt a complete success unless he still had the mother screeching answers when we were half a block away."

The high-strung Cobb had few friends on the team, but Germany, who admired Cobb's competitiveness and craftiness, was one of them. The two were key cogs in Detroit's pennant winners, though Schaefer would be traded late in the 1909 season. "As a drawing card, Herman ranks second only to Cobb," Harry Salsinger wrote in the *Detroit News*. "Schaefer gives the comedy, Cobb the thrills." It was a measure of Schaefer's baseball savvy that, on a roster studded with future managers and Hall of Famers, manager Hugie Jennings named him field captain. This responsibility came with an extra $500, a significant amount of money at the time.

Dollar bills were on Schaefer's mind when, while acting as the players' representative, he asked what seemed to be an inconsequential question at a meeting with baseball officials before the start of the 1907 World Series. "Under the rules, the players share in the gate receipts of the first four games," he said. "If there is a tie game among the first four, do we share in the gate receipts of the fifth game? We think we should because it would be a game that would have to be played over again."

The issue had never come up before. There had never been a tie game in World Series play. Officials huddled and, deciding that the odds of such an occurrence were slim, agreed to the new provision. The very next day, Detroit and Chicago played to a 3–3 tie that umpires called after twelve innings because of darkness. As a result, players pocketed an extra few hundred dollars apiece when officials doled out Series shares. Schaefer later said the question had come to him in a vision, though it was more likely a stupor.

The 1908 campaign was Schaefer's all-around finest as a Tiger. Switching from second base to shortstop, he finished third in the league in runs, stolen bases, and sacrifice hits. That June, during an evening of drinking in the bar of the Brunswick Hotel, a loudmouth disparaging the Tigers took a swat at Schaefer. Germany “lost his usually calm temper” and administered “a thorough beating,” reported the *Free Press.* After sobering up, the victim wrote him a letter, apologizing profusely for his loutish behavior and saying how much he admired the combative team leader.

The Tigers won a second straight pennant in 1908 by beating the White Sox in Chicago on the last day of the season. As always, Germany kept the team loose with his antics. Malcolm Bingay was an admirer of Schaefer's “baseballic madness,” which on one occasion had unintended consequences for teammates George Mullin and Ed Killian.

> One night in front of the Aldine Hotel in Philadelphia Schaef had tried out a new clown stunt for the entertainment of the gang. He had been associating with some low burlesque actors who taught him how knock-about comedians on stage seem to hit each other in the face without being hurt.
>
> They time the slaps so that the one being hit can get his open palm to his face just as the slap comes. The audience does not see that hand going up and it looks as though the victim gets a good stiff poke in the jaw.
>
> Schaefer rehearsed this with little Charlie O'Leary. . . . The act was to have O'Leary sock Schaef and to have Schaef beg for mercy. It all seems silly, and it was, but it was funny on that warm summer evening on Chestnut St.
>
> O'Leary would slap away after a terrific verbal war, then Schaef would cry. The crowds swarmed over the walk onto the pavement. Then the two of them would embrace and do a jig—to the disgust of the spectators who had hopes of seeing a wicked fight.
>
> O'Leary soon tired of the goofy role and Schaef, always the troubadour, induced George Mullin to take his place. The act wasn't so good because Mullin was as big as Schaef. This dampened Schaef's ardor, as a born artist, and he soon followed O'Leary back into the hotel.

> But George . . . wanted to continue "acting." He got Ed Killian to take Schaef's part, being sure he would get as big an audience as Germany did.
>
> Killian agreed to do the slapping. The war of words started and Killian swung on George's jaw as directed.
>
> But poor George forgot that Killian was left-handed!
>
> The sock had all the power Killian possessed and George was jolted to his heels. This made him so mad he took a swing at Killian and this time the crowd got what it had been waiting for. A real fight.

For the second October in a row, the Tigers lost the World Series to the Cubs. Once again, Schaefer had a disappointing series. Overall, he had a paltry .135 batting average across two World Series, failing to knock in a run and scoring just once in ten games. All the same, he remained the mainspring of the infield and was named captain of the 1909 team.

But that August, Schaefer was traded to Washington for second baseman Jim Delahanty. When Germany visited Bennett Park for the first time as a Senator, he was greeted with a warm ovation and a sack containing $100 in gold coins. Although his uniform had changed, his reputation for gambling stayed with him. In the waning days of the pennant race, Ban Johnson ordered him to sit out Washington's final series against Detroit. The American League president was worried that Germany, whom the Tigers had told would receive a World Series share, might be tempted to go less than full-bore against his former teammates. The Tigers clawed their way to a third consecutive pennant. Just before the Series opener against Pittsburgh, Schaefer was spotted trying to get a bet down on his old team. When the action shifted to Detroit, he entered Bennett Park, as always, to loud cheers from the grandstand. Sitting on the Detroit bench, he watched the Tigers lose a third straight World Series.

Schaefer stayed with the Senators for the next five seasons, his stunts and mimicry helping to keep the turnstiles spinning even when the team was losing. He enjoyed his last productive season in

Germany Schaefer spent five gag-filled seasons in Washington. His antics included tightrope-walking the foul lines, making friends with four-legged creatures, and stealing first base in a 1912 game. (Bain Collection/Library of Congress)

1911, when he batted a career-high .334. That summer, in a game against the White Sox, he again stole first base, with the umpire insisting afterward that Schaefer had "a perfect right to go from second back to first." According to a 1912 issue of *Sporting Life*, "Schaefer is such a hit with the crowds that the umpires are giving him every liberty to do as he pleases." As his skills diminished, Germany spent more time on the coaching lines where, apart from the comedy, he remained a first-class sign-stealer. Throughout, pitcher and coach Nick Altrock, his understudy of sorts, assisted Germany in his horseplay. Altrock was a fellow Chicagoan and drinking partner on his way to establishing his own career as a baseball clown. Altrock later famously teamed up with another Washington player-coach, Al Schacht, in a collaboration that ran into the 1930s before they went their separate ways.

Germany worked the vaudeville circuit in the offseason, appearing at Detroit's Temple Theater with Broadway actress Grace Belmont just before Christmas in 1911. During the tour, the vaudevillian-ballplayer shared a compartment on an overnight train, where he drew his fellow passenger's ire for keeping a lamp on while reading. After a prolonged exchange of unkind words, Schaefer turned off the light and plotted his next move in the dark. It wasn't until the following morning, after his antagonist got up, dressed, and left the train, that Germany realized he had thrown his own shoes out the window.

Schaefer never married. He preferred tossing dice, telling stories, and drinking with his buddies to settling down domestically. Like many bachelors, his "best girl" was his mother, whose Chicago flat he often returned to in the offseason. Sophia Schaefer's death had a bit of dark slapstick to it. One Sunday morning in January 1913, the seventy-three-year-old widow, apparently sleepwalking, tumbled out of a third-story window and fractured her skull. The crash woke Herman, who was the first to his mother's side. The grief-stricken Germany wore a black mourning stripe on his uniform all year, first as a Senator, then as a member of a touring all-star team that visited thirteen countries around the world. He was a natural ambassador. In Tokyo, he glibly addressed a crowd of ten thousand Japanese for half an hour. "They had no more idea what he was saying than he did," observed one writer. "But they cheered him wildly."

Schaefer was now in his late thirties. His hair was thinning and his reflexes were slowing. After Washington let him go, he joined Newark, a team in the short-lived Federal League, for the 1915 season. He then worked as a coach for the New York Yankees, managed by former teammate Bill Donovan. With World War I raging and patriotism on the upswing, Schaefer announced he was changing his nickname from Germany to "Liberty" Schaefer. Fans still appreciated his shtick, but sometimes he was feeling too poorly to perform.

In 1918, Schaefer joined the Cleveland Indians as a coach. During the Tigers' home opener against Cleveland, his foghorn voice—once described as able to penetrate six inches of chilled steel—could scarcely be heard by his old friends in the press box. Observers attributed the fall-off in volume and vitality to a cold. In reality, he was dying of tuberculosis. "Even in his later years, when failing health and straitened finances took much of the joy out of life, Schaefer could still see the funny side," Fred Lieb wrote. "Patronage fell off, and to cut expenses Coach Schaefer was let out. 'Now, see what you birds have done,' he said half in anger and half in jest. 'You've run your losing streak so far you've run me right out of a job.'"

Schaefer's oft-stated dream was to one day own a small, cozy neighborhood saloon where every night he could entertain his friends before going upstairs to pass out drunk. But that was not to be. After Cleveland released Schaefer, New York Giants manager John J. McGraw put the sickly prankster on his team's payroll as a scout. On the morning of May 16, 1919, Schaefer was aboard a train in upstate New York when he suffered a brain hemorrhage. He was rushed to a hospital at Saranac Lake, but within an hour baseball's troubadour was dead. He was forty-three years old. Some said there was a trace of a smile on his face.

"Because he was a 'kidder' and a baseball comedian, Schaefer never got full credit for his baseball brains," eulogized the *Free Press*. "He was a good fielder and a fair hitter, but his real strength

Baseball clown Al Schacht entertains the crowd at Detroit's Navin Field before the start of the 1935 World Series. (Walter P. Reuther Library)

was in his baseball brain and in his gameness." More than a century after his passing, Schaefer is best remembered as a ballplayer-entertainer whose shenanigans helped pave the way for Nick Altrock, Al Schacht, Max Patkin, and other baseball clowns, all of whom demonstrated, to fans and owners alike, that comedy could be a profitable part of the ballpark experience.

Schaefer was buried at St. Boniface, a small German Catholic graveyard on Chicago's North Side. He's among fourteen family members crowded under a weathered nineteenth-century monument. The simple inscription, "Herman W. Schaefer," is nearly indecipherable. The stone is badly pitted.

A few months after Schaefer's death, baseball's rules committee issued an overdue clarification: "A baserunner having acquired legal title to a base cannot run bases in reverse order for the purpose of confusing the fielders or making a travesty of the game." The clause was officially known as Rule 52, Section 2. But most people in baseball referred to it as the Germany Schaefer rule.

8

Cigar Central

During Detroit's tobacco heyday, the city's cigar industry—powered principally by young, unskilled women—provided the country with an unending supply of quality nickel and dime smokes.

When looking back over her long life, Josephine Bielawski liked to toss a bit of humor into her mix of reminiscences. "I used to be a stripper," the wry octogenarian would say, waiting a moment or two before explaining, "My job was to operate a machine that stripped tobacco from the stem."

Bielawski's little joke would be lost on today's generation, which has no personal experience of those days when a small army of mostly young women punched the clock at Webster Eisenlohr, Mazur-Cressman, Essex, Bernard Schwartz, and other cigar factories in Detroit, working at tables and machines for up to sixty grueling hours a week.

While a few factories were marginally better than others, offering workers lunchrooms, showers, and even a piano player to help alleviate the strain and monotony, overall the working conditions inside the cigar plants were harsh. Clouds of tobacco dust filled nostrils and settled inside sinuses and lungs. Workers couldn't open windows because the air would dry the stock. Instead, humidifiers ran continuously, turning the factories into damp, smelly sweatshops. Head colds and sore throats were common ailments.

Kidneys took a beating, as those paid by piece resisted lavatory breaks for fear of losing several cigars.

The youngest of eight children born to Polish immigrants, Bielawski (*née* Wasilewski) was three years old when her father died. When she first donned a work apron at a neighborhood cigar plant in 1929, the teenager followed in the footsteps of generations of unskilled women—typically young and unmarried—who accepted the factories as a distasteful but traditional way of contributing to the family income. "I made twenty-five cents an hour," she said. "Each week I gave my whole paycheck to my mother."

Bielawski wound up working a dozen years at various cigar factories. She stayed long enough at the General Cigar Company, maker of White Owl cigars, to earn a silver five-year pin. She was proud of the little keepsake, a memento of a once-thriving industry that went up in smoke after World War II.

To thousands of Detroiters like Bielawski, and more so to the tobacco bosses who employed them, a cigar was much more than just a cigar. For a long stretch beginning in the latter part of the 1800s and continuing well into the twentieth century, manufacturing the pungent wrapped-leaf tubes of tobacco ranked as one of the city's top industries. "Detroit leads the world in the manufacture of cigars that sell for five cents," the *Detroit Free Press* declared in a 1911 article, with precisely "256,271,559 cigars of all kinds . . . shipped to every nook and corner of the country" the previous year. Local boosters liked to brag of the city's reputation for making the higher-quality 10-cent brands, enjoyed by discriminating smokers from coast to coast.

For all the puffing and puffery, today there are very few traces of Detroit's once prominent cigar industry. A handful of former tobacco factories remain, their aromatic old spaces repurposed for twenty-first-century use. Among them are a couple of handsome six-story brick structures built in the late 1880s: the Globe Tobacco Building on East Fort Street, now housing the offices of various tech companies and other small businesses, and the former Brown Brothers factory in Capitol Park, today the Lear Innovation and Design Center.

Another refashioned relic is the former San Telmo factory at 5716 Michigan Avenue, whose thick, century-old wooden floors now accommodate various clinics and offices. The Albert Kahn-designed building is where Theresa Koscielny (*née* Konieczny), then a fourteen-year-old girl growing up on nearby Horatio Street, found employment in 1911. Koscielny vividly recalled how she and others from her westside neighborhood worked steadily at wooden tables, cigar molds at hand. Assembling the typical cigar of filler, binder, and wrapper was labor intensive and required a certain adroitness. Workers who placed tobacco leaves in bunches were known as "bunchers," while those who shaped the tobacco into cigars were called "rollers." A day's production for an experienced worker with deft fingers was about 250 cigars.

Koscielny worked from 7 a.m. to 5 p.m. on weekdays and a half-day on Saturday, the traditional payday. She remembered earning about ten dollars a week, which she dutifully turned over to her immigrant parents.

"You were happy for the work," she said. "You could buy a pound of baloney then for a nickel."

The San Telmo cigar factory in 1916. Ninety percent of the industry's workforce were women, the majority of whom were Polish. (Author's collection)

Or, as the world had discovered, an excellent five-cent cigar. At peak production just prior to World War I, Detroit's army of stogie-stuffers was cranking out more than 1 million cigars each day. That was enough to wrap the planet with a belt of six-inch coronas laid end to end, with plenty left over to provision the city's own population of "human smokestacks."

* * *

Detroit's emergence as a cigar-making center was one of those happy accidents of timing and geography. The first small-scale operation started in 1841 with the opening of George Miller's shop on Woodward Avenue, south of Jefferson. More soon followed, as fledgling cigar makers—many of them German immigrants who transferred their Old World skills to the New—looked to service the town's burgeoning population. When the Civil War cut off the supply of Southern tobacco, the city was able to take advantage of the rich tobacco leaves being grown in southwestern Ontario. Rail and waterway connections helped move finished tobacco products—which also included snuff, cut plug (a sweetened form of chewing tobacco), and the more convenient and increasingly popular "cigar-ettes"—to points near and far. By the early 1880s, Detroit's highly regarded tobacco products crossed oceans, appearing in stores in England and Hawaii.

In the early twentieth century, cigar factories popped up along Grandy Avenue on the near east side and in the Junction-Michigan area on the west side. At the same time, the makeup of the workforce changed. Once composed largely of men, many of whom enjoyed union representation, by 1913 the workforce inside Detroit's ten largest cigar factories was 93 percent female. The vast majority were Polish, a reflection of Poles' standing as the city's largest immigrant group. As in nearly every avenue of American life, the women were paid substantially less than their male counterparts.

Several local cigar makers gained prominence and wealth. Tobacco moguls Merrill I. Mills and John J. Bagley, for example, served as Detroit mayor and Michigan governor, respectively, in the years following the Civil War. Daniel Scotten, creator of the popular

Hiawatha brand, employed 1,200 people by the 1890s. He and his nephew Oren Scotten were multimillionaires at a time when most laborers earned only a few hundred dollars a year.

Ben-Hur, Miss Detroit, and La Azora were just some of the locally produced brands that sold by the tens of millions. Capitalizing on a famous name or newsworthy event was common. Local cigar makers launched a Ty Cobb brand as the Tigers chased the pennant in 1908 and a *Spirit of St. Louis* cigar after Detroit native (and non-smoker) Charles Lindbergh flew the Atlantic in 1927. Wholesalers also made private labels—found in ashtrays throughout the city—for politicians, hotels, and such organizations as the Detroit Athletic Club. The *Free Press* had its own made-to-order line, manufactured by Brown Brothers and called Newsboy Cigars. An 1890s advertising poster published by Detroit's Calvert Lithographic Company survives at the Library of Congress. It depicts a group of young *Free Press* paperboys playing cards and enjoying a smoke, the smoldering butt of a Newsboy nickel cigar on top of the packing crate being used as a table.

The cigar-chomping denizens of Charlie Stubbs's pool hall and tobacco shop in Manistee, Michigan, pose for a photo, circa 1907. Given Detroit's far-reaching reputation for quality smokes, the cigar stand likely carried Ben-Hur, Miss Detroit, La Azora, and other popular brands manufactured in the city's many tobacco plants. (Author's collection)

Mechanization and the Great Depression were a one-two punch, resulting in lost jobs and pay cuts. By the 1930s, many factories had installed giant cigar-making machines requiring a crew of four to operate. One worker was a "feeder" who fed it a constant supply of tobacco. "You can always tell the cigar workers that are feeders because their faces are all marked from the tobacco dust," one employee told a *Detroit News* reporter. "You don't stay pretty long if you work one of those machines." The smudged faces didn't dissuade foremen from making unwelcome advances. Those who resisted the come-ons risked being fired, which kept this harassment a chronic problem.

Despite a major strike in 1916–17 in which workers wrangled an across-the-board pay raise, cigar bosses had generally always dismissed their female employees as docile and unorganized. So factory owners were surprised in early 1937 when workers, upset over wage cuts, speed-ups, unhealthy working conditions, and sexual harassment, and inspired by the historic sit-down strike by autoworkers in Flint, seized and shut down a succession of cigar plants. The first was the Webster Eisenlohr factory at 5535 Grandy Avenue, where women conducted a sit-in on February 16, 1937. Soon some 2,500 workers occupied a half-dozen cigar factories.

Mayor Frank Couzens was unsympathetic to strikers. At General Cigar, organizers narrowly escaped club-wielding goons by jumping out a second-story window. Elsewhere, hundreds of policemen stormed the Bernard Schwartz plant on East Milwaukee Street with orders to forcibly evict the sit-downers. The first cop to come through the door was met by a woman swinging a broom. In a floor-by-floor battle, workers belted the police with heavy wooden cigar molds and anything else that was handy. Outside the plant, picketers hurled rocks, bricks, and snowballs as police dragged strikers out—some by their hair—and loaded them into the waiting paddy wagons. There were several injuries, including a pregnant bystander whom a mounted policeman clubbed in the head.

The brutal crackdown helped turn public opinion against the cigar makers. Four days after the melee at the Bernard Schwartz plant, trade unionists and their supporters held a massive rally

Cigar workers, fed up with wage cuts, poor working conditions, and the lack of union representation, walk the picket line during the 1937 strike. Signs read "Factories Are Not Prisons" and "We Demand Shop Elections." (Walter P. Reuther Library)

in Cadillac Square. Labor organizer Victor Reuther warned cigar bosses that for every subsequent eviction there would be two new plant occupations—no idle threat in a city that saw at least 130 different sites struck by sit-downers in 1937 alone. Eventually the protection and support of the United Auto Workers and the intervention of Governor Frank Murphy forced employers to recognize the United Cigar Workers of America. The women negotiated a 20-percent raise and a 40-hour week. Soon Detroit was producing tens of thousands of boxes of union-labeled cigars.

Workers had won the battle for union representation, but it turned out to be a Pyrrhic victory. Companies continued to leave the city for the South, where labor was cheaper and unorganized. Detroit's cigar industry was already in decline, as automation reduced the need for workers and smokers increasingly preferred cigarettes. By 1956 the number of cigar makers in the city directory had dwindled to just three. Within another dozen years the last of them was stubbed out. A few tangy-scented workplaces remained, along with the occasional whiff of nostalgia over a now-vanished industry.

The flashpoint of the 1967 riot was a predawn raid on a blind pig operating above the Economy Printing Company on 12th Street. (Author's collection)

9

There's Trouble in Detroit

The 12th Street riot of July 1967 came out of nowhere—or did it? Here is a look back at the days of rage that shook a city to its core.

In those years before an explosion of anarchy made "riot" the ugliest four-letter word in Detroit's lexicon, the 12th Street neighborhood was like no other, insists Darryle Buchanan. It was a robust city-within-a-city crowded with attractions ranging from the respectable to the roguish. "There were stores, there were theaters, there were restaurants, I mean, it was a fully self-contained area," recalls the lifelong Detroiter, who grew up on Virginia Park. "There was no reason for you to ever leave that neighborhood to do anything." Hustlers, street vendors, and speakeasies thrived alongside mom-and-pop shops and storefront churches in what was then the most densely populated section of Detroit.

Then came that one hot stretch in July 1967, when the youngster's comfortably circumscribed world fell to ashes. Buchanan remembers indiscriminate looting, raging fires, burning rats fleeing collapsed buildings, and the numbed fascination with which he watched a week of ungraspable chaos unfold. Despite family warnings to stay off 12th Street, he kept returning. "Each time I went back, there was less and less of 12th Street than I remembered," he says. The soundtrack to the ongoing havoc was the "constant drone of sirens that just never went away. After a while, it just started to sound like wailing, like crying. It's almost like the city was dying and it's that crying sound that you heard. It was eerie, you can't forget it, you never forget that."

Revolution? Uprising? Rebellion? While there is an ongoing debate over what to call Detroit's 1967 civil disturbance, there's little disagreement that it remains the seismic event in the city's long history. But was it inevitable? Outsiders generally viewed Detroit in the 1960s as a prosperous if slightly frayed community that, for all of the typical postwar urban woes, seemed to have a handle on its problems. At the time the country's fifth-largest city, it was the legendary home of the automobile industry and the cradle of organized labor, the coupling of which had produced a middle class unimaginable to earlier generations of Americans. The city boasted the country's largest black-owned business in Motown Records and was considered safe and attractive enough to be a serious candidate to host the Olympic Games. But social scientists and historians taking a deeper look have since revealed the city was blithely perched on the cusp of an apocalypse.

In the view of Frank Rashid, whose family owned a store on Linwood that looters sacked during the "insurrection," the violence of July 1967 "was a symptom, not the cause" of a myriad of societal problems that he saw first-hand growing up in a two-family flat at 2511 Lathrop: institutionalized racism, high Black unemployment, and growing disinvestment in the city. "Those conditions were already in place," says Rashid, professor emeritus of English at Marygrove. "The riot just exacerbated them."

This disparity between perception and reality accounts for the shock many people from the era still express over the suddenness with which the city they thought they knew fell to ashes. "I was astounded," says Eileen Glick, who grew up in St. Clair Shores and today lives in Arizona. "I never knew that kind of outburst was brewing. I don't know that anybody knew—except perhaps the people in the area where the riot broke out."

In the selective, sepia-soaked memories of Glick and many others, the Detroit of the 1950s and '60s was a blissful place to live, work, and play. "My childhood was very typical of the babyboom generation," says Glick. "There were a thousand kids in my neighborhood and everybody knew everyone. You felt safe, secure." Her father, a builder, was responsible for many of the new houses popping up in the rapidly expanding suburbs.

Glick spun 45s at backyard record parties, danced at sock hops at Notre Dame and Denby high schools, took excursions to Bob-Lo, Edgewater Park, and Eastland Mall, rode the Jefferson bus downtown, swam in Lake St. Clair, and hung out at the Tastee Freez at 7 Mile and Kelly Street. Upon graduation from Regina High School in 1966, the future marketing professional plopped down a $500 deposit on a new '67 Malibu at Gene Merollis Chevrolet. "It was so cool—metallic gold with a black vinyl top. And it had an AM radio with reverb." Glick's two-door Chevy cost $2,750, roughly half the average annual salary of a full-time American worker.

Detroit's Black middle class was the envy of the country, says James Turner, a Detroit contractor who grew up in Ecorse. "Like many Blacks, my parents came from the South without a high school diploma and still managed to make a good living here," he says. "In many ways, it was a great period to be a youngster. The Temptations and the Supremes were riding high at Motown, and as a kid you really weren't aware of the stress the Black community was under."

The complexion of the city had changed dramatically within a single generation, from 9 percent Black in 1940 to an estimated 40 percent in 1967. Many of the unemployed were poorly educated Southern migrants who continued to view Detroit as an industrial mecca, despite gains in automation that by the mid-1950s were already making many unskilled factory jobs obsolete. Increased competition in the form of smaller, cheaper imports was also beginning to take a bite out of the Big Three automakers' traditional dominance. The closing of Hudson Motors and Packard, as well as drastic labor cuts by Chrysler, the city's largest employer, had eliminated several thousand jobs. Black employees, historically the last hired and the first fired, took the brunt of these layoffs.

Detroit's population peaked at nearly 2 million in 1953, then began a slow slide as the cheaper and more open spaces of the countryside beckoned. Automakers and their suppliers had started building factories in outlying farmland during World War II. By 1966, more than 20,000 White Detroiters a year were moving to the suburbs, their exodus aided by the postwar freeway system that carved up many of the city's stable, existing neighborhoods. "Urban removal," as many Black residents referred to the city's ambitious urban renewal policies, resulted in the paving over many of the traditionally Black neighborhoods on the near east side. Displaced residents poured into the 12th Street neighborhood, making it the most densely populated in the city.

Stoking the growing sense of militant discontent among Black residents was the everyday bigotry they continued to encounter. The Detroit Police Department, which had not integrated its patrol cars until 1959, was notoriously racist, its "Big 4" units of burly enforcers a bitter memory to those they manhandled on a whim.

"As a young Black male, you definitely were targeted," says Turner. Harassment was even worse in Detroit's three largest suburbs—Livonia, Warren, and Dearborn—none of which had more than a dozen Black residents in 1967. "You'd get through Dearborn as fast as possible. You ate or shopped and then got out. No loitering, no lingering."

When a young Irish-Catholic liberal named Jerry Cavanagh became mayor in 1961, the city's population was declining, the tax base was shrinking, and neighborhoods were deteriorating. But as a pet of the Democratic White House, Cavanagh was able to get $42 million in federal funds for various anti-poverty programs. In 1963, he linked arms with the Rev. Martin Luther King Jr. and United Auto Workers President Walter Reuther as 125,000 Black and White Detroiters peacefully marched down Woodward. King capped the "Walk to Freedom" by giving his famous "I Have a Dream" speech for the first time.

As the 1960s marched on, Detroiters by and large remained optimistic—and oblivious. "That sort of thing can't happen here," was the common refrain after the Watts district of Los Angeles, just one of scores of inner-city tinderboxes poised to explode, went up in flames in 1965. But two summers later, it did happen here.

"A few people saw what was going on in Detroit," says Rashid. "Just not enough."

* * *

It all began in the pre-dawn hours of Sunday, July 23, 1967, the start to another scorching summer day. Undercover police from the 10th Precinct conducted a routine raid on an after-hours joint above the Economy Printing Company at the corner of 12th and Clairmount. They expected to find fifteen or twenty people inside the blind pig. Instead, more than eighty partygoers were celebrating the homecoming of two soldiers back from Vietnam. Police let the women go but detained the men. Officers called for paddy wagons to transport the revelers.

A growing crowd of onlookers, initially more curious than confrontational, was milling around when David Bruce and his partner arrived. They were among the first uniformed officers on the scene. There was some good-natured ribbing. A chant went up: "Let 'em go. Let 'em go."

"There was this one guy across the street, he had a green polyester shirt . . . he was the one that was agitating," said Bruce (whose reminiscences, like some others in this narrative, are from the oral histories gathered by the Detroit Historical Museum for its Detroit '67 project). "The auto got there, that was prisoner transport, men started coming down, getting into the prisoner transport. The last one that came down was drunk, I mean he was drunk-drunk. When he went to step onto the auto to go in the back, he fell. Guy across the street—the guy I call Mr. Greensleeves—said, 'Look, they knocked him down.' That's when the bottles and stuff came at us. We started calling for help."

A police lieutenant arrived and took a brick to the head. With that, 12th Street slid into mobocracy. Windows were smashed. Alarms clanged. Sirens sang. Reinforcements came but were instructed to hang back. The hands-off approach emboldened the crowd. Events spiraled out of control. "There was a shoe store there called Cancellation Shoes and they had very good quality shoes, so people were breaking in there, stealing the shoes," Bruce said.

"They were breaking into the restaurants. The thing about it is, White people were helping Black people steal, Black people were helping White people steal, so it definitely wasn't a race thing, it was definitely—I guess they call it a 'civil disobedience.' "

There was an almost carnival atmosphere. "We saw people cutting through the alley carrying couches, carrying chairs, carrying dinette sets, refrigerators," recalled Albert Colbard, who lived a few doors down from Economy Printing. "This one guy had a refrigerator on a dolly. On a dolly!"

Word of the shopping spree raced through the neighborhood. The frenzied ransacking might ordinarily have spent itself as soon as looters emptied all the shelves and the temperature climbed. But soon fires started breaking out. Black youths threw rocks and bricks at responding firefighters, some of whom pulled the lids off garbage cans to use as shields. Commanders sent out an all-Black unit, but it, too, was assaulted. One of the first buildings to go up was a furniture store—a spectacular blaze, said Colbard, who was forced to hose down his roof. "Now it got really, really serious. Because then you have the fire department coming to put the fires out, and somebody started shooting at the fire department. They would leave and just let something burn." It was a breezy day, which helped disperse the fluttering waves of twinkling red embers. Ultimately, fire destroyed 20 percent of the buildings on 12th Street around Virginia Park.

As Sunday wore on, a dirty gray haze spread ominously across the clear blue sky. The crowd watching the Tigers-Yankees doubleheader at Tiger Stadium began to stir. There appeared to be a major fire in the distance. Those listening to the game on WJR were kept in the dark. Announcers Ernie Harwell and Ray Lane were instructed to talk nothing but baseball.

The curl of smoke drifting from the backyard of Alice Nigoghosian's home on Central near West Chicago signaled a good meal in the making as her mother grilled lamb chops on the small brick fireplace. One of the dinner guests had a police scanner in his car. "Do you know what's going on?" he said upon arriving. "There's trouble in Detroit."

Nigoghosian went inside and turned on the television. Nothing. There was a news blackout. "So all afternoon, I kept returning to the car for updates," she says today. "I couldn't believe what I was hearing. You could hear yelling, screaming, firemen were being shot at."

All day Sunday, the rioting spread through the west side—along 14th Street, Linwood, Dexter, Grand River, and Livernois—with looting and fires breaking out on the east side around Mack and Van Dyke. Local Black leaders, including Congressman John Conyers and city councilman Nicholas Hood, were jeered and run off when they tried to calm rioters. "The insurgents were going to do with their neighborhood what they wanted to do," Coleman Young, then a state representative, said in his autobiography, "and to hell with anybody who got in their way." Some business owners scrawled "Soul Brother" and "Afro All the Way" on their storefronts to dissuade looters. Sometimes it worked; often it didn't. Some stores became targets because the owner had a poor reputation with customers.

Mutual respect appears to have saved the Grande Ballroom on Grand River, just a few blocks from the riot's epicenter. The rock

Many Black-owned businesses, hoping to be spared in the wave of arson and looting, painted "Soul Brother" on their storefronts. (Author's collection)

venue's impresario, Dearborn disc jockey Russ Gibb, rushed to the site with two musician friends, hoping to load valuable equipment into a trailer before rioters got to it. Gibb was admittedly scared. To his surprise and relief, rioters touched neither his crew nor the building. According to Gibb, "We had cut a deal with some of the neighbors that we would pick up the mess that our kids made after each show. We tried to treat them as though we were a guest in their community."

Authorities hastily mobilized thousands of police and National Guardsmen, calling many back from vacation. They imposed a 9 p.m. curfew and banned liquor and ammunition sales. Families huddled behind locked doors, away from windows, and tried to process what was happening.

Curiosity got the better of Richard Rybinski, a lifelong Detroiter then living on Hancock. After watching the fires from the roof of his apartment building with friends, he rode his bike down Grand River in the wee hours of Monday for a closer look. He came across a kid, maybe twelve years old, pulling a wagon. In it was a large television set. Rybinski asked if he could bum a cigarette.

"What kind you smoke?" the boy asked.

"Camel."

"Wait a minute," the kid said. "Watch my TV."

"He stepped through the window of this convenience store," Rybinski recalled. "He obviously knew his way around it. Went over to a counter, came out, had a couple of packs with him, and he handed me a pack of Camels." Rybinski thanked him, and both continued on their separate ways.

Not all encounters were so innocuous. The riot's first "official" victim, forty-five-year-old Walter Grzanka, had been shot dead a couple of hours earlier by a shopkeeper while stealing cigars and shoelaces from the Temple Market on Fourth Street. Grzanka was an anomaly; nearly every one of the looters who would die in the next few days were young to middle-aged Black males, several of whom were employed family men caught up in their greed. Their number included two men, both autoworkers, found asphyxiated in the basement of Brown's Drugstore on 12th Street.

Some business owners stubbornly defended their property. One of them, sixty-eight-year-old George Messerlian, was barely five feet tall. Nonetheless, when teens burst into his shoe repair shop on Linwood on the opening day of the riot, he stood his ground. They struck him repeatedly with a thick, thirty-inch club. He died four days later.

Most of the pillaging was over by Sunday night, as authorities deployed groups of National Guardsmen willy-nilly to protect firemen, guard property, man checkpoints, and enforce the curfew. Then the alleged sniping began in earnest. Bullets struck at least a dozen people on Monday. Rumors flew that the sniping was organized, with gunmen brought in from out of town. However, most of the firing was slapdash. One police official dismissed the notion of a cabal of outside agitators as "a damn poor performance for a professional ring, if there is such a thing."

It would later turn out skittish, undertrained, and trigger-happy guardsmen were responsible for much of the gunfire. One member, Jim Atkin of Dearborn, admits today that the state's weekend warriors were unprepared for what they encountered. "Yes, most of the fellows in my unit all had our marksmanship medals and stuff, and we can take orders, we can march, we can do our job, but . . . the street situation? No, it was all new to us."

The result would be numerous tragedies in the coming days. On one occasion, a businesswoman from out of town turned on a lamp inside her motel room window. Bullets flew out of the darkness, killing her. On another, a tank took aim on an apartment where a sniper was supposedly holing up. Machine-gun bullets ripped through the flimsy wooden walls, shredding four-year-old Tanya Blanding. She was the riot's youngest victim. According to the *Detroit Free Press*, which won a Pulitzer Prize for its coverage, guardsmen were involved in at least eleven deaths, nine of them innocent.

Monday, July 24, was Detroit's 266th birthday, an occasion marked by more than 600 alarms and a long string of deaths, mostly looters. Tigers owner John Fetzer offered to have the team play a televised game inside a closed, empty Tiger Stadium, hoping to keep baseball-loving arsonists indoors. Instead, officials moved the scheduled home series with the Orioles to Baltimore. Mickey Lolich couldn't go; the pitcher received instructions to report for National Guard duty.

Law-abiding folks in the affected areas tried to make sense of what was going on. Anita Hadley, then eleven years old, recalls being sequestered at night with siblings and visiting cousins in the basement of the family home on Helen, between Vernor and Charlevoix, as gunshots popped and smoke drifted over the neighborhood. "We had a corner store that was on Vernor," she said, "and they were owned by some Italian people, and they were very good to everybody. They would let you buy stuff and pay for it later, and I remember that my dad and a lot of people got together to protect the guy's store, and said, 'We're going to take care of Al's store. We're not going to let anybody burn or mess with his store.'"

The inferno engulfing Detroit dominated print and broadcast news and was the sole topic of conversation. The images were frightening. There was no denying the city resembled a war zone, complete with tanks, jeeps, and helicopters. Miles from the action, neighbors gathered on lawns, talking in hushed tones while pointing at the sky. Residents brought hunting rifles out of closets. Several suburbs enacted curfews. Orville Hubbard, the unapologetically racist mayor of Dearborn, stationed police all along its border with Detroit. People sat on roofs in the muggy night air and marveled over the soft orange glow in the distance.

Late Monday night, responding to requests by Mayor Cavanagh and Governor George Romney, President Lyndon Johnson went on national television to announce a federal state of emergency now existed in Detroit and that 4,700 members of the 82nd and 101st Airborne would be sent to help restore order. The first contingents of paratroopers, many combat-tested, began arriving early Tuesday. Commanders assigned the airborne units, their ranks thoroughly integrated, to the east side of Woodward. Displaying the kind of breezy self-confidence that comes with jumping out of perfectly good airplanes, they used a light hand in quickly securing that part of town. Richard Rybinski approached one trooper guarding the

Army airborne units rolled into Detroit on the morning of the riot's third day. This sergeant is standing guard while Detroit Edison crews do a damage assessment. (Collections of The Henry Ford)

Detroit Institute of Arts. How did all this compare with Vietnam? "Piece of cake, man," he replied.

On the west side, guardsmen and Detroit and state police continued to employ a heavy, uneven hand. The most infamous incident to emerge from the riot occurred the night of July 25–26. Police and guardsmen stormed the annex of the rundown Algiers Motel on Woodward at Virginia Park. They encountered three Black teens among the occupants—Carl Cooper, Aubrey Pollard, and Fred Temple—and two young White girls, runaways from Ohio. Officers killed the three males with shotgun blasts at close range, though the exact circumstances remain unsettled. The three

Detroit officers ultimately charged with their murders claimed the victims were snipers. John Hersey, author of 1968's *The Algiers Motel Incident*, speculated that the death of Jerry Olshove, the only policeman killed during the riot, may have set the police off.

"Fred was not someone who would handle a gun," insists Michael "Doc" Holbrook, a streetwise Detroiter who was friends with Temple. Holbrook spent part of his childhood in the South and learned to respect the outsized power of a White man with a badge and a grudge. Temple "was in the wrong place at the wrong time," he said. "I know his crime, his sin, was he was there with White girls, and I know how that could go down because I was in a situation similar to that but had the smarts to leave. Wasn't going to stick around and say, 'Well, we're not doing nothing. We have the right.' No. See, that's the type of thing where a lot of people, they get in trouble. And they can easily lose their lives if you don't understand the situation. And when you're looking at someone who has a weapon that can take your life and they have the authority, there's no reasoning, no rational discretion, if they are of the mindset that you are something less than."

Heavy publicity surrounding the case would cause authorities to move the officers' trials outstate. All were acquitted, enraging the Black community. The killings reinforced their belief that July '67 was in a very real sense a "police riot," an unrestrained expansion of the everyday harassment that had helped trigger the riot in the first place. White policemen or guardsmen killed twenty-four Black residents. Many were shot under murky circumstances, where official reports clashed significantly with eyewitness accounts.

Looters and curfew violators accounted for most of the 7,200-plus arrests. Prisoners were stuffed into precinct cells, station house basements and garages, buses, and the elephant cage at the Belle Isle zoo. They ate baloney sandwiches and sweltered in the heat as they waited their turn before a judge. One defendant admitted to torching a building, but only to burn out his cheating girlfriend and lover inside. Another was asked about the new appliance found in his car trunk. "I didn't loot that," he argued. "I bought it from a guy at a traffic stop. I gave him a five-dollar bill for a washing machine."

Only 3 percent of the cases ever went to trial, and just half of those wound up in convictions. Not a single person was convicted of sniping.

As the week wore on, firefighters struggled to contain the seemingly endless number of blazes. "I learned a great respect for firemen at that time," Jim Atkin said, "because it didn't matter what the color was of the area. If there was a fire, they went to put out the fire." By the time firefighters doused the last of the 1,600 fires, more than 1,700 firefighters from Detroit and forty-four nearby communities, including Windsor, had risked their lives. Two Detroit firemen died. One was struck by a stray bullet; the other was electrocuted.

By Thursday, July 27, some 17,000 soldiers and policemen were keeping the peace. Police shot dead the last looter the previous night, a young White man who had been caught stealing a four-dollar part in an auto junkyard on Joseph Campau. The city had finally calmed down. Authorities released thousands of prisoners and ordered guardsmen to unload their weapons and sheath their bayonets. There was a general air of exhaustion, even among suburbanites who had done nothing more stressful than watch news coverage all week with a pellet rifle propped up against the sofa. Federal troops began to withdraw on Friday. Camera-toting gawkers toured gutted neighborhoods, auguring Detroit's future as a destination for ruin-porn aficionados. The last victims of the violence lingered in hospital beds. The final death was Roy Banks, who succumbed August 14 to gunshot wounds received three weeks earlier. The forty-six-year-old deaf-mute had been walking to work when police mistook him for a looter, one of many dubious claims made by officers in fatal shootings.

To this day, many people in the Black community believe the riot's death toll was higher than authorities reported, insisting that an unknown number of bodies were cremated inside burning buildings, dumped into sewers, or secretly buried. The official figure stands at forty-three deaths: thirty-three Black residents and ten White residents. Property damage was in the range of $40 million to $80 million. About 2,500 stores were looted or burned, and 690 buildings had to be torn down. The riot left nearly 400 families homeless. Many businesses never reopened or moved, a blow to devastated neighborhoods. Price gouging was rampant.

Sociologists and urban historians generally regard the 12th Street riot as an opportunistic uprising against society's ingrained inequalities. From a child's simple perspective, the "revolt" was as incomprehensible as it was overwhelming. "It was a bad summer for us kids," said Anita Hadley, recalling the widespread despair left in its wake. "Everything you knew that was familiar was gone . . . the dry cleaners, the grocery stores, meat market, and everything was just burnt and gone. To this day it's still gone . . . it was always so nice because these people that we shopped with, they knew us kids, they knew us by name, and a lot of them were White. Italians, Jewish people, most of the people that owned the businesses were White people. But, it was sad . . . we wouldn't see them again, they wouldn't see us. We didn't understand, but everything that we knew that was familiar wasn't there anymore."

Various public and private initiatives arose in response to the riot, including a state housing act that was stronger than existing federal law and aggressive minority hiring programs. The Detroit Police Department doubled its number of Black officers while the State Police hired the first Black trooper in its fifty-year history. Programs like FOCUS: Hope and New Detroit arose to address social and economic inequities. Nothing stemmed the exodus of families, businesses, and tax dollars from the polarized city, a migration that accelerated with the election of its first Black mayor six years later. "I was taking over the administration of Detroit because the White people didn't want the damn thing anymore," Coleman Young claimed. The seminal event in Detroit's long history would remain the country's deadliest riot until Los Angeles blew up over the acquittal of police officers in the Rodney King case in 1992.

Twelfth Street was renamed Rosa Parks Boulevard in 1976. Its scorched contours have been ponderously reworked beyond recognition. Stripped of its name and its personality but not its past, it occupies a bittersweet spot in Darryle Buchanan's heart. It once was the city's most vibrant neighborhood, and then suddenly it wasn't, he said. "It was like it just died, and it never, ever came back."

In the immediate aftermath of the riot, sixteen-year-old Detroiter Phil Cherner took photographs of his devastated surroundings, including this image of charred trees and smoldering rubble on Pingree Street. (Phil Cherner)

The Victims

The official death toll of the 12th Street riot is forty-three people, with all but three of the fatalities males. The deadliest day was July 24—Detroit's 266th birthday—with seventeen people either shot or electrocuted.

Sunday, July 23

Krikor "George" Messerlian (68, White). Storeowner beaten by teens at about 4 p.m. while defending his shoe repair shop at 7711 Linwood. Died on July 27 at Henry Ford Hospital.

Sheren George (23, White). Car passenger struck in the chest by an unknown shooter at 11:30 p.m. as her husband tried to drive past a mob at Woodward and Melbourne. The mother of two, reportedly pregnant, died overnight at Highland Park General Hospital.

Willie Hunter (26, Black) and **Price Williams** (32, Black). Apparent looters trapped by fire in the basement of Brown's Drugstore on 12th Street and asphyxiated. They were last seen together on Sunday evening. Their charred, decomposing bodies were discovered on July 26. Although time of death was impossible to determine, it's very possible they were the first victims of the riot.

Monday, July 24

Walter Grzanka (45, White). Shot about midnight by shopkeeper while looting Temple Market on 4th Street. Pronounced dead at 12:25 a.m. at Detroit General Hospital, the first official fatality of the riot. (Sheren George would die an hour later.)

Clifton Pryor (23, White). Alleged rooftop sniper killed by National Guardsman at 2:45 a.m. Witnesses maintain the unarmed victim was one of several tenants at 667 West Alexandrine guarding against sparks from nearby fires.

John Ashby (24, White). Detroit fireman electrocuted at 3:30 a.m. when his metal helmet touched a high-voltage line while fighting a blaze at Canton and Lafayette. Died August 5 at Detroit General Hospital.

Fred Williams (49, Black). Homeowner electrocuted at about 7 a.m. by a downed power line in the alley behind his burning residence at 9541 Goodwin.

Herman Ector (30, Black). Shot at 9:45 a.m. by Waverly Solomon, an unlicensed security guard who claimed that his rifle went off when Ector tried to grab it.

Daniel Jennings (36, Black). Killed by storeowner during a noontime break-in at Stanley Meszczenski's drugstore at 6000 John R.

Robert Beal (49, Black). Shot dead at 1:25 p.m. by police while looting Rite-Way Auto Parts at 9335 Oakland.

Joseph Chandler (34, Black). Looter fatally wounded by Detroit police after fleeing the Food Time Market on Second Street. Pronounced dead at 1:45 p.m.

Herman Canty (46, Black). Shot in the neck by police at about 2:30 p.m. as he drove off in a van with goods stolen from the Bi-Lo Supermarket on West Grand Boulevard.

Alfred Peachlum (35, Black). Killed by police at about 4 p.m. while looting the A & P supermarket at 3430 Joy Road.

Alphonso Smith (35, Black). Shot by police at 4:15 p.m. inside the Standard Food Market at 9750 Dexter.

Nathaniel Edmunds (23, Black). Edmunds, an Army veteran and Ford worker, was shot dead at 4:30 p.m. on Baldwin near Harper by a White man, Richard Paul Shugar, who accused him of breaking into a nearby store. Shugar was later convicted by an all-White jury of second-degree murder.

Edward Kemp (35, Black). Looter shot in the back by police and National Guardsmen at 5:20 p.m. as he fled Borghi Brothers market on Mack.

Richard Sims (35, Black). Shot by police in a neighbor's driveway at about 8:30 p.m. after he was spotted trying to break into the Hobby Bar at Linwood and Buena Vista.

Frank Tanner (19, Black). Mortally wounded by police on Monday evening after he ran from a pharmacy at East Grand Boulevard and Helen. Tenants of the building where he collapsed ignored his groans and didn't call for help. Tanner was finally taken to Detroit General Hospital the following morning and pronounced dead at 8:05 a.m.

Carl Smith (30, White). Detroit fireman shot through the head at 11:30 p.m. at the corner of St. Jean and Mack, during a period of heavy rifle fire. The fatal shot, initially attributed to a sniper, was likely fired by a National Guardsman.

Manuel Cosby (26, Black). Killed by police at around midnight as he ran from N & T Grocery at 4441 East Nevada.

Tuesday, July 25

Henry Denson (27, Black). Shot dead by a guardsman at about 1 a.m. after the car he was riding in allegedly ran a checkpoint on Mack near East Grand Boulevard. Witnesses disputed official reports that the driver had tried to run down police and guardsmen.

Julius Dorsey (55, Black). Security guard accidentally shot outside the fruit market he was protecting at 1000 Field. The guardsman who killed him at about 1:30 a.m. was responding to reports of looters in the vicinity.

Jerome Olshove (32, White). The only policeman to die was shot in the stomach when another officer's shotgun discharged during a struggle with a looter. The incident took place at about 3 a.m. outside the A & P store at 121 Holbrook.

Roy Banks (46, Black). A deaf and mute person shot at 4:30 a.m. while walking to work on Crane Street, near Rohns. Guardsmen maintained they spotted him looting a bar at Mack and Rohns. Died on August 14.

Ronald Evans (24, Black) and **William Jones** (28, Black). Killed by multiple gunshots from Detroit police and guardsmen early Tuesday after being caught stealing beer from Bob's Market at 4100 Pennsylvania. Several witnesses disputed the police officers' claims that the men, both drunk and unarmed, tried to flee.

Arthur Johnson (36, Black) and **Perry Williams** (36, Black). Killed by Detroit police at about 3 p.m. inside Sherman's Loans at 1401 Holbrook.

Jack Sydnor (38, Black). The only known sniper to die was killed by police at 9:45 p.m. Sydnor was drunk when he started shooting his pistol out the window of his third-floor apartment on Hazelhurst. He managed to wound one policeman before being killed.

Tanya Blanding (4, Black). Killed on Tuesday night by .50-caliber machine-gun fire directed against her family's second-floor apartment at 1756 West Euclid. The National Guard tank commander who ordered the bursts believed sniper fire originated from the building.

John LeRoy (30, Black). Among a carload of men fired on by National Guardsmen shortly before midnight as they drove on Lycaste, near Charlevoix. Died on July 28 at Detroit General Hospital.

Wednesday, July 26

Helen Hall (51, White). Shot through the heart at about 1 a.m. as she opened the drapes of her fourth-floor room at the Harlan House Motel at 6500 John Lodge Freeway. Evidence indicated a National Guard or police bullet killed the Connecticut businesswoman.

Aubrey Pollard (19, Black), **Carl Cooper** (17, Black), and **Fred Temple** (18, Black). Killed during an overnight raid on the Algiers Motel at Woodward and Virginia Park. Each was shot at close range with a shotgun. The Detroit officers charged with murder and conspiracy in their deaths were later acquitted.

The three teenagers who were shot dead by police inside the Algiers Motel on July 26, 1967. From left: Fred Temple, Aubrey Pollard, and Carl Cooper. (Author's collection)

Larry Post (26, White). The only National Guardsman to die was accidentally killed by fellow guardsmen opening fire on a car that reportedly ran a roadblock at Dexter and Richton early Wednesday morning. The curfew violators, three White men in their early twenties, claimed they were beaten with Blackjacks inside a locked room by 10th Precinct officers; one suffered a broken jaw.

Willie McDaniels (23, Black). Shot in the head by police at about 2:30 p.m. after fleeing the Domestic Outfitting store at 6858 Gratiot. Died the following evening.

George Talbert (20, Black). Unarmed pedestrian shot at about 5 p.m. by a guardsman as he walked on LaSalle Gardens South, near 12th Street. Died on August 5 at Henry Ford Hospital. The

National Guard said he was shot for refusing to obey an order to halt.

Julius Lust (26, White). Shot dead by police at about 9:30 p.m. while trying to steal a water pump at the G & W Auto Parts junkyard at 17130 Joseph Campau.

Albert Robinson (38, Black). Shot and bayoneted by National Guardsmen Wednesday evening after they stormed an apartment building at Davison and La Salle in search of snipers. Died on August 5 at Detroit General Hospital.

Friday, July 28

William N. Dalton (19, Black). Suspected arsonist shot by an unidentified policeman shortly after midnight. Witnesses said officers took him into an alley on Grand River near Arcadia and goaded him into running.

Saturday, July 29

Ernest Roquemore (19, Black). Shot in the back by a paratrooper who was allegedly aiming at an armed suspect fleeing a raided flat at 3484 St. Jean. Pronounced dead at 7:40 p.m.

Henry and Edsel Ford at the introduction of the 1928 Model A that replaced the iconic Model T. "Henry," said a rival automaker, "I don't envy you a damn thing except that boy of yours." (Collections of The Henry Ford)

10

The Edsel Enigma

He was an inspired auto stylist, an aviation pioneer, a generous benefactor of the arts, a visionary industrialist, and a fixture of society. So why is Edsel "the forgotten Ford"?

One day in 1933, several members of the Senate committee investigating the banking crisis in Detroit stood in front of the Senate Office Building. A member of Washington's press corps, looking to take a photograph of this self-important group, lowered his Speed Graphic just long enough to shoo a wiry, elegantly attired fellow out of the frame.

"Bud, would you mind?" he said. "This is just for big shots."

Edsel Ford, who had just testified before the committee, didn't mind. Once again, the son of the richest and most famous person on the planet obligingly dissolved into the background. Throughout his life, it was a spot where his accommodating nature routinely and comfortably placed him.

Edsel has been correctly labeled "the forgotten Ford." In histories and public memory, the outsize personalities of his father Henry, the fabled "Flivver King," and the equally colorful Henry Ford II, Edsel's oldest son, too often overshadow the accomplishments of this quiet, good man. Today, when his name pops up at all, it's usually as a metaphor for colossal failure. Ford launched the midsize Edsel with the horse-collar grille in 1957, in the midst of a severe economic recession, and it became a disaster of timing and design. Critics called it the New Coke of the Eisenhower era.

This association with failure is especially galling to those who know of the character and achievements of Henry's only child. Of his creativity in designing such cars as the Model A and Lincoln Zephyr, of his pioneering work in aviation, and of his many philanthropies, particularly his patronage of the Detroit Institute of Arts. There, his most visible contribution to the city—Diego Rivera's homage to the assembly line, *Detroit Industry*—continues to draw admiration in the museum's courtyard.

Edsel's own father must take much of the blame for history's neglect. According to "Cast Iron Charlie" Sorenson, the company's longtime production chief, Henry's treatment of Edsel was Ford's "greatest tragedy"—an assessment that nobody close to the family drama would dare challenge.

Because of the rank and file's hatred of Henry and his handpicked security chief, a bull-necked Svengali named Harry Bennett, "some of that feeling rubbed off on Edsel," said Paul Boatin, a former autoworker and union official whose face appears in one of the Rivera murals. "Edsel Ford had a kind of funny image with workers. There wasn't a hell of a lot of negative stuff written or said about him."

Boatin admitted that his own view softened after he heard rumors of Edsel's prior treatment at the hands of old Henry. He also came to admire his staunch support of Rivera's controversial murals, which cloaked ordinary working men in unaccustomed dignity.

"Poor Edsel," Boatin said. "Throughout his life he was never given much credit."

Getting to know Edsel Ford has never been easy. In a quarter century as president of the company, he never conducted a single business press conference. When reporters approached him for a quote, he politely steered them away. "See Father," he'd say. They always did.

At the Ford Archives in Dearborn, the repository for most documents relating to the company, his personal files are distressingly threadbare. One day in the early 1960s, Henry II had the files purged. He also removed the family's medical records from Henry Ford Hospital. "Hank the Deuce"—who before his death would destroy his own personal papers to thwart biographers—was determined that nobody ever would examine his life, or the life of his unsung father, in great detail. The lack of primary source material so frustrated bestselling biographer Robert Lacey when he came to Grosse Pointe that he gave up his original notion of exploring Edsel's life and instead turned to a full-blown study of the Ford Family.

Odds are that there was nothing eye-opening or salacious in the pitched files. Edsel was averse to scandal and self-promotion, which helps explain why his story has never been grist for mainstream publishers. Niche publishers have put out the smattering of books about him with small print runs. Retired engineer and Ford historian Henry Dominguez collaborated with legendary designer E. T. "Bob" Gregorie on one such title for the Society of Automotive Engineers. "I wish there was something spicy about Edsel Ford that we could put in this chapter, you know, liven it up a little," Gregorie told Dominguez at one point. "But there isn't anything. Edsel Ford was a nice man, a gentleman, and that's it."

Intimates like Gregorie viewed Edsel as a sensitive, creative soul whom, despite his loyalty to his meddlesome father and the company, years of tension and conflict finally beat down. These closet dramas typically pitted him against the old man and Harry Bennett. When Edsel died in the prime of life in 1943, the media reported that he had succumbed to stomach cancer. Those of a more melodramatic nature reckoned he died of a broken heart.

* * *

Henry Ford was still two and a half years from driving his "quadricycle" through the cobblestone streets of Detroit when Clara Ford gave birth to their first and only child on November 6, 1893. Edsel was named after one of his father's grade-school friends, Edsel Ruddiman. He was literally raised on the smell of gasoline. On Christmas Eve, 1893, while his son slept in the next room, Ford clamped his first gas engine to the kitchen sink and started it up. The ungodly noise and noxious fumes caused Clara to scoop up the seven-week-old baby and carry him upstairs. The incident evidently didn't unsettle the boy. Even before he started kindergarten,

Clara Ford and two-year-old Edsel in front of their Detroit home in 1895, years before unimaginable fame, riches—and stress—came the family's way. (Collections of The Henry Ford)

he was accompanying his father on rides aboard various experimental cars. Within a few years the schoolboy was driving them himself.

When Edsel was born, Ford was an obscure engineer making about seventy-five dollars a month at the Edison Illuminating Company. The fame and wealth waiting just down the road were as unfathomable to him as to the poor youngster who penned the following letter one Christmas:

> *Dear Santa Claus, I haven't had Any Christmas Tree in four years and I Have Broken all my trimmings and I want some more and I Want a Pair of Roller Skates and a Book and I Can't Think Of Anything more I want You to Think of something more. Good By Edsel Ford.*

Edsel grew into a curious, even-tempered boy of slight build and dark complexion. He attended public schools and, after the money started rolling into the household, the private Detroit University

School. He often worked after class at his father's factory, helping with the mail or fooling around in the experimental lab. "If that kid can only continue the way he is going," Ford happily told an associate. "I've got a boy I can be proud of."

Although he possessed a fine mechanical mind, Edsel preferred designing cars to tinkering with them, keeping a scrapbook filled with pictures of automobile styling. In high school, he tricked out his own, one-of-a-kind hot rod. Edsel had the ability, ambition, and resources to attend college, but instead went straight to work for his father following graduation in 1912. By then, Ford was a multimillionaire and a folk hero, thanks to his creation of the Model T.

Edsel watched this phenomenon unfold in front of his eyes. His father's strategy of concentrating on a simple car that ordinary folks could afford, a "family horse," wasn't unique among automakers. And contrary to legend, he didn't invent the assembly line. His genius lay in improving mass-production techniques and then passing on the savings to customers. As the time required to build a Model T continued to drop, so did its price, from $850 in 1908 to $290 in 1924. At one point every other car on the road was a Model T. By the time production ended in 1927, more than 15 million of the beloved "flivvers" had rolled off the assembly line.

Edsel shared in the bonanza. One day in 1914, he and his father walked into a Detroit bank. "Bill," Henry told the banker, "I have a million dollars in gold here. This is Edsel's twenty-first birthday and I want him to have it." Visibly shaken, Edsel might have been forgiven for taking the rest of the day off to celebrate—or to recuperate. Instead, the sole heir to the world's greatest fortune went back to his factory office and spent his birthday working behind the desk. He did admit later, however, that he'd never made as many mistakes as he did that day.

Edsel displayed a level of maturity and sense of responsibility not often found among other children of the nouveau riche. Detroit's auto pioneers, mechanics turned millionaires, were a hard-boiled lot, but Edsel succeeded in winning over even the crustiest of them. "Henry," said one, "I don't envy you a damn thing except that boy of yours."

In 1918, with America at war, Edsel initially refused to ask for a draft deferment. By now he was married with a child and was obviously worth more to the war effort running a manufacturing company, but he did not want preferential treatment. But Ford, a pacifist who had drawn considerable ridicule for his failed "Peace Ship" mission to Europe three years earlier, browbeat Edsel into requesting a deferment, which was then granted. Predictably, many labeled him a coward and a slacker. Some people close to the situation couldn't understand why Edsel didn't simply allow himself to be drafted and then assigned to the Ford Motor Company. "I don't want to don a uniform with the assurance that I will be expected to do nothing but sit in a swivel chair," he retorted. "There is one job in this war I do not want and will not take, and that is the job of a rich man's son."

In 1919, after Ford bought out the last of the shareholders, he made Edsel president of the company. He was just twenty-five and his father fifty-six. Although Edsel—whom company executives referred to as "Mr. Edsel" to differentiate him from the other Mr. Ford—stayed in that position until his death, everybody understood who really ran the show.

As Model T after Model T rolled out of the Highland Park plant, the press burnished Ford's image as a paternalistic captain of industry, someone for whom his workers' welfare was of paramount concern. His famous sociological department sought to educate and Americanize workers and their families, though it included such heavy-handed tactics as spying on and firing those employees whose lifestyle choices—drinking, gambling, whoring—the department judged unsatisfactory.

Throughout the 1920s, throngs of hungry, unskilled but hopeful men from Poland, Italy, Syria, and elsewhere continued to flock to Detroit to take advantage of Ford's famous "Five-Dollar Day," first announced in 1914. Detroit's swelling population, which had the highest percentage of foreign-born in the country, included Paul Boatin, an Italian immigrant who followed his father into the

Rouge plant in 1925. The largest industrial complex in the world employed 120,000 workers at its peak.

"The working conditions were dehumanizing," Boatin said. "You couldn't talk to another worker, couldn't even say hello without getting fired. There was no laughing, no smoking. You had to get permission to get a drink of water or go to the toilet. You'd sit and eat your lunch by your machine because the servicemen wouldn't allow any groups."

Edsel came to understand, at the hand of his own father, something of the terrorism workers experienced on the shop floor. Ford loved his only son, but as the years went by he began to realize that he'd had little success in molding him in his own image. With no stockholders to answer to and his son a bit of a disappointment in his eyes, Henry became increasingly narrow-minded, mean-spirited, and imperious. As the industry became more competitive with the rise of General Motors and Chrysler, he had great trouble accepting views different from his own on practically every subject.

Many of their differences were minor but telling. Edsel enjoyed reading *The New Yorker*, Ford found humor in *Little Orphan Annie* cartoons. Edsel smoked and drank; Ford was a teetotaler who did not allow smoking on company property. Edsel was a philanthropist; Ford didn't believe in charity. Other points of contention revolved around industry issues. Edsel, for example, wanted to develop an eight-cylinder car; Ford contended that "a motor car should not have more spark plugs than a cow has teats."

Time and again, Henry thwarted his son's ideas, sometimes in humiliating and brutal ways. On one occasion, having disagreed with Edsel's decision to construct some coke ovens at the Rouge, Ford waited until they were built and then demolished them. During an executive meeting in which Edsel proposed the need for modern hydraulic brakes, he shouted, "Edsel, you shut up!" before storming out of the room.

After the 1920s, one of the biggest challenges facing carmakers was that almost everyone already owned an automobile, no small obstacle in those non-disposable times. Edsel eventually convinced his father that his beloved Model T was obsolete. Henry may not have trusted his son's instincts, but when Chevrolet began taking away market share with its cheaper, option-laden six-cylinder vehicles, commerce convinced him. Edsel was instrumental in designing its more fashionable successor, the Model A, which won back drivers when it was unveiled in 1927 to great acclaim.

Edsel had a keen sense of automotive styling, an important attribute as the demand for luxury automobiles grew. To capture these new customers, Edsel convinced Henry to purchase the Lincoln Motor Company in 1922. "Edsel's eye for detail and exacting personality compelled him to analyze every new design down to the minutest detail," Henry Dominguez wrote of his influence in the design studio. His elegant sensibilities would become fully evident in the 1930s with the introduction of the Zephyr, the first truly streamlined car, and the Continental, which Frank Lloyd Wright called the most beautiful car ever built.

In addition to his work in styling and engineering, Edsel assumed responsibility for administering the company's far-flung business concerns. He deserved credit for overseeing the Rouge's massive and complicated expansion between 1919 and 1925, as well as for the opening of overseas plants, making Ford the first global car manufacturer. Always a progressive thinker, he convinced his father to extend credit to new car buyers. But far more often than not, the sole owner of the Ford empire got the last word. Ford

The streamlined Zephyr was one of Edsel's design successes. (Author's collection)

arbitrarily fired executives loyal to Edsel, countermanded directives, and ridiculed his suggestions. This was his version of tough love. In his opinion, Edsel was "too soft." He hoped these cruel put-downs would instill backbone.

Despite the constant belittlement, Edsel remained loyal and respectful. Edsel "was a gentleman in the finest, fullest meaning of the word," said Charlie Sorenson. "I never heard anyone who knew him speak of him except in the highest terms."

Unless, of course, the person talking was Harry Bennett.

* * *

Harry Bennett was the son Henry Ford never had. Bennett, nearly two years older than Edsel, was an Ann Arbor native whose father had been killed in a barroom brawl when Harry was an infant. Bernie Ghers introduced him to Ford in 1916. The New York columnist had admired the way the sawed-off, heavily tattooed sailor just discharged from the Navy had handled himself in a fight. Ghers knew that Ford was looking for a tough guy to oversee security at the Rouge plant, then under construction.

Bennett did all sorts of odd jobs for Ford, carrying out orders with dispatch and efficiency, no questions asked. Ford liked his belligerence. "Many times in critical situations," Bennett recalled, "his attitude was 'Harry, let's you and him have a fight.'"

Bennett pandered to Ford's fear of kidnapping, a crime much in vogue in the 1920s and '30s. Bennett's men shadowed Edsel's children when they went to school, looking to prevent the same kind of tragedy that befell aviator Charles Lindbergh, whose infant son was kidnapped and found dead in 1932. To keep informed of potential threats on members of the Ford family, Bennett forged links with various underworld types, getting involved in various escapades that Ford loved hearing about. On one occasion, a shotgun blast blew out the windshield of Bennett's car as he drove home from the Rouge. On another, an unidentified gunman shot through the front door of his Ann Arbor home, striking one of his daughters.

The strongman was colorful, keeping lions as pets and once shooting a foul-smelling cigar out of the mouth of a visitor who refused his request to put it out. He was an above-average artist and could play several instruments. Anne Morrow Lindbergh, taken with the service chief's charm, thought him "a troubadour." Bennett dressed fashionably but practically, always wearing a bowtie because, as he explained, an opponent could grab a tie in a fight.

Mark Beltaire, the longtime "Town Crier" columnist for the *Detroit Free Press*, recalled attending a party once at the Book-Cadillac Hotel. "There was a lot of drinking going on in the suites," he said. "When I went to the men's room, I stumbled over a body." It was Bennett, passed out drunk. That is, Beltaire and everybody else who gingerly stepped around the crumpled heap thought he was drunk. "I heard later that he had a habit of doing that so he could listen in on conversations."

Any person who would play possum on the floor of a public lavatory deserves to be taken seriously. Bennett most certainly was. The little man flexed a muscle far out of proportion to his stocky five-foot-five frame (which made him one inch shorter than Edsel). "Do you really want to get rid of Hitler?" Ford asked an Englishman on the eve of World War II. "I'll send Harry over with six of his men. They'll get rid of Hitler for you in no time."

Bennett roamed the office hallways, factory aisles, and back alleys of the Ford empire at will, turning Ford's whimsy into policy with the kind of head-cracking efficiency Ford had always desired in Edsel. "I became his most intimate companion," Bennett bragged in his old age, "closer to him even than his own son." As the years passed, Bennett, emboldened by his growing influence with Ford, didn't try to hide his contempt for Edsel. Bennett referred to him as "the weakling" in his conversations with other executives.

Nowhere was the difference between Ford's "good" and "bad" surrogate son more pronounced than in the area of labor relations. As the organized labor movement gathered momentum with the advent of hard times, Edsel favored a conciliatory approach. Bennett, with Henry's blessing, stressed intimidation.

Ford originally created the Service Department to provide plant security during World War I, when industrial sabotage was a very real concern. By the early 1920s, however, Bennett had built the

Harry Bennett in 1938. (Author's collection)

department into the world's largest private security force: 3,000 plug-uglies recruited from local gyms, college football teams, and prisons. Stooges were everywhere, peeping even into Edsel's design department.

"They were all rotten, no-good sons-of-bitches!" exclaimed Al Bardelli, who despite his advanced age practically flew off the couch when asked about Bennett's goons. The Dearborn resident, who first entered the Rouge in 1927, remembered how armed servicemen would follow him home, to the market, and to organizing meetings in Walter Reuther's basement.

In the winter of 1931–32, during the depths of the Depression, three-quarters of the Rouge workforce was unemployed. On the afternoon of March 7, 1932, about 2,500 desperate people staged a "Hunger March" on the Rouge. They were met by an army of servicemen and police, who opened fire on the demonstrators. Bardelli, one of the fortunate few to still be working, returned home to find friends frantically tallying the score. "Bennett's men killed five marchers and wounded twenty or so others," Bardelli said. One of the victims fell dead over Bennett, who had been knocked unconscious by a thrown chunk of slag when he went out to confront the mob. Like Bardelli, Edsel was sickened by the violence, which helped solidify Bennett's standing with his obstinate father.

* * *

In contrast to Bennett, an aficionado of pornography who married three times and enjoyed moving in seedier circles, Edsel lived a stable, if Gatsby-esque life. He married Eleanor Lowthian Clay on November 1, 1916, uniting two of the city's most prominent families. Eleanor, an engaging young lady remembered by one acquaintance as "a brilliant woman with a shrewd mind," was the niece of Joseph L. Hudson, founder of the city's largest department store. They had met at a dance while teenagers.

The newlyweds, ignoring Henry's constant entreaties to live near him in Dearborn, first resided in a house in Indian Village. Henry II was born in 1917, followed by Benson (1919), Josephine (1923), and William (1925). In 1926, Edsel commissioned Albert Kahn, architect of the Rouge and other Ford factories, to design their dream home at Gaukler Point, a prime piece of lakefront property in Grosse Pointe Shores.

Edsel and Eleanor had no interest in an auto tycoon's gaudy showplace palace or a Bennett-style fortress. (Bennett's Ann Arbor "castle" included gun turrets and secret passageways with mismatched steps to trip up unsuspecting intruders. He also owned

Eleanor Clay Ford as a young bride in 1916. (Library of Congress)

several recreational properties, the security measures including machine guns and explosive devices.) The young couple wanted a large, elegant, tasteful home to service a comfortable family life and a hectic social one. Kahn patterned the rambling estate at 1100 Lake Shore Drive after the stone houses of England's Cotswold district.

Centuries-old fireplaces and staircases were reassembled in the sprawling 30,000-square-foot house.

In 1929, after three years of design and construction, Edsel, Eleanor, and the kids moved in. Admittedly, the three-story, sixty-room house was extraordinary, with as many as fifty-two servants and maintenance people required to keep the estate running smoothly. But for all its imposing size and lavish appointments, there was an undeniable warmth and intimacy. Employees were treated well and were extremely loyal, with many staying several decades. The site included 3,000 feet of Lake St. Clair shoreline, along with an artificial lagoon, which provided mooring for a veritable armada of vessels. Edsel was an avid sailor, owning several sloops and an eighty-eight-foot schooner. On nice summer days he often piloted his speedboat up the Detroit and Rouge rivers to work.

As might be expected, the couple hosted many of the day's movers and shakers. One night the guest list might include Detroit Tigers catcher-manager Mickey Cochrane and his wife, Mary, and the conversation could stray to a new slugger named Joe DiMaggio or a mutual literary favorite, Rudyard Kipling. Another evening it might be polar explorer Admiral Richard E. Byrd or artist John Carroll, exchanging small talk with some of Detroit's young rich: the Books, Calkins, Jacksons, Porters, and Macauleys. After assembling in the drawing room filled with eighteenth-century French furniture, guests would move into the dining room, which glowed with the warm light of candles. To ensure atmosphere, workers had been forbidden to install electrical outlets in the room. Afterward, the ladies retired to the intimate morning room for coffee (and a look at van Gogh's *Portrait of the Postman Joseph Roulin*) while the men gathered in the study for cigars and liqueurs. The Elizabethan oak-paneled study was Edsel's favorite room and today remains virtually intact from the last time he was in it. Lining the walls are photographs of Douglas Fairbanks Sr., Mary Pickford, John D. Rockefeller, and other notables. Most of the images were a testament to Edsel's skills as an amateur photographer (he kept a darkroom in the study) and the glamorous circles he traveled in.

Meanwhile, the elder Ford, quietly ensconced with Clara in their Fair Lane estate in the woods of west Dearborn, remained openly disdainful of his son's social life. Once during the Prohibition years, when he knew Edsel and Eleanor were away, he had Bennett drive him to Gaukler Point, where he proceeded to destroy their stash of liquor.

Edsel doted on his children, with the grounds at Gaukler Point (laid out by renowned landscape designer Jens Jensen) providing an expansive playground for them as they grew. He worked off tension by organizing a baseball or touch football game when he got home. Henry built the boys miniature motorized cars, which they joyfully drove around—and occasionally through—the property's hundreds of trees and shrubs. Lest Josephine feel slighted as an only daughter, Edsel enlisted Kahn to build a $15,000 miniature playhouse, complete with scaled-down furniture and a fireplace, for her seventh birthday.

As a man of means, Edsel could easily bring bandleader Tommy Dorsey, tap-dancer Paul Draper, and an up-and-coming crooner

Edsel on the beach at Seal Harbor, Maine, in 1921 with sons Henry II (*left*) and Benson. He and Eleanor built a summer estate there. (Collections of The Henry Ford)

An avid boater, Edsel indulged himself with a variety of watercraft, including sailboats, motorboats, yachts, and an elaborate houseboat used as a winter retreat in Hobe Sound, Florida. He often drove a speedboat to commute between his estate on Lake St. Clair and the Rouge plant. (Collections of The Henry Ford)

named Frank Sinatra to town to entertain at Henry II's twenty-first birthday in 1938. He could afford a summer estate in Seal Harbor, Maine; a winter retreat in Hobe Sound, Florida; and a combination lodge and farm on three thousand acres near White Lake Township. Being much closer to home, Edsel considered Haven Hill his "nerve retreat," a place he, Eleanor, and the children visited at all times of the year. Here the family swam, rode horses, played tennis, and took long hikes in the rolling countryside. These three properties cost Edsel more than $6 million. Coupled with the $3 million spent on the Gaukler Point estate, the total outlay for the four properties was roughly $160 million in today's dollars.

Edsel's wealth allowed him to pursue varied interests, many of which he helped support financially. His underwriting of Admiral Byrd's pioneering flights over the North and South poles in the late 1920s was a natural outgrowth of his interest in aviation. (In gratitude, Byrd named his plane the *Josephine Ford* after his sponsor's daughter and a 150-mile range in Antarctica the Edsel Ford

Mountains.) As a teenager, Edsel had received his father's permission to build—but not fly—an experimental aircraft powered by a Model T engine. In the 1920s, he was involved in opening the world's first modern airport on Oakwood Boulevard in Dearborn, soon a hub of commercial and passenger traffic carried aloft in the famous all-steel Ford Tri-Motor aircraft. Edsel's many air-minded activities included donating $50,000 and a huge trophy for a 1,775-mile reliability tour that for several years began and ended there. To aid cross-country pilots in their navigation, he insisted that all Ford dealers paint a big northward-pointing arrow and the name of their town on the roof.

Edsel supported art in all forms, with Eleanor and Detroit Institute of Arts director William Valentiner schooling him on painting, sculpture, and furniture. By 1932, he was sufficiently enlightened to pay Diego Rivera's $22,000 commission to decorate the walls of the DIA's interior courtyard with a series of frescoes depicting Detroit's industrial might. Rivera, one of the leaders of the Mexican muralist movement and a known Marxist, immediately hit it off with his corporate benefactor. "They had a mutual interest in art, engineering, and design," explained Linda Downs, former curator of education at the DIA and a Rivera expert. "Rivera was fascinated with the Rouge complex. Edsel opened up the plant completely to him."

Rivera's commission came on the heels of the Hunger March massacre. It was largely left to Rivera to decide on a motif. He spent his first three months in Detroit exploring the Rouge and making sketches. His political sympathies became obvious as work began and progressed through 1933 on *Detroit Industry*. The chubby cigar-smoking artist created twenty-seven panels in eight months, a rigorous pace that caused him to shed one hundred pounds. In the two main panels, on the north and south walls of the courtyard, the unsmiling workers are straining at their tasks, watched over by the omnipresent servicemen. "Rivera knew, he identified with the workers," said Paul Boatin.

Lucienne Bloch, the only one of Rivera's eight assistants still living, remembers Edsel observing the artist and his helpers at work. "I had the feeling he was a little confused about what we were

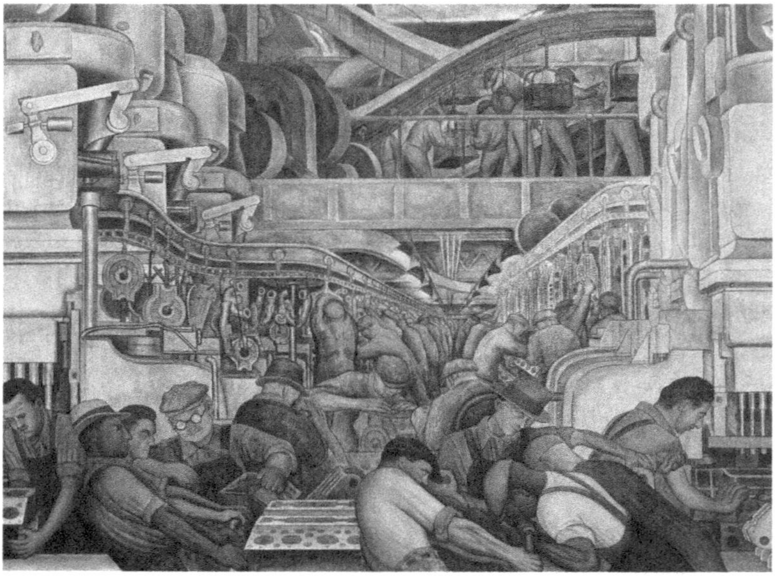

Details from Diego Rivera's *Detroit Industry*. This mural, one of twenty-seven panels painted over an eight-month period in 1932–33, is on the north wall of the Detroit Institute of Art's courtyard. Edsel Ford paid the artist's $22,000 fee, just one of many significant contributions he and Eleanor made to the museum over the years. (Detroit Institute of Arts)

doing," said Bloch from her northern California home. Many civic and religious leaders howled over the murals' supposedly sacrilegious and anticapitalistic themes. Nonetheless, Bloch says, their patron "courageously" stilled the cries for whitewash voiced by alarmed citizens. He arranged classes for visitors to be educated in Rivera's work—how it depicted the inter-connectedness of worker and boss, of art and industry—and formally accepted the murals for the museum. *Detroit Industry* has since been designated a National Historic Landmark, joining the similarly honored Rouge complex and the Edsel and Eleanor Ford House at Gaukler Point.

* * *

By the spring of 1937, organized labor was on a roll. Successful sit-down strikes in Flint and Detroit had helped the United Auto Workers forge historic contracts with General Motors and Chrysler.

Henry Ford, however, vowed that he would close his plants before negotiating with a union. He openly thumbed his nose at the Wagner Act, federal legislation that had given workers the legal right to organize on the job.

One day that May, several UAW organizers, including Richard Frankensteen and Walter Reuther, climbed the Miller Road overpass outside Gate 4 of the Rouge plant. Their announced intention was to hand out leaflets urging workers to join the union. As they smiled and lined up for some photos, a cadre of servicemen suddenly moved in.

Bill May was a young reporter for the International News Service. Now retired and living in North Muskegon, he is one of the few surviving eyewitnesses to what was to become a seminal moment in the history of the company and of the labor movement: "The Battle of the Overpass."

"They had their targets all picked out, that was obvious," he recalled. "I had my eyes glued on Frankensteen, probably because I knew him best. They pulled his jacket up around his head and started letting him have it in the gut. Meanwhile, Reuther was on the ground. He was a small guy and he wasn't putting up too much resistance. They got Frankensteen up on the rail, as if they were going to drop him off the overpass onto the sidewalk below. I distinctly remember one of the fellas who was doing the beating say, 'No, don't do that, we'll kill the guy.' So they started booting him down the steps. It was all over in about five minutes."

Actually, the uproar had just begun. Bennett explained with a straight face that the beatings had been administered not by his servicemen, but by workers who didn't want a union. He felt safe with this fiction, knowing that authorities had absolved the company of all blame in the Hunger March massacre five years earlier, and thinking that in any case his thugs had seized all of the cameras recording the beatdown.

However, a couple of photographers had managed to flee the scene with their film. The photos that survived clearly identified known underworld types. The damning evidence of Henry Ford's violent opposition to the law appeared on the pages of newspapers and national magazines. Once a hero to the working class, the man behind the Five-Dollar Day was now exposed as perhaps its most ardent enemy.

Despite the swing in public opinion against Ford, and a National Labor Relations Board ruling that the company was in violation of the Wagner Act, Henry continued to resist organization attempts for four more chaotic years. The UAW stepped up its efforts inside and outside Ford plants. Henry, ignoring the advice of Edsel, relied on Bennett to identify, intimidate, and fire union activists.

Working conditions remained brutal. Al Bardelli recalls the infamous "Ford speedup," which stretched a man's ability to keep up with the pace of assembly. "I'd come home so tired and irritated, I'd take it out on my wife and my kids," he said, curling his gnarled hand into a fist. "What I really wanted to do was beat the shit out Bennett. That's what we all wanted to do."

Meanwhile Henry grew more erratic, more stubborn. No one can determine exactly when his senility began to set in. There are indications that he suffered a series of small strokes as early as 1938. But it's clear that in the years leading up to World War II, he was gradually losing his grip. He seemed more determined than ever not to relinquish power. Bennett either drove out top executives loyal to Edsel, or they left of their own accord, unwilling to wait any longer for the aging Henry to surrender the crown to his son. "You always figured there was one gentleman here," recalled an engineer loyal to Edsel, "and that someday he was going to run the place, and that it would be a fine place to work when he was running it."

Despite Bennett's strong-arm tactics, the UAW continued to sign up more members. The matter came to an explosive head on April 1, 1941, when eight workers were fired for union activities. A general strike followed, with tens of thousands of pickets wrapped like a giant boa constrictor around the Rouge. Cars were parked three and four deep down every street. Nobody could get into the plant. Bardelli, then a picket captain, joyfully remembers workers picking up a car containing half a dozen servicemen and turning it back in the direction from which it came. Now *this* was solidarity.

Edsel, who had been ill and was trying to regain his health in Florida, flew to Detroit to argue his case with Henry. Edsel was weak, thin, and pale, and perhaps for this reason his father reluctantly caved in to his plea to accommodate the workers. Over the objections of Bennett, Ford agreed to allow a National Labor Relations Board election, which in his delusional state he believed would result in his workers rejecting a union. Instead, only 2.5 percent of the Rouge's 80,000 workers voted his way; the rest demanded the right to collective bargaining. Ford, the onetime paterfamilias of autoworkers, was crushed by this overwhelming rejection. He refused to sign a formal agreement, yelling that he would close the plant if he had to.

The prospect of renewed picket-line violence caused Clara Ford to finally confront her husband. If Henry would not recognize the union and put an end to years of suffering experienced by not only the rank and file, but by their own son, she would sell her share of Ford stock and leave him.

Henry, now seventy-eight and weary, was rocked by Clara's ultimatum. He surprised everybody by suddenly capitulating. He instructed Bennett to negotiate a historic contract with the UAW that was even more favorable than the ones it had signed with General Motors and Chrysler. "Never underestimate the power of a woman," Henry told an associate.

World War II was at hand, with Ford shifting production to jeeps, tank engines, gliders, bombers, and other vital war materials. The stress and strain on Edsel were immense. By the fall of 1942, he had undergone surgery twice for recurring stomach ulcers. He gulped pills and changed his diet. Henry blamed his son's declining health on his "high living" and listening to "ear piddlers," his term for gossip-mongers. A food faddist ("You can live as long as you want," he declared about this time, "as long as you only eat cracked wheat"), he thought drinking unpasteurized milk from his farm would help settle Edsel's stomach. Instead, he came down with undulant fever, which aggravated his condition.

Gaunt and weak, Edsel nonetheless attempted to tend to company business. All along Bennett stymied him, his machinations continually backed by the increasingly senile Ford. One day, after

Scenes from the 1941 Ford strike: Thousands of workers surrounded the Rouge plant while skirmishes occasionally broke out on the picket line. (Collections of The Henry Ford)

losing a confrontation over the firing of a longtime, loyal associate, Edsel decided he'd had enough. He privately told Charlie Sorenson that he was going to leave the company.

He did, in the manner many had feared—feet first. Doctors had misdiagnosed his chronic abdominal problems and botched his treatment. An operation in late 1942 revealed metastasized stomach cancer. Benson, for one, had no trouble identifying the cause of his father's illness. "Grandfather is responsible for Father's sickness," he raged after learning that it was terminal, "and I'm through with him!" All along Henry expressed no sympathy for his son, who was plainly disintegrating but still attempting to soldier on.

In May 1943, Edsel was moved into the third-floor infirmary at Gaukler Point. Morphine eased his agony. According to one of the doctors who attended him, "he didn't complain and he wasn't morose. He knew that the end was near and that he couldn't do anything about it." By the evening of May 25, 1943, he was in a coma. He died at 1:10 the following morning, his hand in Eleanor's. It was exactly six years to the day that Bennett had so brutally enforced his father's will on the Miller Road overpass.

The community mourned Edsel's passing. One of the most moving moments was when hundreds of factory hands, ordinary men who might have stepped out of a certain mural, came to pay their respects. Bennett, refusing to be a hypocrite, did not attend the funeral. "I knew that Edsel had despised me," he later explained, "and felt that the honest thing to do was to stay away."

Henry, weeks from turning eighty, sagged with grief. The old man ordered the entire organization to shut down on the day of the funeral and observe a brief spell of respectful silence.

Ford R. Bryan was working inside the Rouge plant's magnesium foundry, next to the powerhouse, the afternoon Edsel was laid to rest at Woodlawn Cemetery. "My recollection is that it was very strange," said the Dearborn resident, who in retirement has written several Ford-related books. "Everything stopped. Having been accustomed to hearing all the banging, all the machinery roaring all the time, the silence was eerie. The only sound was the boiling of the furnaces, which were kept on."

Industry can wait only so long for any man, regardless of station. After five minutes, the Rouge and the rest of the Ford empire roared back to life.

Over the next several months, Ford alternately mourned and raged. He blamed the cows, the doctors, himself. He sought solace in his long-held conviction that all living things are reincarnated. "Well, Harry," he'd say hopefully to Bennett, "you know my belief—Edsel isn't dead."

But he was, and Ford couldn't shake the feeling that he bore the brunt of the responsibility. Regret flooded out. He brooded constantly upon the nature of their relationship, once asking Bennett if he had been cruel to Edsel.

"Well, cruel, no," Bennett answered. "But unfair, yes. If that had been me, I'd have got mad."

"That's what I wanted him to do," mused Ford. "Get mad."

* * *

Henry Ford, born the year the battle of Gettysburg was fought, named himself president of a company that had been retooled to fight World War II. The move disheartened the US government, already concerned with the firm's uneven production of vital war material, particularly at the huge Willow Run bomber plant. There was even speculation that President Roosevelt—a man Henry despised—would order the nationalization of the company. Historians think that only FDR's friendship with Edsel kept it from happening.

Into the picture stepped Henry II, whom the Navy discharged to help restore order to a company beset with internal chaos. Edsel's twenty-three-year-old son was not Henry's choice to succeed him as president; Bennett was. But the Ford women closed ranks behind Henry II in the fall of 1945. Rumors suggest that Eleanor issued an ultimatum: Unless old Henry handed power over to his young namesake, she was going to create the first public offering of Ford stock by selling off her shares. "He killed my husband, and he's not going to kill my son," she reportedly said.

Henry II soon cleaned house of Bennett and a thousand of his cronies, firing many of them personally. By the time Henry Ford died in 1947 at age eighty-four, Hank the Deuce was well on his way to turning the company around. "I could see in him an effort to be more socially accepted by the workers," said Paul Boatin, who met the new company president about this time. "I think in a way he was trying to fill the void left by his father."

The manner of Bennett's leaving has several versions. The most plausible is also the most anti-climactic. Weeks before the board meeting that named Henry II president, Bennett realized that he too would be "retired" along with his enfeebled benefactor of the last twenty-nine years. Management neither fired him in an angry confrontation nor showed him the door at the point of a gun, though either scenario would have pleased countless people.

Outside of testifying in 1951 before the Kefauver Commission investigating organized crime, Bennett never returned to Detroit. Characteristically, he prepared for the hearing by digging up as much dirt on Senator Estes Kefauver as he could. "He never knew how much I had on him, but it would have embarrassed him," he gloated years later. Bennett lived out West until his death in a nursing home in 1979. In his final years he took to painting his shoes silver to compensate for his failing eyesight.

The symbols of Edsel Ford's corporate, public, and private sides exist much as they did during his lifetime—at the Rouge, the courtyard of the DIA, and the house at Gaukler Point, where the fireplace inside his study has not been lit since his death. If one believes in reincarnation, as Henry Ford so desperately did, everything is in place for a good man and a loyal son to return home.

This wartime poster featured one of Joe Louis's most memorable quotes. (National Archives)

11

The Brown Bomber Goes to War

Heavyweight champion Joe Louis transformed into a symbol of national resolve as he took the fight to the enemy—both foreign and domestic—during World War II.

Reflecting on the Japanese attack on Pearl Harbor in 1941, history's greatest heavyweight fighter described how he felt about the event that suddenly thrust him and millions of fellow Americans into World War II.

"I was mad, I was furious, you name it," Joe Louis said. "Hell, this is my country. Don't come around sneaking up and attacking it. If a fighter had done that to me, I would have smashed him. I'm strictly for fair deals and open fighting."

Twenty-seven years old and in his boxing prime when America entered the war, Joe Louis had already been an international figure for years. In 1935, as concerns grew over Italy's bullying (and eventual invasion) of Abyssinia, he had methodically chopped down the sequoia-sized Primo Carnera in the ring, dealing a symbolic blow to Mussolini's blackshirts. Three years later, Detroit's "Brown Bomber" famously avenged his sole professional defeat by destroying German fighter Max Schmeling in a first-round flurry of punches that served as an allegorical prelude to World War II. President Franklin Roosevelt squeezed Joe's bicep at the White House and declared that his were the kind of muscles the country was going to need to beat the Nazis.

Early in 1941, Louis had registered for the peacetime draft, and been classified 1-A by a Chicago draft board. As the sole supporter of his wife, mother, and several family members, he might have qualified for a deferment. But he had no intention of avoiding conscription as heavyweight champ Jack Dempsey had controversially done during World War I.

The war could not have come at a more inopportune time for Louis. Although Joe was not the type to think in such terms, his longtime manager, Mike Jacobs, was. He realized Joe's career would likely be put on hold for the duration of the war, and nobody knew how long that would be. Jacobs came up with an idea that was both patriotic and self-serving. He asked Louis if he would be willing to put his title on the line at a charity boxing event, with all his winnings going to the Navy Relief Society. The organization aided the families of sailors killed in combat. Without hesitation, Joe said yes.

It was just like Jacobs to capitalize on the country's patriotic fervor, and just like Joe not to give a second thought to risking his championship for zilch. Of course, Louis didn't view it that way. "Ain't fighting for nothing," he told reporters. "I'm fighting for my country."

At this point in his career, Joe had a 54–1 ring record and was into his fifth year as heavyweight champ. He had everything to lose and nothing to gain. His remarkable gesture inspired a fresh flush of affection among his countrymen. "You don't see a shipyard owner risking his entire business," Jimmy Powers wrote in the *New York Daily News*. "If the government wants a battleship, the government doesn't ask him to donate it. The government pays him a fat profit. . . . The more I think of it, the greater guy I see in this Joe Louis."

Madison Square Garden was awash in red, white, and blue bunting the night of January 9, 1942. Joe's opponent was Buddy Baer, a six-foot-six-inch, 250-pounder he had beaten the previous spring. A crowd of 16,889 endured a drawn-out program of introductions and speeches, including one by Wendell Wilkie. Joe had actively supported the liberal-minded Republican in his unsuccessful 1940 presidential campaign because he felt FDR had not fulfilled his promises to Black Americans.

With a national radio audience listening in, Louis then proceeded to snap Baer's head back with a succession of fast, accurate punches, knocking him down three times. Baer was still trying to pull himself up by the ropes when the referee counted him out with four seconds left in the opening round. "The only way I could have beaten Joe that night was with a baseball bat," he later said.

The winner's share of the purse was $65,200. After deducting his training expenses, Louis donated the balance of $47,500 to Navy Relief. Baer chipped in a portion of his purse and Jacobs contributed $37,229, making for a total contribution of $88,807.

The next day, Louis enlisted in the Army. He took his physical, then reported for duty (via a chauffeured limousine) at Camp Upton on Long Island, New York. There he participated in a staged scene for the newsreels. As a clerk nervously typed out a form, he looked up and asked, "What's your occupation?" "Fighting," Louis replied, "and let us at them Japs."

But first, the Army—jealous over the publicity the Navy had received—wanted him to fight for *its* pet charity. While Joe underwent basic training with a segregated company, Mike Jacobs lined up an opponent. He signed Abe Simon to meet Joe at Madison Square Garden on March 27, 1942. Once again, the champ would risk his title with all proceeds going to charity, causing one newspaper to gush that "from almost any angle you can consider, there has never been a champion like Joe Louis."

At a dinner given by the Navy Relief Society on March 10 at the Garden, Joe uttered one of the most memorable lines of the war. Wearing his private's uniform, he nervously stood at the dais placed in the center of a boxing ring and honored a request to say a few words. "I have only done what any red-blooded American would do," he said. "We gonna do our part, and we will win, because we are on God's side."

Joe's extemporaneous corruption of the familiar phrase that "God is on our side" brought a standing ovation and practically overnight leaped into popular usage. President Roosevelt sent a telegram complimenting his choice of words. It inspired a popular recruiting poster ("We'll win because we're on God's side") as well as a poem by ad man Carl Byoir, "Joe Louis Named the War," which enjoyed wide circulation.

Joe trained for the fight at Fort Dix, New Jersey. Having repeatedly turned down offers of an officer's commission before enlisting, he enjoyed interacting with the ordinary GIs who came to watch him work out. The Army's policy of segregation, however, bothered him. Here were Black Americans willing to risk their lives, "but they can't sleep in the same barracks with the White guys or go to the same movies or hardly get in officers' training."

On fight night, Louis kayoed Simon in the sixth round. Ring announcer Don Dunphy used the knockout to symbolize the country's resolve to defeat Japan and Germany, enemies who in early 1942 clearly had the upper hand. "We won't stop punching, just as Louis does, 'til we win," Dunphy declared.

From his purse of $45,882, Joe deducted expenses and gave $36,146 to Army Relief. Contributions from Jacobs and Simon brought the total donation to $55,000.

Joe's largesse was remarkable when considering his staggering debts. At the time, the $21-a-month private owed $217,000, more than half of which the IRS claimed for back taxes. Jacobs, who regularly advanced his fighters large sums against future purses, Louis owed $60,000, and another of his clients, Billy Conn, owed $34,500.

Nervous that he would never get repaid, Jacobs proposed a blockbuster charity bout to pull everybody out of the hole. Louis and Conn would meet in a rematch of their storied 1941 title bout. In that fight, the underdog Conn was winning on points until he got cocky and tried knocking the champ out. Instead it was Conn who hit the canvas.

Jacobs easily sold the War Department on Louis-Conn II, tentatively scheduled for Yankee Stadium in October 1942. By late September, advance ticket sales and a record broadcast deal were pointing to a million-dollar gate.

But, to the consternation of Secretary of War Henry Stimson, someone had altered the original deal to allow the two fighters to deduct the money they owed Jacobs from the receipts. In addition, Jacobs demanded control of the first 20 rows of seats, an audacious money grab. Even with these modifications, the fight still would have produced as much as $750,000 for Army Relief. Nonetheless, Stimson abruptly called the fight off, explaining that it wouldn't be fair to the millions of other GIs who weren't given similar opportunities to work off their debts while serving their country. He soon banned all similar projects for relief agencies.

Despite the contributions of millions of Black citizens to the war effort, America's ingrained racism proved difficult to eradicate. Even Louis had to contend with some of the same problems faced by ordinary Black soldiers. Once, as he and fellow boxer Sugar Ray Robinson were waiting for a bus at Camp Siebert in Alabama, a White military policeman told them to move to the "colored" station.

"What's my color got to do with it?" said Joe, choking back his anger. "I'm wearing a uniform like you."

"Down here," the military police officer (MP) responded, "you do as you're told." With that, he poked Joe in the ribs with his billy club.

In a flash, Robinson jumped on the policeman's back and all hell broke loose. MPs hustled Louis and Robinson over to the jailhouse, where a colonel listened to their stories. The arresting MP was bawled out and the boxers released. Meanwhile, word had gotten around the base. To diffuse the growing racial tension, Joe and Sugar Ray drove around in a jeep to show that everything was okay.

It really wasn't, of course. But Joe's approach to dealing with the prejudice he encountered, especially in the Deep South, was to tacitly accept Jim Crow restrictions off base, since he figured he'd have little success challenging local ordinances or customs.

However, on base he quietly but firmly used his position to effect change. He would privately demand of a commanding officer that the crowd attending one of his exhibitions be integrated or else he would refuse to box. When he came across a particularly egregious example of racism, he would place calls to highly placed friends in Washington, DC. In terms of Joe's activism, the brouhaha at Camp Siebert was unusual in that it got into the newspapers. But the publicity had a positive effect. Soon after the incident, the Army ordered all military buses to be desegregated.

* * *

In June 1942, Joe used his connections to get assigned to Fort Riley, Kansas, a cavalry post. His well-known love of horses wouldn't be enough to delay the outdated unit's replacement by a mechanized unit. But he was able to use his influence to better the conditions of Black soldiers on the base, including a former All-American football player from UCLA named Jackie Robinson.

Robinson, destined to break major league baseball's color line after the war, was drafted just a few weeks before Joe's arrival at Fort Riley. Robinson and several other Black soldiers had applied for Officer Candidate School, but the base's White command ignored official Army policy, which called for qualified Black candidates to be trained in integrated facilities. Instead, officials privately told rejected candidates that they lacked leadership ability.

Robinson approached Louis about leap-frogging the chain of command and for the fighter—now a corporal—in effect to pull rank on the base commander, a general. Joe called Truman Gibson, an attorney friend who was now a top aide at the War Department. Gibson came to Fort Riley to hear the Black candidates' grievance. Within a few days, Robinson and eighteen other Black candidates were enrolled in OCS.

But Robinson, never one to close his eyes to racism, almost didn't make it out of school. When a White officer used a racial epithet in his presence, Robinson "practically knocked every tooth out of that officer's head," Gibson recalled. Joe, Gibson added, was "very persuasive" in getting the base commander to drop charges and allow Robinson to graduate. By that, Gibson meant Joe had bribed the general with a selection of fine gifts. But that was acceptable to Louis—that's what money was for. When Robinson's class graduated, Joe bought all of the newly commissioned second lieutenants tailored uniforms.

Louis was the centerpiece of arguably the most influential US propaganda film to come out of the war, *The Negro Soldier.* In 1943, the War Department, under fire for its discriminatory practices, ordered Colonel Frank Capra to produce a documentary that would educate all servicemen, especially Whites, about the accomplishments of Black figures throughout American history. Capra, who'd won three Academy Awards for Best Director before becoming chief of the Army Pictorial Service, was a populist who was a master at injecting mild social commentary into his films.

Capra turned the proselytizing up several notches for *The Negro Soldier.* In fact, he presented the forty-minute documentary in the form of a preacher delivering a sermon. In the film, the preacher tells his flock that he'd been at the second Louis-Schmeling fight, which he presents as an allegory for the war. Over footage of the two opponents in the ring and then in military training, he says: "In one minute and 49 seconds, an American fist won a victory. . . . This time it's a fight not between man and man, but between nation and nation. A fight for the real championship of the world, to determine which way of life shall survive."

In terms of audience size, *The Negro Soldier* rivaled any of Capra's previous box-office hits. The Army released it free to more than 3,500 commercial theaters, and it was required viewing for all members of the armed forces. While it's impossible to gauge the short film's impact on promoting racial tolerance, it received overwhelmingly positive reviews—especially from the initially skeptical Black press, accustomed as it was to Hollywood stereotypes. Abe Hill of the *Amsterdam News* marveled: "Who on earth thought such a thing could be done so accurately. . . . The movie succeeds in proving that this is the Negro's war. He is too deeply rooted in the making of this great country—he has as much at stake in its destiny as any other waver of the red, white, and blue."

Joe, who eventually rose to the rank of sergeant, spent most of the war staging exhibition bouts and visiting hospitals across the United States and overseas. Although he was never a combatant, he had his share of close calls. He survived several days of V-2 rocket attacks in London and an emergency landing aboard a crippled

Sergeant Joe Louis in 1944. During World War II, the heavyweight champ donated his proceeds from two title fights to service charities and fought ninety-six exhibitions before the troops. (Author's collection)

bomber. Once photographers captured him pulling the lanyard of an artillery piece in Italy; the next day, it malfunctioned and the barrel exploded, killing several soldiers.

The war officially ended on September 2, 1945, with Japan's surrender. On October 1, the Army discharged Joe at Camp Shanks, New York. Except for the occasional ugly incident, Detroit's famous Brown Bomber had enjoyed being just plain old GI Joe during his forty-five months of duty. Free from his handlers, he was forced to become more self-reliant.

"When I didn't have them around to think for me and tell me what to eat and when to go to bed, I had to figure things out myself," he said later. "I grew up in the Army."

He had also grown in the nation's consciousness and in its esteem. No longer was he the inscrutable, racially stereotyped "sepia slugger" of prewar days. The needs of a country at war had humanized him, transforming him into a friendly, dignified, and reassuring symbol of national resolve and "a quiet parable in racial good will," as one national magazine put it. He was awarded the Legion of Merit "for exceptionally meritorious service," an honor rarely given to enlisted men. He'd traveled more than 70,000 miles, fought ninety-six exhibitions, and been seen in person by about 5 million service members. Tens of millions of others had seen him featured in newsreels and films and on recruiting posters. Millions of Americans, even those who didn't follow boxing, would always remember that he had donated the purses of two title fights and had "named the war."

There would be a few dings in the prizefighter's public image during the second half of his life. But when he died in 1981, there was no question of where he would be buried. Sergeant Joseph Louis Barrow rests at Arlington National Cemetery, in the company of patriots and heroes.

Detroit in 1910: "Detroit has much to be proud of and undoubtedly has a great future," said one impressed visitor to the city. (Author's collection)

12

Slogan for a City

With Detroit popping its buttons over its growing size and importance, boosters promoted a catchphrase that captured the city's zeitgeist.

Is life really worth living in Detroit?

As with any community of a certain size and vintage, over the years there have been some doubts. But in the early 1900s, there were few reservations about hanging one's hat in Detroit, either as a day-tripper or as a permanent resident. A respected name as a manufacturer of stoves, shoes, paints, seeds, pharmaceuticals, ships, rolling stock, cigars, and those newfangled automobiles, the nation's thirteenth-largest city in the 1900 census—and rapidly gaining on those ranked above it—also was known for its eye-pleasing avenues, vibrant downtown, and cool lake breezes.

"Having visited some of the most beautiful cities in Europe, I unhesitatingly can say that Detroit is one of the finest residential cities I have ever been in," an Englishman named Oswald Williams commented after a 1907 visit. "With your splendid river and great lake trade increasing annually and its ranking as one of the greatest automobile manufacturing centers in the world, with glorious Belle Isle . . . as a rendezvous for your pleasure seekers, Detroit has much to be proud of and undoubtedly has a great future."

The city of some 300,000 citizens was on the verge of greatness, but what was needed was a catchy slogan to wrap around this bundle of natural and man-made gifts. Local boosters got cracking. Henry T. Ewald, a young publicity man for a local steamship company, was a driving force behind the effort. Ewald, described as a "persistent plugger," had been born in a room over his father's east-side saloon. He was only twenty years old when he founded the Adcraft Club, an organization of local advertising executives, in 1905. The public-spirited Detroiter would go on to co-found the Campbell-Ewald ad agency and become one of the city's leading philanthropists, lauded by newspaperman Malcolm Bingay as someone who sought to suffuse a city of stone and steel with something just as vital: *soul*.

City slogans were a bit of a fad in the years before World War I, with seemingly every community, whether a village or a metropolis, feeling the need to trumpet its worth. They were a reflection of local pride, to be sure, but also a marketing tool designed to attract new families, businesses, conventions, tourists, and investors.

Detroit already had an official city motto, adopted after fire destroyed it in 1805: "We hope for better things; it shall rise from the ashes." That was fine for the municipal seal found in Mayor William Thompson's office. But the solemn sentiment—in Latin, no less—was hardly the kind of punchy messaging to be fitted on a convention badge or a souvenir pillowcase.

In 1906, the Adcraft Club formed a "civic improvement" committee to explore ways of generating publicity for Detroit. Among its most active members was Alfred M. "Mark" Woodward, of the Acme White Lead & Color Works, the largest paint and varnish factory in the world. A toastmaster type brimming with ideas, the forty-five-year-old English immigrant had risen to assistant secretary at Acme by aggressively promoting the virtues of lead paint.

Adcrafters worked up a loosely coordinated campaign with the Detroit Board of Trade, with a yet-to-be-determined motto as its centerpiece. Unlike other communities, which typically held a slogan contest in conjunction with the local newspaper or chamber of commerce, organizers didn't invite Detroiters to submit suggestions or ask them to vote for their favorite. On March 4, 1907, residents woke up to discover that, through absolutely no effort

Henry T. Ewald, the public-spirited founder of the Adcraft Club and co-founder of the Campbell-Ewald ad agency, was the driving force behind Detroit's most famous slogan. (Author's collection)

on their part, the city suddenly had a new quasi-official slogan: "In Detroit Life Is Worth Living." Woodward was credited as the author.

Actually, the expression had been floating around town for a while, though the words were not always strung together in that precise order. Silas Farmer's popular street guide had boasted that "our advantages are many and exceptional—in Detroit, where life is worth living." And Stroh's brewery had used a similar phrase in its beer ads, urging Detroiters to "take a bottle . . . out of the ice box and make life worth living."

On cue, the following morning's *Detroit Free Press* had a poem by Edgar Guest, who, not coincidentally, was also an active Adcrafter.

In Detroit, Life's Worth Living,
Every day;
In Detroit, we are giving
Joys away.
In Detroit, it is true,
That our skies are always blue,
There's a smile for me and you,
Blithe and gay.

As part of the rollout, businesses ranging from Electric Park to Leonard's Reliable Storage Company incorporated the catchphrase into ad copy. Organizers encouraged local journalists to use it as a synonym for Detroit or as a tagline, a practice out-of-town newspapers soon picked up. Real estate developers and tourist bureaus heavily promoted it. The slogan was prominently spelled out in flowers in Grand Circus Park—the heart of the retail district—and on City Hall's front lawn. The floral displays made for colorful postcards that found their way into countless albums around the country.

Meanwhile, footloose Detroiters road-tested it. A traveling salesman took to signing hotel registers along the East Coast as "George Ringle, Where Life Is Worth Living." Another wag, vacationing in Mexico, mailed a postcard to a friend that he addressed to "Where life is worth living, USA." The post office knew exactly where to send it.

In this era of parlor pianos and nickel sheet music, a song naturally was called for. Enter Charles A. Parker, a principal of the Curtis Advertising Company, basso of the Jefferson Avenue Presbyterian Church, and an enthusiastic Adcrafter. Parker wrote the words and music to "In Detroit Life Is Worth Living," which he unveiled during the club's annual moonlight lake outing in July 1907.

You take your best girl and away you whirl
For an automobile ride,
As far as you please, 'mid flowers and trees,
On the boulevards you glide;
Then you take in the sights and electric lights
At night when the avenue's gay,
And join in the song, with the rest of the throng,
When the band begins to play.

(Chorus)

In Detroit life is worth living each minute of
ev'ry year,
Who could wish for anything more than we
have right here,
We ought to be happy in this old town with
pleasures ashore and afloat,
In Detroit, life is worth L-I-V-I-N-G, that is
the popular vote.

There were several verses, with the lyrics favorably comparing Detroit to such places as New York, Cleveland, New Orleans, Washington, St. Louis, Chicago, Buffalo, and "the town that's famed for beans," Boston.

The campaign's timing was serendipitous. It was launched just as Ty Cobb was leading the Tigers into the first of three straight World Series; the following year, Henry Ford's first Model Ts hit the streets. Baseball's greatest attraction and the media-savvy creator of the most popular car on the planet brought even more exposure and prestige to the city. In 1908, Ewald, Joseph L. Hudson, and other leading citizens formed the Detroit City Service League, devoted to "arousing a spirit of civic pride." Membership was automatic with the purchase of a button that bore the slogan.

George Lewis, owner of the Lewis Institute, a nationally known school for stutterers, was among those who caught the fever. He announced sending out 1 million circulars and other printed matter

Sheet music for "In Detroit Life Is Worth Living," a song released by the Adcraft Club in 1907 to help promote the city's new catchphrase. (Author's collection)

featuring the watchword, "In Detroit, Life is Worth Living." At the same time, he released to local newspapers a long poem carrying the motto as its title. A sampling of its verses:

Famed for her factories,
In which turn great wheels;
Famed for her drugs,
For her automobiles;

Famed for her seeds,
For her stoves, for her schools,
Famed for her foundries,
Where men work with tools!
Detroit for conventions,
Detroit for all classes,
Detroit for Detroit,
Detroit for the masses!
No other city under the sun,
Can compare with Detroit
Our city the one!

Ewald would later claim that the Adcrafters' effort to promote Detroit was "the first advertising campaign ever prepared for any municipality." Whether this was true or not, other towns around

Pennants, pillowcases, postcards, and pinbacks were just a few of the souvenir items bearing some version of Detroit's slogan. (Author's collection)

the state followed Detroit's lead, with boosters coining such slogans as "Grand Rapids Knows How," "In Kalamazoo We Do," and "Belding—Bigger and Better."

As all ad campaigns do, this one eventually ran its course, with Detroit's disorderly growth through the World War I years and beyond making the motto seem more ironic than iconic. Was life really worth living in an urban center where traffic, housing, pollution, crime, and racial and ethnic tensions were serious concerns? One million people—and counting—apparently thought so. In the 1920s, the teeming motorcar capital leapfrogged all but New York, Chicago, and Philadelphia in population while also making its mark in such varied fields as aviation, music, radio, architecture, and sports. "We have the biggest of nearly everything," the 1925–26 city directory bragged, "the tallest building, the biggest electric sign, the longest bridge, the most money."

By then, observers considered the once ubiquitous catchphrase—so evocative of the leafy midsized community from which it sprang—quaint. The sooty, sprawling industrial powerhouse now carried a label that better captured its mad charge into the front rank of cities: "Dynamic Detroit."

Seeing Detroit

More than one hundred years ago, the most popular way of seeing Detroit was Seeing Detroit. The oversized Packards operated by A. C. Dietsche were everywhere. Whenever a "rubbernecking wagon" of Elks, Masons, or realtors rumbled past City Hall or the floral clock at Waterworks Park, odds were great that it belonged to the savvy, über-connected German American entrepreneur. The attractive and comprehensive brochure Dietsche gave each customer was given boasted that the company's fleet of open-air vehicles were "The Only Way to See Detroit," capable of providing up to thirty-five passengers with "a quick, restful, and inexpensive way of seeing Detroit and its famous Belle Isle Park, the most magnificent island park in this country, its beautiful river, grand boulevards, handsome residences, and great buildings."

On all Dietsche tours, "competent lecturers" were on hand to "point out and explain all points of interest."

Detroit's sightseeing heyday was the turn of the twentieth century, when it enjoyed a reputation as a highly desirable tourist and convention destination. A variety of operators, large and small, sprang up to service the burgeoning trade in out-of-town day trippers with regularly scheduled runs and special charters. The Metropolitan Sight Seeing Company conducted business from its main location inside the Oxford Hotel downtown. The Detroit Urban Railway promised that a ride on its special "Yolanda" electric streetcar would show a stranger the best of Detroit in two hours. B. J. Sturn offered the "Finest Sight Seeing Cars In Detroit" from his Woodward location. On August 26, 1910, one satisfied Sturn customer, a tourist from Cleveland, wrote her mother and sister on a postcard provided by the operator: "We are now in Waterworks Park after having had an auto ride in this large car for 25 miles. It is sinfully grand. Wish you could both be here."

However, for many years nobody cornered the market like A. C. Dietsche. Rivals grumbled about his "in" with the German aldermen and mayors who dominated local politics during this era. In 1915, Frank Wells complained that Seeing Detroit vehicles were allowed to idle all day and night in a prime location on Woodward by the Opera House, squeezing out competitors like himself. "Two of the cars stand there all the time; they don't move at all," he told the city attorney. "One at the lower end catches the passengers walking up the avenue and the other at the upper end gets those strolling down." Once a car was loaded, Wells said, "they pull a third one up alongside and transfer the passengers across. It means we smaller fellows can't get a stand in there because there isn't enough room."

Dietsche maintained the city's best-stocked souvenir shop in the downtown cigar store he'd been operating since 1904. The store at the corner of Woodward and Larned also served as a waiting room for Seeing Detroit's scheduled hourly departures. Before or after their trip, tourists could pick up a pennant, ashtray, plate, glass, or some other Detroit-centric memento. Lapel buttons declaring "In Detroit Life Is Worth Living" were popular. Out-of-towners anxious to share their experiences in the City by the Strait could choose between hundreds of different mass-produced postcards. Or they could visit the adjacent studio and pose behind a whimsically painted backdrop, such as a wheelbarrow or automobile, for a one-of-a-kind "real photo" postcard to mail to a friend or stick in an album. Dietsche produced many of the commercial postcards he sold, including sets of the pennant-winning Tigers that are highly prized among baseball memorabilia collectors.

In an era when millions of people had yet to set foot inside a car, the novelty of doing so inside an automobile heightened the excitement of taking in such sights as the Belle Isle aquarium, Henry Ford's famous Model T plant, the giant spruce log in Palmer Park, and the world's largest stove on Jefferson. For many Seeing Detroit customers, it was their first ride in a motorcar. For at least one, however, it was her last. "No more autos for me," Myrtle Campbell of Duluth, Minnesota, declared one June afternoon in 1907, after the sightseeing car she and her family were riding in collided with a Third Avenue trolley. "I've had enough of them. Somebody get a carriage to take us home."

Each day a small fleet of A. C. Dietsche sightseeing buses carried hundreds of day-trippers, conventioneers, traveling salesmen, and out-of-town relatives on a scenic drive around Detroit. For many tourists, the experience was their first-ever ride in a motorcar. (Author's collection)

13

No Running Away

In 1961, Del Shannon scored a "Runaway" hit. But as the years passed and his star fell, the song's heartbreak mirrored the singer's very real pain.

It's been said that if you plant your scuffed suede bucks on the spot where the Hi-Lo Club once stood, squeeze your eyes tight, and concentrate really, *really* hard, you can hear the cloud-scraping falsetto and creepily cascading Musitron solo.

And I wonder, I wah-wah-wah-wah wonder. . . .

It's an evening sometime in the fall of 1960, your imagination tells you, and within the walls of the dingy, smoke-shrouded lounge you're on the sticky ground floor of pop-music history.

My little runaway, a-run-run-run-run runaway. . . .

Alas, the feeble attempt at time travel doesn't work. Sixty years on, there's nothing to hear but the mumble of traffic at the corner of Hamblin and Capital avenues in downtown Battle Creek, Michigan. The Hi-Lo Club and the faded hotel that housed it are long gone. In their place is a green and gold state historical marker, informing the occasional interested passerby that this is where Charles Weedon Westover—better known to the public as Del Shannon—first performed early versions of what became the international hit called "Runaway."

"Runaway" was released in March 1961, and over the coming months nobody within earshot of a radio, record player, or jukebox could escape its driving and hauntingly distinctive sound. In the years since, some two hundred artists have covered "Runaway," everybody from Elvis Presley and Lawrence Welk to the Small Faces and Bonnie Raitt. It's been featured in such popular films as *American Graffiti* and *Born on the Fourth of July* and was the theme of a hit network television crime drama. The song was a phenomenal success for an earnest but tormented singer-songwriter from rural Michigan whose anguished oeuvre grew to include follow-up hits like "Two Kinds of Teardrops," "Keep Searchin'," and "Stranger in Town." "Del's songs were refreshing," says Tony Press, a British fan whose first record, "Runaway," was a gift on his fourteenth birthday. The lyrics were never particularly deep, the Bristol accountant concedes. "But we could all relate to teenage heartbreak and relationships that foundered."

Chart-topping success would prove impossible to sustain, however, and whatever internal demons the singer was battling ultimately won out. "It's a tough deal, that music business," reflects Earl Meerman, a lifelong pal. "It's not all gravy. You're riding number one today, and the next day you're a nobody. Things got a little tough for him. Life got more than he could handle. He's thinking, 'There's only one way out of this, baby.' "

* * *

Long before there was Del Shannon, there was Chuck Westover, a small-town boy with jug-handle ears and a mischievous grin. Born on December 30, 1934, in Grand Rapids, he grew up in the snoozy farming community of Coopersville, Michigan. Despite the inevitable onset of subdivisions and industrial parks, agriculture still accounts for much of the land in and around Coopersville.

"Most older people around here know him as Chuck, or Charlie," says Meerman, who lives on five acres outside of town. A large man with gray, cropped hair, the retired Greyhound employee grew up across from the Westovers' farmhouse on 48th Street. "I guess you could say Chuck was a little hell-raiser in school. But kids are kids. We played softball, played on the football team together. He was a grade ahead of me. Everywhere he went he had that damn guitar."

Chuck had two younger sisters. According to one of them, Blanche Dykehouse, the family was not the least bit musical. "Mom got Chuck an Arthur Godfrey ukulele one Christmas," says the Fruitport resident, who bears a startling resemblance to her brother. "He was about thirteen when he got his first guitar. He bought it out of the Sears catalog for, I think, five dollars."

Chuck's dad, Bert, drove for the road commission. "He knew every mailbox that had a beer in it," Meerman says. The head of the Westover household was hardly supportive of his son's obsession. "You get that goddamn guitar outta here," Bert would say.

"Maybe if he hadn't said 'get that guitar outta here,' I wouldn't have been interested in playing," the shy but determined youngster would say years later. "Maybe instead I'd be driving a truck."

The boy's mother was more understanding. "It's okay, son," Leone Westover would say. "You can sing for me."

Chuck sang and played for anyone who would listen, and for more than a few who had no choice. He lugged his guitar down school hallways, into lavatories (where he learned "bathroom acoustics"), and inside the locker room. He was an indifferent student, though he exhibited a knack for writing. He was already experiencing some of the feelings of alienation that would later color his songs. "I was an outcast growing up with a bunch of Christian people," he once told the *Los Angeles Times*. "My father didn't go to church and that was not good news if you lived right in the middle of it." Another formative experience was getting dumped by his prom date for his rival.

While in high school, he met a bright and lively farm girl named Shirley Nash, who agreed to a date after he gave her the first flowers she had ever received from a boy. "I didn't like him at first," Shirley Westover says today. "I thought he was kind of pushy."

But in 1954 they married. He was nineteen, she was seventeen. Chuck entered the army and the newlyweds soon found themselves in Stuttgart, Germany. There Private Westover won a talent contest and played guitar in a band called the Cool Flames. He was discharged in 1957, but after having no luck finding a good job back home, he enlisted in the Air Force with the provision he be stationed at Camp Custer in Battle Creek. He stayed in uniform until receiving a hardship discharge because of his father's brain cancer.

Now raising a young family in Battle Creek, he worked at a carpet store during the day and at night played rhythm guitar for a small group at the Hi-Lo Club, a honky-tonk frequented by workers from the nearby Kellogg's plant. "It was the kind of place roughnecks felt comfortable in," recalls Max Crook. Soon Chuck Westover was the group's singer and leader. He called himself Charlie Johnson and renamed the trio the Big Little Show Band. A local disc jockey named Charlie Marsh shopped around tapes of some of Westover's original tunes, such numbers as "Hi-Lo Boogie" and "Hi-Lo Blues," with no luck.

Crook, a young keyboardist who had formed a band called the White Bucks while attending college in Kalamazoo, joined the group in 1959, setting up on stage an odd-looking homemade machine he dubbed the Musitron. It was an early version of a synthesizer, made of tubes, wires, resistors, amplifiers, and appliance parts, and it produced some wonderfully futuristic electronic sounds.

Crook convinced a friend, Ann Arbor disc jockey Ollie McLaughlin, to come out and hear them play. McLaughlin was impressed. He took some demos to Harry Balk and Irving Micahnik, who operated an independent production company on Alexander Street in Detroit. Balk, a jazz aficionado and former pool-hall hustler, had a knack for discovering talent and fine-tuning an artist's work in the studio. Micahnik, who'd gone bankrupt as a furrier in Pennsylvania and had a serious gambling problem, had no background in music but handled the financial and marketing end of things. Among their successes were such artists as Little Willie John and Johnny and the Hurricanes.

Balk saw potential in Westover and Crook, and signed both to five-year contracts in July 1960. But there was the matter of Westover's name. Balk asked him to change it to something more dynamic. Always an admirer of Detroit iron, the singer coupled a contraction for the Cadillac Coupe de Ville to the name of a wrestler he knew named Mark Shannon. The newly minted "Del Shannon" would always be only his stage name; his legal name would remain Chuck Westover.

Balk and Micahnik had a production arrangement with New York's Big Top Records. Following a disappointing recording session in New York, where producers deemed none of his efforts good enough to release, Shannon was encouraged to rework one of his earlier unfinished songs, a more up-tempo number using Crook's Musitron as the lead instrument.

Shannon later recalled the genesis of what became his signature hit. It was a Friday night in October 1960. "We were on stage, and Max hit an A minor and a G and I said, 'Max, play that again, it's a great change.'" After about fifteen minutes of playing the unusual chord change over and over, the exasperated manager of the Hi-Lo Club bellowed, "Knock it off, play something else."

Shannon, inspired, wrote some lyrics the next day at the carpet store. A friend, Wes Kilbourne, happened to drop by that Saturday. "I recall Del's original title of the song was 'Little Runaway,'" Kilbourne said. "He was working out lyrics like 'I'm a-walkin' in the storm' and 'I'm a-walkin' beneath the clouds.' Things like that. In fact, he had an entire second verse that he wrote but totally scrapped because it didn't fit in as well as the first verse: 'Something-something-something, I see the image of my love, I'm a-walkin' in the rain. . . .'"

"That night," said Shannon, "I went back to the club and I told Max to play an instrumental on his Musitron for the middle part, and when he played that solo, we had 'Runaway.'"

Not quite. There still was plenty of tweaking. "By the time it came out," Shirley says, "it was already an oldie-but-goodie to me, because he played it constantly."

"Runaway," along with three other songs, was recorded in a single three-hour session at Bell Sound Studios in New York on January 21, 1961. Balk supervised the session, and one of his edicts was that Shannon—a self-taught but accomplished guitarist—would supply only the vocals. In fact, Balk never allowed Shannon to play the guitar in studio or on stage, insisting the singer adopt the finger-snapping style then in vogue. Shannon was nervous and sang flat, so in order to bring his vocals into key, Balk had the tape speeded

Del Shannon in his prime. Between 1961 and 1966 he charted sixteen singles, though the British invasion caused the hits to dry up. (Author's collection)

up. When Shannon first heard the finished song in Detroit, he protested: "That doesn't even sound like me!"

"Yeah, but Del," Balk responded, "nobody knows what the hell you sound like!"

That quickly changed. Before engineers mixed and mastered the song, someone played a rough version over the telephone to distributors around the country. Orders poured in. "We had a hit even before the record was pressed," Crook says. After a radio station in Miami played the song, Big Top received an order from one vendor for an unprecedented 39,000 copies. On the strength of "Runaway" and its B-side, "Jody" (which actually would remain Shannon's favorite among all of his songs), Shannon opened at the Paramount Theater in Brooklyn, New York, on March 31, where he sang "Runaway" four times a day. Boosted by his appearance on *American Bandstand* ten days later, followed by a whirlwind tour of the East Coast and Canada, "Runaway" charged up the *Billboard* charts, selling as many as 80,000 copies in a single day. According to Crook, who later turned to gospel and spiritual music and today lives in New Mexico, the song's main appeal was its novelty. "It was unorthodox, a 'hook' song," he says. "You've got the chord progressions, the falsetto, the Musitron."

"Runaway" hit number one in late April and stayed there for four weeks. *Billboard* later named it the Song of the Year. Shannon followed up "Runaway" with "Hats Off To Larry," which he wrote while backstage at the Paramount with Dion and Bobby Vee. The song peaked at number five that summer. Two other songs cracked the Top 40 in 1961: "So Long Baby" and "Hey! Little Girl."

Shannon was overwhelmed by the attention he was receiving. "The screaming kids . . . when I got to number one, Lord, the fear was so great," he recalled. "I wanted to go back to Coopersville where I was picking strawberries. I said, 'What am I doing here?'" When he finally did get back to Coopersville, his friends and neighbors honored him, but local officials decided against holding a concert. They were afraid his music was too raucous. He wound up staging an impromptu gig in the back of a pickup truck.

When "Runaway" took off, Shannon was a married twenty-six-year-old army veteran with two kids and a third on the way, living in a house trailer. As one of the music industry's newest faces, managers instructed him to shave five years off his age and to tell reporters he was single. Micahnik tried to get the singer's "girlfriend" to dress more sophisticatedly—perhaps a fur coat. "I said I didn't want to play dress-up in my mother's clothes," says Shirley, one of thirteen children raised with a minimum of frills on the family farm. "But overall, we let managers make decisions for us. We were kind of immature. I figured that's what we had to do to make it." Despite his managers' best efforts, Shannon was miscast as a teen idol. A stocky five-foot-six and already fretting about his hairline, he was pleasant looking but no dreamboat in the Ricky Nelson or Frankie Avalon mode.

Desperate to get a start in the business, Shannon had signed a contract that gave Balk and Micahnik the bulk of the profits and allowed them to deduct expenses from his earnings. Nonetheless, the few pennies he made in royalties on every record sold quickly piled up, and Shannon was able to move his young family into a new ranch home in Southfield, outside Detroit. He also bought himself a white Cadillac convertible. "The pot of gold at the end of the rainbow is real," declared a Battle Creek columnist, attributing the local boy's success to persistence and "Detroit promotion."

Shannon continued to chart with "Little Town Flirt" and "The Swiss Maid" in 1962. He was extremely popular in England, where he performed with Chubby Checker and other top American acts in the British film comedy, *It's Trad, Dad!* In 1963, he shared a London bill with the up-and-coming Beatles. He asked to record "From Me to You," making him the first American to cover a Beatles song. For their part, the Fab Four loved "Runaway." Years later, Paul McCartney remembered thinking "how great and different that song was from the others of the time." McCartney and John Lennon "took the lovely A-minor chord we heard in 'Runaway' and inserted it in 'From Me to You.' It was just funny when Del recorded the song, because part of the influence came from him."

Unlike most artists at the time, Shannon wrote or co-wrote much of his own material. There always was a strain of hurt, loss, and betrayal in his songs, the product of him pulling inspiration out of some dark corner of his being. He rarely used the word "love" in his lyrics. "I usually write when I'm in a great place," he once explained. "When I'm depressed, I don't usually write. So I take all of when I'm depressed and throw it into when I'm feeling good. Weird, I guess." One of his compositions, a breakup ballad called "I Go to Pieces," was recorded by Peter and Gordon and became a big seller in the United States and the United Kingdom. Shannon always regretted not releasing the song himself at the time. The hits were starting to dry up.

Meanwhile, he had a falling-out with his Detroit managers over royalty payments. Balk attributed the shortfall to delinquent distributors, but the real issue was Micahnik diverting money owed artists and recording studios to pay his heavy gambling debts in Detroit and New York. When Shannon sued and formed his own record label, Micahnik responded by attempting to blackball him in the industry. It was a tangled mess, with nobody getting paid except the lawyers, and ultimately Balk, Micahnik, and Shannon decided it was in everybody's best interests to settle up and go their separate ways.

Shannon and his family moved from Southfield to Van Nuys, California, in 1966, just as he was about to enter the least productive stretch of his career. Having charted sixteen singles between 1961 and 1966, including "Keep Searchin' (We'll Follow the Sun)" and "Stranger in Town," he then virtually vanished. His experimental efforts—an album of hardcore Hank Williams honky-tonk and a psychedelic-flavored LP called *The Further Adventures of*

"Detroit promotion" in the form of producers Harry Balk (*left*) and Irving Micahnik (*right*) enabled Shannon, on the strength of his breakout hit "Runaway," to leave a trailer in Battle Creek for a roomy ranch home in Southfield. The managers even picked out the house for the singer and his family. It wasn't long, however, before arguments over royalties broke up the team. (Author's collection)

Charles Westover—generated critical praise but lukewarm sales. He found some success as an independent producer. In 1969 he took the obscure Los Angeles band Smith under his wing and arranged a soulful remake of the old Shirelles tune, "Baby, It's You." The reworked version sold more than a million copies. He was friends with former teen idol Brian Hyland and in 1970 produced a couple of the singer's comeback hits, including a cover of "Gypsy Woman." That also went gold.

For the most part, the 1970s were a rudderless blur. Now entering his forties, Shannon sported snug-fitting bell-bottoms, bushy muttonchops, and an unconvincing combover. Although he always hated traveling, he toured England, Australia, and the Philippines, countries where he enjoyed a more loyal following than at home. Just a few years removed from being lauded as an original, he was in danger of becoming a rock-and-roll cliché: aging, dissipated, and irrelevant. He smoked weed, snorted cocaine, and popped pills while retaining his old-school vices of tobacco and alcohol. He often was drunk before noon. "I hated the taste of booze," he once told the *Los Angeles Times*, "but I liked where it took me—into oblivion."

"Chuck came from a long line of alcoholics," says Shirley Westover, who admits that their own three children grew up to have problems with substance abuse. "A lot of it is genetic. But alcoholism is a lonely disease. He'd get so wired on stage he could never sleep. He'd go down in the hotel bar or, if he wanted to get away from the fans, he'd drink in his room."

In 1978, following detox at a Los Angeles hospital, Shannon joined Alcoholics Anonymous. He surprised many by quitting the bottle for good and getting back into shape. Concurrent with his newfound sobriety was an up-tick in his professional fortunes. One of his Detroit friends, Dan Bourgoise, had helped with his move west and was now his manager. Bourgoise's new L.A.-based company, Bug Music, aggressively tracked down and collected Shannon's royalties while pitching songs from his catalog for placement in film and television.

Tom Petty, who was ten years old when "Runaway" came out, was a longtime fan. In 1981, he produced *Drop Down and Get Me,*

Shannon's first album in nearly a decade, with Petty and his Heartbreakers backing him in the studio. Shannon's version of "Sea of Love" was released as a single, putting him back on the pop charts for the first time in fifteen years. In 1986, another longtime fan, *Miami Vice* producer Michael Mann, made "Runaway" (with reworked lyrics) the theme of his stylish new television series, *Crime Story*. A quarter-century after he had introduced his signature song to the country on *American Bandstand*, the fifty-one-year-old rocker gave a spirited performance for a new generation on *Late Night with David Letterman*, with Paul Shaffer handling Max Crook's solos on the keyboard.

Bookings and royalties allowed Shannon to enjoy a comfortable, if far from opulent, lifestyle. He and Shirley owned a home in Sand Canyon, a one-acre property shaded by maple and oak trees. Shannon drove a Honda Gold Wing and bought a new Cadillac every other year. Throughout all the vagaries of his profession, he remained essentially the same person who had once picked strawberries and sold carpeting in western Michigan.

"I remember when Chuck would fly into Grand Rapids," Earl Meerman says. "I worked at a gas station then. He'd get a limo and visit, and we'd chew the fat for a couple hours. He never changed." Shannon bought his mother a house in California, close to his, after his father died.

"Chuck was very generous," Shirley says. "When he was with AA, he'd always leave food baskets on porches—you know, knock and run. He'd put a hundred-dollar bill in people's cars while they were inside at a meeting." The singer "reached out to friends and strangers alike, taking a genuine interest in their well-being," remembered music writer Dawn Eden. "But the flip side of sensitivity is vulnerability, something he knew only too well."

His creativity sprang from a melancholic core. Too often he resembled the restless and frustrated characters he sang about. "You could see it in the way he went from record company to record company, artist to artist, during his career," Crook says. "He was always very self-critical. He was never really satisfied with his work." All told, Shannon recorded for eight different labels. He belatedly came to accept that his pop-rock classics were what the public was most interested in.

"So I do me, and me is my hits," he told a reporter backstage at an oldies concert in 1989. "I'm out there really to satisfy the people." More than one reviewer commented that, unlike many of his contemporaries on the nostalgia circuit of nightclubs, state fairs, amusement parks, and reunion shows, Shannon didn't appear jaded, even as he performed "Runaway" for the umpteenth time.

Shirley Westover, along with some others who knew Shannon intimately, today describes him as manic-depressive, a major affective disorder thought to be more prevalent among creative types. "He was always up or down," she says from her Las Vegas home. "There was never a middle with him. I just didn't recognize it at the time. Then with the alcohol and the drugs—it affected his behavior, so you would attribute his mood swings to that."

Tired of her husband's addictions, affairs, and near-constant touring, she had wanted out of the marriage for a long time. "But I could never leave him until he was sober. I was very afraid that he was suicidal." She finally left in 1985, ending thirty-one years of marriage. "At first we separated. He didn't really mind the separation until he realized that I wasn't coming back, that we were getting a divorce."

Shirley remained worried about his bouts of despondency even as they went their separate ways. In late 1987, the singer remarried. The new bride was LeAnne Gutierrez, a neighbor's daughter who was half his age and had a young daughter of her own. "He still loved Shirley," Crook says. "He couldn't let go."

The divorced couple regularly talked on the phone, but a rapprochement was out of the question, at least as far as Shirley was concerned. "Chuck told LeAnne that he'd leave her if I ever decided to come back," she says. "I think she drove him to the bullet."

Shannon's last performance was foreboding. On February 3, 1990, he played at a memorial concert for Buddy Holly, Ritchie Valens, and J. P. ("Big Bopper") Richardson in Fargo, North Dakota. The three rockers had perished in a plane crash one winter evening in 1959, a tragedy immortalized by songwriter Don McLean as "the day the music died."

Five nights later, on February 8, 1990, Shannon's wife and step-daughter came home from shopping. About 11:25 p.m., LeAnne stepped into the darkened den, a room filled with gold records and expensive instruments. She found the fifty-five-year-old singer slumped sideways in a chair, facing the doorway.

"He was wearing only a bathrobe, and his hairpiece was missing," reported the medical examiner dispatched to the scene. "There was a hole in his right temple from a .22-caliber rifle, which was lying beside him on the floor. His eye sockets were, as expected, black and blue from the trauma. He had been dead for a few hours."

There was no suicide note, leaving others to ponder what dark impulse had taken hold of him. Del and LeAnne had just moved into their $260,000 house on Saddleback Road in Canyon Country, about thirty-five miles north of Los Angeles. Shannon, who had visited a psychologist two days before his death, seemed disoriented in the new surroundings. Over the last couple weeks of his life, he had appeared increasingly lethargic. He'd lost weight and his zest for playing music. He canceled an upcoming tour in England. Associates said he was worried about an upcoming IRS audit and also suffering from a stubborn sinus infection. Later, there were rumors that he had found out that he would not, as some had thought, be invited to replace the late Roy Orbison in the Traveling Wilburys, a super-group whose other members were Tom Petty, Bob Dylan, George Harrison, and Jeff Lynne. (The group recorded a version of "Runaway" in his honor, and Petty finished the album he had been producing for Shannon.)

The autopsy revealed no alcohol or illegal drugs in his system. However, in mid-January, he had visited a psychiatrist, hoping to break out of his funk. He came home with a prescription for a new antidepressant, introduced just three years earlier, which was more effective. It didn't produce the same side effects of other drugs, such as weight gain and high blood pressure.

"It's not really a drug, it's a chemical," he told LeAnne. "It'll help me over the hump I'm in."

The psychiatrist had prescribed Prozac. His young widow sued the drug maker, Eli Lilly. "I watched him turn into somebody who was agitated, pacing, had trembling hands, insomnia and couldn't function," she said at the time.

The suit, one of many filed by the families of Prozac patients who had experienced suicidal fantasies or committed violence upon themselves or others, was later dropped. In 2004, the Food and Drug Administration started requiring pharmaceutical companies to include label warnings on their antipsychotic drugs. This was cold comfort to Shannon's fans, friends, and family members.

To this day, some people close to Shannon believe he was murdered, though homicide detectives found no evidence of foul play. "It had to be impulsive," Dan Bourgoise said of his friend's suicide. "In the end, he must have felt alone. All the paranoid things that made him write those songs he wrote, like 'Runaway.' I think he just ended up being that lonely guy."

More than sixty years after "Runaway" topped the charts in twenty-one countries, it remains one of the most instantly recognizable songs on the planet. Among other accolades, the Grammy Hall of Fame enshrined the recording, and *Rolling Stone* named it one of the greatest songs of all time. In 1999, the Rock and Roll Hall of Fame posthumously inducted Shannon, ostensibly for a lifetime's work but principally on the strength of that one song. Airplay and downloads of "Runaway" continue to generate royalties in the low six-figure range each year, a haul divided between his heirs and co-writer Max Crook.

There is no gravesite for Chuck Westover. He was cremated, and mourners spread his ashes from the back of a motorcycle speeding across the Nevada desert. Due to the nature of music in this digital age, he is assured a form of immortality unimaginable to the small-town kid who lugged his five-dollar guitar everywhere he went. "Del Shannon was many years ahead of his time," one critic observed upon the singer's passing. "He never imitated anybody, and he never sounded like anybody but Del Shannon."

14

The Little Sufferers

The Tilden School fire was the deadliest Yuletide tragedy of nineteenth-century Detroit and the worst calamity in the history of local schools.

On the bitterly cold afternoon of March 5, 1890, Carrie Bentliff slipped away, the last of the Detroit schoolgirls to die. It had been just a few weeks since she burst through the doors of Tilden School, a screaming and wild-eyed mass of flames. Somebody on that awful December day, most likely a workingman passing by, had thrown her to the ground and beaten out the fire, but not before her chest, shoulders, and neck had been roasted raw and her bountiful head of hair singed to the scalp. Amid the tumult and the horror—other girls were ablaze, clawing madly at their clothes—she had then gotten up and tried to stagger home, but managed only a few steps before collapsing in shock. While several of her classmates quickly succumbed to their terrible burns, the plucky seventeen-year-old had hung on, inspiring doctors and giving her family hope, until she finally gave in to fever and internal injuries inside her Fourth Street home.

Mourners laid the schoolgirl to rest in a handsome white casket entwined with shiny green tendrils of smilax. "Many and touching were the allusions to the suffering child's heroism and patience during her long sickness," observed a reporter at the funeral service at St. Andrew's Episcopal Church, where the deceased once sang in

Christmas morning as depicted in this 1889 stereo card. That December, a number of badly burned schoolchildren were fighting for their lives inside their joyless Detroit homes. (Library of Congress)

the choir. As the tributes continued, "many eyes were dimmed with sympathetic tears."

Although the Tilden School fire has been lost to time, it remains the worst catastrophe in the history of Detroit's schools and ranks as the city's deadliest Yuletide tragedy of the nineteenth century. In all, nine schoolgirls died from their burns, and several survivors were scarred for life in what the *Detroit Free Press* called "one of the saddest and most desolating calamities Detroit has ever known."

Many years later, music teacher Florence Marsh, a contemporary of the victims, remembered it as "a sad happening for the close of a prosperous and cheerful decade." She expressed the hope that it would remain the only one of its kind "ever connected with our schools." That proved to be the case, as officials put measures in place to prevent a re-occurrence. However, the changes came too late for Carrie Bentliff and her fellow "little sufferers," whose agonizing struggle for life captivated Detroiters during the Christmas season of 1889.

* * *

That December in Detroit was among the dreariest in memory. There was no snow on the ground and no nip in the air. Rain, mud, and forty-degree temperatures kept many shoppers at home and dampened overall enthusiasm for the holiday. Nonetheless, in schools across the city, light-hearted preparations continued on the Yuletide programs traditionally performed on the last day of class before everybody adjourned for a two-week recess.

On Thursday, December 19, 1889, a small group of teachers and pupils gathered inside Room A of Tilden School, located at the northwest corner of Kirby Avenue and Seventh Street. They were staging a final dress rehearsal of their Christmas cantata, called "Santa Claus at Play." The performance included twenty students, most of them teenage girls dressed in whimsical costumes made of cotton batting and mosquito netting.

Helping to direct the after-school session was Maud Priest. The twenty-year-old teacher had grown up loving books and saw education as her life's work. In 1888, she graduated from Detroit Normal School (a teachers' training program administered by the city's only high school) and, armed with enthusiasm and her diploma, immediately began teaching. Joining Priest in the second-floor classroom were two other young instructors, Hattie Sanders and Dora Woodsworth.

The room grew darker as the afternoon wore on. Someone brought a candle out of a cupboard and lit it. One of the boys dutifully held the candleholder near the piano as Miss Woodsworth played. Sometime around five o'clock, something happened that caused the glowing taper to graze the costume of Bessie Seely. Either there was a momentary lapse of concentration on the boy's part or a girl accidentally struck the candle while waving a wand.

In an eye-blink, twelve-year-old Bessie was ablaze. Classmates instinctively flocked to the screaming youngster, trying to beat out the spreading flames, only to have their own costumes catch fire. In mere seconds, the harmonious chorus that had filled the room turned into inconsonant shrieks of terror. As Priest later related, it was "absolutely impossible to control the pupils after their lives were imperiled. They became panic-stricken, and a number ran right by a penstock in the hallway to get at water in the basement of the building." Priest grabbed a piano cover and tried to smother the flames on several girls, scorching her own hands in the process.

Several girls ran out of the building, a stampede of screeching human torches that startled passersby. Quick-thinking men tackled and rolled the blazing victims in the muddy street. Alarms brought horse-drawn ambulances and a fire wagon racing to the scene. Word spread that the school was burning down (though firefighters quickly extinguished any smoldering piles of clothes, resulting in scant property damage). In short order, the streets of the working-class neighborhood were lined with frantic parents.

Marshall P. Thatcher was buying cigars at a downtown shop when he casually asked a friend entering the store what was new.

"Nothing," the man replied, "unless it is that several children at one of the schools were badly burned."

Thatcher bolted out of the store and ran practically all the way home. His heart sank when he saw the ambulance parked at the curb. Rescuers had taken his vivacious thirteen-year-old daughter, Nellie, a star pupil, inside. Her left arm and side were charred and her neck was raw from the flames.

All of the boys and teachers in Room A had suffered minor burns helping to extinguish the fire. Alexander McMillan and Eddie Wheeler—described as "brave boy pupils who were burned in tearing off the blazing costumes of some of the girls"—acted heroically, ripping down draperies and flags to keep the flames from spreading.

Remarkably, a couple of the girls escaped with only singed costumes. However, fourteen other students, all girls between the ages of twelve and eighteen, were grievously burned, most of them on their hands, arms, upper torso, neck, and face. Their scorched hair fell out in clumps. There were no dedicated burn units then, though one mildly burned victim was taken to Harper Hospital. The others were rushed home or to the closest physician's office. (Most doctors then worked out of their residence.) Rescuers brought those too critically injured into the nearest welcoming household, where they were tended to by sympathetic neighbors until a nurse, doctor, or family members arrived.

Many of the victims were barely conscious and had rapid but feeble pulses. Standard procedure called for immediately administering stimulants, such as placing ammonia under the nose and hot water bottles by the feet and sides of the body. For those whose stomach could handle it, doctors gave whiskey in milk.

Inside the Thatchers' modest corner house at Hancock and Seventh, Nellie tossed her head from side to side, moaning deliriously. She had several paroxysms of vomiting. "She is a terribly burned child," said the doctor attending her, "and I fear the worst."

At the time, doctors did not use the system of classifying burns according to their level of severity. However, contemporary descriptions indicate many of the schoolchildren had suffered what today would be graded as third-degree burns, characterized by deep tissue damage and black, charred skin. Some had fourth-degree burns, where the fire not only destroyed the skin and nerve endings but also underlying muscles, tendons, and ligaments. Then, as now, fourth-degree burns usually resulted in death.

Among those clinging to life was Jennie Lankshear, whom rescuers carried into the nearby home of Joseph Miller. "When the half-dead girl was placed on a bed in Mr. Miller's house it was found that everything had been burned off her, except her shoes," reported the *Free Press*. "She was in the greatest agony and in various portions of her body the flesh dropped off in large pieces." A doctor did what he could, applying dressings of linseed oil, lint, and powdered chalk to the raw flesh. "All during the evening the suffering girl could be heard in an adjoining room, praying God to give relief." It finally came at ten o'clock that night, when the fifteen-year-old died after five hours of excruciating pain.

Early Friday morning, twelve hours of torment ended for Bertha Moody when the fourteen-year-old slipped quietly away inside her home on Trumbull. "Her whole body, excepting her feet, was burned to a crisp," observed a visitor, "and the shock to her nervous system was enough of itself to cause death." The girl's father was the Rev. Edward B. Moody, a traveling evangelist who was frantically trying to arrange transportation back to Detroit when she died.

Later that day, Edith Wheeler succumbed to shock and smoke inhalation. A janitor had thrown a bucket of water over the eighteen-year-old as she ran screaming from Room A, but by then the flames had burned off all of her clothes except her corset and shoes. Long shreds of skin had peeled off her body and hung from her fingertips as her brother Edward, who had taken the part of Santa Claus in the play, helped her into a doctor's office on West Warren. Before dying, she "inquired solicitously after her schoolmates, whom she knew were in the school room when the panic occurred."

The death toll climbed to four on Saturday, when Florence Westgate died at home, attended by her physician father. The thirteen-year-old had been badly burned about her face, arms, and upper torso, but was thought to be in survivable condition. However, she had also inhaled flames, scorching her lungs and leading to her sudden collapse.

On Sunday, December 22, the first funerals were held. As was customary then, the deceased were laid out at home before being taken to the cemetery. The parlors overflowed with flowers and mourners, including mayor-elect Hazen Pingree. Large groups of students, teachers, and school officials hurried from one service to the next. The weather was appropriately funereal: cold, windy, overcast.

The next day, local Baptist ministers held their weekly meeting. "Resolutions of sympathy were passed for the sufferers by the

Tilden School fire and especially with Brother Moody in the loss of his daughter," an attendee noted. The evangelists stressed their belief that the rewards of the righteous would last through eternity. Rev. Moody and his wife would need such moral sustenance. Over the next two winters, they would bury two more children alongside Bertha: one a stillborn baby and the other a week-old infant girl.

Nellie Thatcher, whose injuries were so severe that doctors admitted she would be permanently crippled if she survived, died on December 23, surrounded by family members. "She would gaze intently into one face, then into another, striving by scanning the countenances to ascertain just how they regarded her condition," said A. W. Hilliard, who was present for her final moments. "Each one strove to appear natural and free from apprehension but it is doubtful the eager eyes of the dying girl were in the least misled." Her family was devastated. "She was the light of our household," Marshall Thatcher said, "and sad indeed it will ever seem with the sunlight of her presence gone for all time from our midst."

* * *

The day before Christmas was a dry Tuesday. With better weather came swarms of last-minute shoppers, keeping Woodward Avenue merchants happy and post offices busy. In the display window of Newcomb, Endicott & Co., the city's leading retailer, a jovial Santa Claus entertained the jostling crowds of passersby. Inside a dozen scattered homes, however, the mood was somber, as the fire victims continued to fight for their lives. "In the midst of all the festivities of this season," the *Free Press* reminded its readers on Christmas Eve, "a thought of the sufferers by the Tilden School fire and the stricken friends of the dead is seemly."

The thoughts and prayers appeared to work, if only briefly. For nearly the entirety of Christmas week, there were no new deaths to report. Doctors had stabilized the patients, their bodies and heads swathed in oil-soaked cloth bandages. The bandages needed to be kept moist so that the cloth wouldn't stick to the burned surface. They had to be regularly changed, a procedure that could take three or four hours. Pieces of mortified flesh were softened with warm water for half an hour or so before being carefully cut away with scissors. Doctors administered laudanum and other opiates to help alleviate the mind-bending pain and to induce sleep.

Georgette "Georgie" Horner passed in and out of consciousness. "We have admitted no one to see our child since she was brought home, except those immediately concerned," said the twelve-year-old's father. "She is burned much worse than has been stated, and for the first time the doctor gave us a little hope. But it is only a little. He thinks she has reached the turning point in the case, but is far from being out of danger. She passed a bad night last night, and a very bad day today, with sinking spells at frequent intervals. Oh, it is terrible."

Meanwhile, the school board bought space in *Scientific American* magazine, soliciting bids to install chemical fire extinguishers in all Detroit public schools.

By early January, doctors were preparing to perform skin grafting on Bessie Seely, the girl whose dress first caught fire, using skin from the arm of her sister. Carrie Bentliff seemed much improved, and soon she too would undergo her first skin graft. One of her younger sisters would be the donor.

However, all of the victims of what the press had labeled "the school holocaust" were highly susceptible to fevers, infections, and pneumonia. Several remained in critical condition. Edna Fonda, thirteen, had been burned to the bone in several places and had a deep burn over her jugular. By December 31, death was imminent. "Her flesh is like leather where she was burned," her nurse said, "and the charred pieces still remain undisturbed. The physician hoped that he could remove the burned flesh today, but he could not. She takes little nourishment, and now it seems absolutely impossible for her to recover." Edna died before midnight rang in a new year and a new decade, the sixth victim of the fire.

Two days later, on January 2, 1890, Bessie Bamford, whose entire front portion of her body was described as "a hard and blackened cinder," became the seventh. Observers praised the Bannisters, the neighborhood couple who had taken the fourteen-year-old into their house at 136 Langley, close to the school, for "the unselfish

Maud Priest in 1888. She was just starting her long career as an educator when disaster struck. (Author's collection)

devotion and watchfulness with which they cared for the little sufferer during the two weeks of agony she passed under their hospitable roof . . . everything that was possible to do to ease her pain or in any way make her more comfortable was cheerfully done."

Early the following morning, Lucy Remshaw's ordeal also ended when the fifteen-year-old died inside the family home on Wabash.

Some criticized the teachers involved in the calamity. Reporters attempted to interview Hattie Sanders at her residence, but were turned away. The young teacher, who had suffered minor burns and smoke inhalation, was racked by guilt. A coroner's inquest revealed that it was Sanders who had brought the candle out of a storage cabinet, though all of the teachers were negligent in not following the unofficial school policy prohibiting any flame except a closed lantern inside the classroom.

"I don't see how anyone can be so unkind as to blame the teachers in the slightest degree," one of the victim's mothers said in defense. "They had the interests of the children at heart, were affectionately disposed toward them all, gave of their own money to help along such entertainments as the cantata they were rehearsing, and now that this dreadful calamity has come upon us I dare say no one is any more grief-stricken than these same teachers."

Two weeks after the fire, the school's twenty-nine-year-old principal, Ella Sheeran, still was in shock and unable to leave her apartment. "As yet she knows nothing of the affair, comparatively, and has not been informed of the death of any of the children," said W. E. Robinson, superintendent of Detroit Public Schools.

When school reopened on January 6, the continued absences of Sanders and Sheeran, the bandaged burns and anguished faces of the teachers who did report, and the many empty desks contributed to the overall air of solemnity. "The little ones were visibly affected by their recent bereavement," noted a visitor to the school. "They gathered in groups and talked in low voices and walked with light steps as if they were in the chamber of death." But there continued to be hope for some of the more seriously burned victims. Late that evening, the doctor visited Georgie Horner and reported her condition "greatly improved."

At a school board meeting on January 23, an investigative committee released its report. The panel found "no blame resting anywhere," but recommended a formal district-wide policy banning the use of flammable costumes and open flame in school recitals. In February, the board approved payments totaling $2,118.18 in medical, burial, and incidental expenses associated with the tragedy.

By the end of February, more than two months after the fire, several of the survivors had recovered sufficiently to return to class, although two girls remained bedridden. Superintendent Robinson described Mildred Raquet as "considerably disfigured" and in grave condition. But the doughty fifteen-year-old, tenderly looked after by her widowed mother and siblings, surprised everyone by eventually recovering from the burns to her face, back, and arms.

Conversely, Carrie Bentliff, who "lay through the long days of pain propped up in an armchair in her room," took an unexpected turn for the worse. She died on the afternoon of March 5, conscious to the end, her devastated parents and sisters at her bedside. She was the last of nine names on the drawn-out list of fatalities. In reporting the girl's passing, the *Free Press* observed that "the memory of the fire, in the rapid pressure of events, has now fairly faded from the public mind." In late August, the school board voted to pay an additional $1,174.78 in expenses associated with the victims' care to "close the matter up" before the new school year began.

The traumatized survivors faced harrowing futures, physically and emotionally. Their bodies were still maturing, meaning they would literally grow out of their skin for several more years. The ongoing treatment of adolescent burn victims in terms of skin grafting, reconstructive surgery, antibiotics, rehabilitative physical therapy, and psychological counseling was nothing like it is today. The usual teenage concerns revolving around body image and self-esteem were exacerbated by the patchwork of scars that each of them wore like a sordid undergarment.

But Detroit's little sufferers showed remarkable resiliency, gradually re-entering the world of social activities they had enjoyed before the catastrophe. Within a few years, some were marrying and starting families. Georgie Horner, for example, married the son of the founder of the Beecher, Peck & Lewis paper company; together they produced four daughters and enjoyed a comfortable lifestyle. She passed away three days before Christmas in 1936, having just marked the anniversary of a distant, darker holiday.

Others never married, either by choice or as a consequence of their disfigurement. Bessie Seely made education her life's work, beginning as a forty-five-dollar-a-month teacher at Poe Elementary in 1897. She took courses when she could, eventually earning her bachelor's degree when she was fifty-seven years old. When she traveled to England, her passport noted "scars under chin" as distinguishing marks. She was always generous at Christmas time, donating a dress or money to her favorite children's charities. The retired schoolteacher was eighty-three when she died, still living at her childhood home on Englewood Avenue. One wonders if she was aware of a cruel coincidence. In 1945, a twenty-five-year-old woman with the exact same name, along with her three young children, perished in a house fire in Woodburn, Oregon. The tragedy occurred on December 19, the fifty-sixth anniversary of the Tilden fire.

Mildred Raquet, who in middle age moved to California with her mother, also remained single while outliving all other survivors.

Tilden School in the 1930s. Arsonists burned it in 1963. (Author's collection)

She was eighty-six years old when a motorist fatally struck her in Santa Monica in 1960.

Maud Priest, only a couple of years older than some of her pupils, went on to spend thirty years in Detroit's public schools as a teacher and principal, gaining prominence as a tireless advocate of school libraries and teacher pensions. The dedicated educator with the scarred hands remained "Miss Priest" to the very end, never marrying and leaving no relatives when she died of liver cancer at forty-eight. The district named an elementary school after her, and today the familiar commotion of youngsters at study and at play fills the worn but still vital building on Wagner Street on the city's west side.

Christmas, above all else, is a season of memories, but recollections of Detroit's worst Yuletide tragedy were too distressing to endure through the years. Tilden School is long gone—ironically destroyed by teenage arsonists in 1963—while the names of the schoolgirls who perished in the 1889 fire have been lost in the collective amnesia of old graveyards like Elmwood and Woodmere. Forgotten, too, are the gifts the students of Room A planned to present to their teachers before the capricious flutter of a flame turned the world upside down. One was a book, titled *Burned as by Fire*. The other was a decorative candlestick.

Players and coaches assemble outside the Northland Hotel in Marquette, Michigan, during the Detroit Red Wings' 1954 trip to play the local prison team. (Author's collection)

15

Pen Pals

In the midst of another successful Stanley Cup season, the Detroit Red Wings squared off against a squad of hockey-mad inmates at Marquette Prison.

It was, insists Leonard "Oakie" Brumm, the damnedest hockey game ever played. Here it was, in the dead of winter and smack-dab in the middle of the 1953–54 National Hockey League season, and the Detroit Red Wings chartered a plane to fly hundreds of miles to the rugged northern reaches of Michigan in order to slap around a rubber disc with a group of spaghetti-legged kidnappers, murderers, burglars, and arsonists.

Gordie Howe. Ted Lindsay. Red Kelly. Terry Sawchuk. What were these future Hall of Famers doing squaring off on an outdoor rink against the likes of Bugsy Wisocki and an assortment of other four- and five-time losers? According to Brumm, it was the result of a promise Red Wings general manager Jack Adams had made to the officials of Marquette Prison. "Build it," Jolly Jack had said in a spurt of offhand largesse, or words to that effect, "and we will come."

"It" was a walled, regulation-sized hockey rink, something no prison in the country ever had. But thanks to the efforts of Brumm—the prison's first athletic director and a top-drawer contractor to boot—workers built the rink. And, remarkably, the Red Wings did come—to a tough and dreary maximum-security prison justifiably known as "Alcatraz of the North."

The teams played the game on the afternoon of February 2, 1954. But the story really begins many years earlier, back in 1927, when Adams arrived in the Motor City as the new coach of the Detroit Cougars, as the Red Wings originally were called. Prohibition made the 1920s an uproarious decade, and nowhere was the uproar louder than in Detroit, whose proximity to Canada made it the perfect conduit for illegal booze.

The city's most notorious bootleggers were a loosely organized band of young punks who grew up together on the near east side. Dubbed the Purple Gang by the press, they were known as flashy men-about-town who enjoyed rubbing shoulders with Detroit's sporting elite. The Purples could be seen taking in baseball games at Navin Field, boxing matches at neighborhood gyms, and hockey games at the brand-new Olympia Stadium on Grand River Avenue. Somewhere along the line the ringleaders—Ray Bernstein, Irving Milberg, and Harry Keywell—made the acquaintance of Adams, who had enough sense to just smile, shake hands, and politely turn down all invitations to join the boys for a night out on the town.

That, of course, was a wise decision. In 1931, authorities sent several Purples to Jackson State Prison for their part in the Collingwood Massacre, a triple homicide inside an apartment building on Collingwood Avenue in Detroit. The gangsters' influence extended beyond prison walls, however, as seen by the baseball-loving Bernstein's ability to coax Tigers star Hank Greenberg to once play in an exhibition game at Jackson. The imprisoned Purples also continued their murderous ways, arranging for the infamous slaying of state Senator Warren G. Hooper in 1945. For their suspected involvement in the Hooper case, authorities shipped the Purples to Marquette Prison.

"You didn't get into Marquette," Brumm said, "unless you've screwed up several times."

Marquette was where inmates did the hardest time imaginable: sequestered in cramped cells with no toilets and forced to endure the interminable, bone-numbing winters without long johns because the warden was afraid they'd give escapees an edge in the wilderness. And this was where Adams, touring the grounds as a guest of warden Emery Jacques one day in 1953, unexpectedly ran into a pair of old acquaintances, Bernstein and Keywell.

"Say, Jack," the old Purples said, "how about bringing the Red Wings up for a scrimmage someday?"

"Sure, no problem," replied Adams, knowing the prison had no facility or team.

Not to be outdone, the warden piped in: "Anytime at all, Jack. Just let us know and we'll be ready."

Adams returned to Detroit and promptly forgot the matter. He didn't realize what his casual conversation had set in motion. Jacques firmly believed that organized recreation helped inmates blow off steam that might otherwise be channeled into the riot that ripped apart Jackson Prison the previous year.

Unbeknownst to Adams, the warden was in the process of hiring Oakie Brumm as the prison's first athletic director. Brumm, a member of the University of Michigan's 1948 NCAA championship hockey team, had just come home to his native Marquette from the University of Alaska, where he had directed the hockey program and built the school's rink.

"Practically all I heard from inmates from the time I got hired by Jacques was, 'The Red Wings are coming! The Red Wings are coming!' " Brumm said. "And all I could think was, 'How am I supposed to get together some kind of team to play them?' "

Brumm spent four years as the prison's athletic director, during which time he developed football, baseball, hockey, golf, and other recreational programs. He remembers how prison athletes, huffing and puffing their way through football and hockey practices, would nonetheless constantly smoke throughout the sessions. One goalie even installed an ashtray on top of his net. Inmates were known to throw a game for three cartons of cigarettes, conceal homemade weapons inside their uniforms (one convict was stabbed during a pileup), and honor the criminal's code to never snitch—even when opponents blithely robbed them of their equipment.

Since Marquette was designed for older prisoners (a convict had to be at least twenty-eight years old to be assigned there), most of the inmates who tried out for Brumm's hockey team in late 1953 were in their thirties and forties. Few could skate very well. Most exhibited minimum hockey ability. And Brumm had to fight to get hockey sticks for the players. For years, the prison had disallowed sticks, fearing that inmates would use them to attack guards or each other. Instead of ice hockey, inmates had played kick hockey, a kind of soccer on ice.

Brumm used his construction know-how and material donated by his father, a building contractor, to erect a walled rink in a corner of the prison yard. Jacques kept Adams apprised of Brumm's progress. When informed that the inmates had no pads, skates, or goaltending equipment, Adams donated all of the equipment of the Omaha Knights, which had just ceased being a Wings farm club. As a joke, he had "Emery's Boys," in honor of the warden, sewn on the front of each jersey.

Brumm relentlessly drilled his squad of inmates over the winter of 1953–54. They scheduled games against teams from the "free world" and did surprisingly well against them. With a few such games under their belt, Emery's Boys finally felt confident enough to challenge the Wings.

At this point, Adams may very well have regretted ever having met the Purple Gang or making such an off-the-cuff remark in front of a courtyard of prisoners. But, true to his word, on the morning of February 2, 1954, the entire Wings squad arrived at Marquette County Airport via a twin-prop DC-3 that cost the semipro Marquette Sentinels (the sponsor of the trip) $1,800 to charter. The Wings were fresh off a pair of home-and-home victories over the Chicago Blackhawks. After checking into the Northland Hotel and enjoying a light lunch, organizers took the Wings to the old brownstone prison. Some of the Detroit players, tough guys on the ice, were understandably apprehensive.

"The prison game generated all kinds of interest," Brumm said. "No one knew the caliber of the players or how the Wings and inmates would react to each other. Jack Adams got some criticism at the time. It was one thing to fight at Olympia against other real hockey players. But what would they do in a fight on the ice at

Coach Leonard "Oakie" Brumm (*standing at far right*) and his prison hockey team named Emery's Boys after the warden. They are pictured at the ice rink inside Marquette Prison. (Author's collection)

Marquette Prison with someone who had already probably killed a couple of people? Not to mention being surrounded by hundreds of the toughest, most volatile 'fans' in the country."

The rousing reception the visitors got quickly put their fears to rest. After dressing in the carpenter's shack (the only building with a shower large enough to enable it to serve as a locker room) and being patted down by guards, the Wings trooped onto the immaculately manicured ice, accompanied by shouts of encouragement and recognition from the assembled cons.

"Most of them were great hockey fans," recalled left winger Johnny Wilson. "They listened to all the games on the radio. They knew all the boys and were cheering us on, which was kind of nice."

Dutch Reibel, centering a line that included Lindsay and Howe, took the opening face-off at 1:30 that afternoon. The entire prison population of 600 convicts (minus those in solitary confinement) stood around the boards. The weather was perfect for hockey: about 21 degrees, overcast, and no wind. Not that Adams's troops needed any meteorological advantage.

For the first several minutes, nary an inmate touched the puck. The Wings freely passed it back and forth several times on each rush, skating around the cons as if they were pylons. After about a minute of this dazzling stickwork, someone would finally pop the puck past the prisoners' goalie, Bugsy Wisocki, a habitual thief whom guards released from solitary confinement specifically for this game.

"Howe would get the puck and circle the net three times before putting it in," Wilson said. "It was funny to watch."

After ten minutes, the Wings had a 10–0 lead. By the fifteen-minute mark the score had grown to 15–0. It easily could have been 50–0. "The only time I touched the puck," lamented Brumm, who installed himself on defense, "was when I pulled it out of the back of the net."

Terry Sawchuk, bored by the inactivity at his end of the ice, sat atop his lonesome net. When he spied the puck finally coming his way, he raced up to it and took it halfway down the ice himself. After enduring several more minutes of idleness, he deliberately tripped one of Emery's Boys so referees would send him to the penalty box to sign a few autographs. Meanwhile, the inmates and guards were hooting and hollering at the overmatched cons and imploring the Wings to pour it on.

At one point Lindsay handed the puck to the cons' best player, Ed Rilley. "Go, man, go," the Wings's captain told him.

Rilley, who had been embarrassed enough, thank you, looked Terrible Ted square in the face. "Screw you, Ted," he said. "I ain't going." Everyone within earshot of this exchange roared with laughter.

Later, some of the Wings donned the prisoners' green jerseys to even up the sides. Lindsay skated up to prison officials seated in the primitive press box. "We'll win this one, see," he said in his best James Cagney impersonation, "and be outta here in two years."

For Emery's Boys, it only seemed like two years. The first period ended with an 18–0 Wings lead, after which nobody bothered to keep score. Everyone was engrossed watching the Wings's pinpoint passing, crisp shots, and graceful skating. It was a skills exhibition that had the inmates on the ice standing in their tracks, leaning on their sticks, and whistling in admiration. Defenseman Bob Goldham earned the cons' respect as perhaps the bravest man on the ice, as he repeatedly dropped in front of shots and blocked them with his special belly pad.

"They've won the Stanley Cup and a lot of other big prizes," Brumm said at the end of the exhibition, "but now the Red Wings will receive an award no other hockey team can ever claim." With that he handed Adams and coach Tommy Ivan a "honey bucket," a pail that prisoners used in their cells in lieu of a toilet.

"This is a great day," proclaimed Adams, hoisting the bucket high for all to see. "I'm proud to have such a fine 'farm' team up here in the north. The only trouble is, you guys sure have made it tough for me to recruit any of you."

After showering, the Wings enjoyed dinner with the convict team and several guests from both sides of the prison walls. Inmates gave

Jack Adams hoists the Red Wings's newly won trophy—a "honey bucket"—to the amusement of players on both teams, including Detroit captain Ted Lindsay. (Author's collection)

each Wing a hand-tooled wallet with his name and winged-wheel logo on it. Gordie Howe, who earlier had pronounced the ice surface the best he had ever skated on, gave a talk, as did the warden and Adams. Then at six o'clock it was off to the hotel, where the Wings rested an hour before playing another exhibition game at the indoor Marquette Palestra against the semipro Sentinels.

The Wings toyed with the Sentinels, beating them soundly in front of a full house of 3,000 fans. Brumm, who earlier had played with Emery's Boys, took a regular shift with the Sentinels. This confused Wings defenseman Jim "Red Eye" Hay, who skated up to Brumm shortly after the puck dropped at 8:30 p.m.

"He said, 'How the hell did you get out to play down here tonight?' " Brumm recalled with a laugh. "I guess throughout the entire afternoon he never realized I was working at the prison instead of doing time!"

The next morning, when it came time to board the plane for home, it was so cold the engines wouldn't start. "We sat on the runway and froze," Johnny Wilson remembered. "Meanwhile Jack was afraid half of his boys would get sick." The propellers finally turned, and the first—and so far, the only—NHL team to play inside a maximum-security prison headed back to Detroit, leaving a considerable share of equipment and goodwill behind. Ten weeks later, the Wings defeated Montreal to win their third Stanley Cup of the decade. The following year they won a fourth, cheered on by the residents of the largest penalty box any of the Wings would ever see.

The prison game's success made many wonder why officials didn't schedule more.

"We tried," Brumm said, "but not very hard. Somebody should've gone to Detroit, sat down with Jack Adams, and ironed out a plan. But he got busy, we got busy, and for some reason it never happened."

Adams continued to donate equipment for the prison's hockey program, however, even after Brumm left the prison in 1957 to work in his family's construction business. For the next thirty years, Brumm moved around the world as a construction project manager. Throughout, memories of the one-of-a-kind game remained fresh. He recounted it with gusto in a book he wrote, wryly titled *We Only Played Home Games.*

"I'll tell you what it was," he said. "It was a hell of an entertaining game from this perspective: when the best team in hockey played the worst, you saw all the skills, the passing and skating ability, that you missed in a tight-checking NHL game. In a game like ours, you realized just how good those Red Wing teams of the '50s really were."

An electric message board in downtown Detroit flashes the shocking news: John F. Kennedy is dead. (Walter P. Reuther Library)

16

Black November

The assassination of President John F. Kennedy sent the country into a state of shock, disbelief, and despair. Decades later, the tragedy continues to evoke a strong emotional response in Detroiters.

The church and the hall were booked, the food, liquor, cake, and flowers ordered. Staff were attending to last-minute details. Flashing back to that distant Friday, Vanda Skuras remembers that she had the day off from work to prepare for her Saturday wedding, but still needed to drop by the office. "I was working for a brokerage firm in the Penobscot Building," the Grosse Pointe Woods resident recalls. "It was payday, so I swung by to pick up my check."

Instead of encountering a final round of congratulations and good-natured ribbing from her co-workers, the twenty-two-year-old bride-to-be came upon a cluster of employees with shocked and drawn faces. "Everybody was huddled around the stock ticker. I asked what was going on and they said President Kennedy had been shot."

Vanda's fiancé, English teacher Deno Skuras, was being feted in the teachers' lounge at Eastern High School when word came over the PA system. "The party stopped immediately," says Deno, today an attorney. "Everything stopped." Vanda drove home to Trenton. "I took Jefferson and there was no traffic," she says. "It was quiet, very eerie. I was listening to the radio all the way and that's when I learned the president had died. It seemed like the end of the world."

The following morning, at St. Joseph Catholic Church in Trenton, the freshly minted Vanda Skuras was a vision in white, stepping out into a world suddenly trimmed in black. "We decided we weren't going to change our plans," Deno says. Fifty of the anticipated three hundred guests didn't show up to celebrate the newlyweds at Roma Hall. "There was a pall," he says. "But it was still relatively exciting." Vanda adds: "It was an Italian and Greek wedding with a large number of immigrants. With this group of people, the president's death was very emotional."

Every generation or so, America has a punched-in-the-gut moment, a tragedy so overwhelming and culturally significant that a date stamp is indelibly branded into the national psyche. Pearl Harbor Sunday, December 7, 1941, is remembered as "a date which will live in infamy" and the kickoff to the country's all-out fight in World War II. The scope and horror of the terrorist attacks of September 11, 2001, are reduced to the shorthand of "9/11."

Sandwiched between these two events is the assassination of President John F. Kennedy on November 22, 1963, an equally profound moment that, several decades on, seems to resonate most strongly with the baby boomers who were too young to vote him into office. "I remember that day, that whole weekend, like it was yesterday," says Royal Oak resident Nadine Scodellaro, then a sixth-grader growing up in Southfield. "So much sadness and tears—just unbelievable. And anger. It still makes me cry when I think about it. I was eleven and President Kennedy was killed on my brother's thirteenth birthday. All of us were glued to the TV all weekend. The first time I ever saw my dad cry was during the president's funeral."

JFK and the Kennedy years exist in that sweet spot of history, a time when America's "greatest generation" had saved the world, then strived to rebuild it in its image. Citizens still believed in their leaders and institutions. The charismatic president personified the country's optimism and energy, daring others to dream big, whether it was NASA engineers putting a man on the moon or college students bringing water to an African village. He was "the man for Young America"—a war hero, a Pulitzer Prize–winning author, and the possessor of a keen wit and intellect.

During JFK's 1960 presidential run, Ann Spybrook belonged to that small army of straw-hatted campaign workers known as "Kennedy girls," a term that didn't seem suggestive then, thanks to the media's turning a blind eye to the Massachusetts senator's many dalliances. "I remember when he walked through the door of the Book Cadillac," says the Roseville resident, then a twenty-one-year-old student at Mercy College. "He was much taller than I thought he'd be—and so handsome."

Kennedy drew an estimated 50,000 people at the traditional Labor Day rally in Detroit's Cadillac Square. A few weeks later, during a brief, extemporaneous midnight speech at the University of Michigan in Ann Arbor, he asked idealistic students to consider volunteering their services overseas—a challenge that begat the Peace Corps. On election day, Detroiters went for JFK at a higher rate than voters in any other big city in the country. At forty-three, Kennedy was the youngest man ever to be elected president. The following November, Detroit attorney Jerry Cavanagh, an Irish-Catholic Democrat in the mold of Kennedy, was elected mayor. At thirty-three, he was the city's youngest mayor.

The first president born in the twentieth century was blessed with an almost impossibly photogenic family: his smart, elegant wife Jackie and toddlers Caroline and John Jr., nicknamed "John-John." The images of "Camelot" (a term that actually wasn't used until after his assassination) helped deflect criticism of Kennedy as he gingerly handled such thorny issues as the exploding Civil Rights Movement and America's deepening involvement in Southeast Asia. By the fall of 1963, he was gearing up for another presidential campaign. Part of that included a two-day trip to Texas, a state whose history of violence worried JFK's aides. Assuming he won reelection—his average approval rating was 70 percent, which remains the highest of any post–World War II president—his second term would end in January 1969. There would be plenty of time to fulfill the administration's expectations of great accomplishments.

* * *

Friday, November 22, 1963, was a bleak autumn day in Detroit. Trees were bare. Here and there, piles of wet leaves waited to be burned at curbside and in the alleys. Temperatures were in the fifties. Ex-governor John Swainson, lunching downtown, described a sky filled with "low, foreboding black-gray clouds, and strange cloud formations." That morning, in a meeting of shareholders at the Statler-Hilton, William Clay Ford bought the Detroit Lions for $6 million; some observers thought the price too steep for a team six years removed from its last championship. The final weekend of the college football season was at hand, with Michigan set to host Ohio State on Saturday while Michigan State prepared to meet Illinois in East Lansing, the winner going to the Rose Bowl.

In other news, *Wards Automotive* reported that the US auto industry was on pace to set a new single-year record for vehicle production. Michigan Governor George Romney slammed fellow Republican (and presidential hopeful) Barry Goldwater for his support of right-to-work legislation. In the classifieds, the Detroit Police Department advertised for recruits (starting salary: $5,650), Stu Evans Lincoln-Mercury offered to put car buyers in a new '64 Comet for $2,115, Robert Hall featured boys' suits "in the newest fall shades" for under $12, and a pair of denim "western dungarees" could be found at Shopper's Fair for $1.97. The top attractions at local theaters and drive-ins were *The V.I.P.s*, starring Richard Burton and Elizabeth Taylor, and John Wayne's latest western, *McClintock*. WKNR ("Keener 13") had just delivered the new music guide to record stores, hi-fi shops, and department chains like Korvette's and Federal's. At No. 1 for the week of November 21–28 was the Kingsmen's "Louie, Louie." The Dearborn station's "Key Song of the Week" was by an obscure local girls group called the Chevells. The new 45-RPM record had a foreboding title: "Another Tear Must Fall." The flip side was "It's Goodbye."

A thousand miles and a time zone away, large, friendly crowds greeted the presidential motorcade in downtown Dallas. The forty-six-year-old president and Jackie Kennedy were seated in the back of the presidential limo: a 1961 Lincoln Continental convertible, built in Wixom, with $200,000 worth of customizations. In the jump seat ahead of the Kennedys were Texas Governor John Connally and his wife. There was no armor plating or bullet-proof glass. The portable bubble top wasn't attached because the air conditioning didn't work well when it was in place.

It was 12:30 p.m. in Texas—1:30 Eastern Standard Time (EST) in Detroit—when pandemonium broke out. "We heard a shot and the president jumped up in his seat," said a young man standing within a few feet of the passing limousine. "I thought it scared him because I thought it was a firecracker." Seven minutes later, Detroiters watching *As the World Turns* on WJBK-TV (Channel 2) were startled when the screen abruptly switched from the live soap opera to a stark CBS Bulletin notice, accompanied by Walter Cronkite's voiceover: "Bulletin . . . In Dallas, Texas, three shots were fired at President Kennedy's motorcade. The first reports say the President was seriously wounded, that he slumped over in Mrs. Kennedy's lap, she cried out, 'Oh, no!' and the motorcade went on. . . . The wounds perhaps could be fatal." Quickly, sobersided newsmen began appearing on every television channel and weighty voices broke into radio programming, all relaying the same awful, unfathomable news.

Ed Golick was a second-grader at Logan Elementary on the city's west side. "We were all watching a live program on Channel 56, the PBS station," recalls Golick, today a media specialist for Detroit Public Schools. "We were half paying attention to the TV instructor when another man appeared on the screen and interrupted him, saying that President Kennedy had been shot. I remember there being an uncomfortable silence, then some of my classmates started sobbing, and then my teacher started crying, too. An announcement was made over the PA system that school was dismissed for the day, and that we should all go directly home."

There was confusion and disbelief as the first sketchy reports came in. Windsor station CKLW-TV was jammed with callers on both sides of the Detroit River wanting to know if popular movie-show host Bill Kennedy had been shot. Motorists listening on their car radio pulled over or drove aimlessly around. "I was in a dime store when they announced it over a loudspeaker," councilwoman Mary Beck told the press. "People just stopped in their tracks, stunned. A lot of them couldn't believe it. Some said, 'No, no.'" People instinctively called family members and friends until the flood of calls caused Michigan Bell's switchboards to crash. John Swainson was finishing lunch at Schweitzer's when a Republican friend passed the word. The lifelong Democrat considered the source and convinced himself it was simply a poor joke—until he returned to his Lansing home and saw televised images of Jackie Kennedy "in her pink dress with the splotches of blood on it."

There never was the slightest chance that the team of doctors frantically tending to the president could save his life. He had been shot through the throat and, moments later, suffered a massive head wound. (Governor Connally, also struck, would survive wounds to his chest, thigh, and wrist.) At 2:38 p.m. EST, after a flurry of ominous but unofficial reports from Parkland Hospital, everybody's worst fear was confirmed. The electronic message ribbon crawling across the front of the Detroit Bank & Trust Building informed passersby: JOHN F. KENNEDY IS DEAD. He had officially died at 2 o'clock, Detroit time. "Within minutes there were no smiles on the downtown streets, where shoppers stood in shocked silence among the newly erected decorations for the season of peace and good will," Louis Cook wrote in the next day's *Free Press*. "Suddenly, everything else seemed unimportant. Letters lay half-finished in the typewriters. The auto lines ground on, but the men turning down the bolts worked on in heavy silence."

People oblivious to the day's events walked into stores to find clusters of sobbing clerks and dazed customers. "I asked what was wrong," one shopper told a reporter. "They told me the president had been killed. I went outside then, and I just walked around for a long time. What can you say?" The City Planning Commission was in the middle of a closed-door meeting when a member was called from the room to take a phone call. He returned with the news. "One man just burst out crying," said commission member

Students at this Detroit Catholic school filled church pews to pray for the slain president—and his assassin. (Author's collection)

John Bigelow. "The rest of us just sat there. Then we all got up and walked away. I don't even know whether we officially adjourned or not. We just walked away." When an elevator operator told Pearly Lashley, an employee at Hudson's, what had happened, "I just stood there holding my stomach," she said. "Nobody got any work done that day and it didn't simmer down the next day either."

The wave of shock rolled over people of all ages, races, and denominations, but the grief seemed especially keen among Metro Detroit's million-plus Catholics. Fay Dutka was inside a fourth-grade classroom at Epiphany Catholic Grade School on Detroit's west side. "I remember the nuns were crying, so it was serious. Nuns didn't cry in front of kids." In parishes from Sacred Heart in Dearborn to Most Holy Trinity in Corktown, uniformed schoolchildren filed into church in orderly fashion. They said a rosary for the president, then prayed for his assassin. St. Aloysius on Washington Boulevard was "a scene of hushed and somber grief," the *Free Press* reported, with several women wearing black mourning babushkas.

As pews filled up and votive cups were lit, others struggled to get through the rest of the work day. The cast of *Hello, Dolly* resumed their rehearsal at the Fisher Theater, but it finally was canceled along with the evening's performance. "We tried to go on," said headliner Carol Channing, "but we just couldn't." Berry Gordy, president of Motown Records, sat stunned inside his closed office. Distraught, he nonetheless kept his scheduled meeting with singer Marvin Gaye. Gaye also was upset—upset that more wasn't being done to promote his new single, "Can I Get a Witness." Words grew heated. Gordy finally ended the argument by sweeping everything off the top of his desk and yelling, "Don't you realize that the president was killed today?"

Officials flew the coffin bearing Kennedy's body to Washington. En route, vice-president Lyndon Johnson was hurriedly sworn in as the thirty-sixth president. Most weekend events were postponed: the Ice Follies at Olympia, comedian Dick Gregory's show at the University of Detroit, the entire college football schedule. The annual Goodfellows high school championship game went on as planned, with Denby beating Notre Dame, 7–0, on a misty Friday evening in half-empty Tiger Stadium. However, networks preempted the usual television and radio coverage of the game, as well as all other regular programming

Employees at J. L. Hudson's quickly assembled a memorial inside a display window at the downtown store. (Walter P. Reuther Library)

through Monday night. Tom Oren of Silver Spring, Maryland, then living in Warren, was at the game. "I was twelve, and Mom worked at Denby. She was proud as a single mom to take me and my younger brother to that game. I remember it—and the whole weekend—as surreal. What were we doing at a football game? It was absurd."

Within hours of the assassination, the country learned a prime suspect was in custody. Lee Harvey Oswald initially was arrested for gunning down Dallas policeman J. D. Tippit about forty-five minutes after the president was shot. Investigators soon determined that he matched the description of the man seen leaving the Texas School Book Depository, from where the shots fired on the motorcade originated and investigators found a scoped rifle belonging to Oswald. Oswald, who worked at the depository, was a twenty-four-year-old high school dropout and self-proclaimed Marxist who had spent three years in Russia before returning to the United States in 1962 with a Russian wife. On Friday evening, Americans got their first look at Oswald, who denied to shouting reporters that he had killed the president or Tippit.

As Saturday brought more news about the suspected assassin and his background, Andy Sobieralski, a twenty-seven-year-old Warren mechanic, realized he was the same Lee Oswald he had served with in the Marine Corps a few years earlier. The men had trained as radar operators and were in the same air control squadron at Atsugi, Japan. "He was one of the weakest men in the barracks," Sobieralski says today. "Lazy. But he had a mouth on him." The Marines court-martialed Oswald twice: once for accidentally shooting himself in the elbow with a handgun inside the barracks, and again for assaulting a sergeant in a bar. In Sobieralski's view, Oswald was "fully capable" of killing the president, both from a philosophical and a practical standpoint. "We all thought he was an oddball. I'd walk past him every day. 'What you reading, Ozzie?' It was always a book about Marxism." Asked whether Oswald could have fired three aimed shots with a bolt-action rifle at a moving car within a span of five seconds—a feat that some believe was beyond Oswald's ability—Sobieralski responds, "Marksmanship training in the Marines is about as good as it gets."

Due to his brush with history, Sobieralski has read extensively about Oswald. He believes there was a second shooter in Dallas, positioned on the now infamous "grassy knoll," the sloped area directly to the right of the president's car when the bullets hit. He also thinks Oswald likely was part of some plot involving America's Cold War enemies.

He recalls a 1958 incident when the squadron was in the Philippines. One night, officers rousted Sobieralski out of his bunk and ordered him to replace a Marine sentry named Schrand, whom guards had just found dead at his post. Investigators thought that the hangar being guarded housed one of America's highly secret U-2 spy planes. Although investigators eventually ruled that Schrand's gunshot wound was accidental and self-inflicted, rumors persisted that the squadron's resident Marxist, who knew Schrand, was somehow involved. Was Oswald, who was already planning his defection, looking for information that would ingratiate him with Russian officials?

"Maybe he was poking around and was discovered," Sobieralski suggests. The enigmatic Oswald would carry many mysteries to an early grave.

On Sunday, November 24, the president's body was moved with somber pageantry from the White House to the Capitol rotunda, where it would lay in state until Monday's funeral. Tens of millions of television viewers watched the horse-drawn caisson bearing the flag-draped coffin slowly move down Pennsylvania Avenue. Later they saw Jackie Kennedy and Caroline Kennedy, just three days short of her sixth birthday, kneeling to kiss the coffin's flag. The lines of mourners stretched for miles, with hundreds of thousands standing in the damp weather for hours for the opportunity to walk past the closed casket.

In Dallas, Oswald was escorted through the basement of police headquarters to an armored truck waiting to transfer him to the county jail. It was 12:21 p.m. EST when Detroiters watching WWJ-TV (Channel 4), the NBC affiliate, saw a dark blur rush across their television screens. Ann Spybrook remembers that she was leaving for church when a family member cried out, "Oh my Lord! He's been shot!"

A stocky figure in a suit and fedora, later identified as fifty-two-year-old Dallas nightclub owner Jack Ruby, had just lunged at Oswald with a snub-nose revolver and fired it point-blank into his stomach. NBC was the only network to air the shooting as it happened, but the other networks quickly shifted their coverage from Washington to Dallas. CBS used its new slow-motion technology to replay the shooting, frame by agonizing frame—a surrealistic choreography that by dint of its horror and endless repetition burned itself into the national psyche. Oswald was pronounced dead at 2:07 p.m. The country seemed to be unraveling. The president had been killed, and now millions had just watched his presumed assassin gunned down in the first murder ever committed on live television.

As the networks switched back and forth between the solemn ritualism in Washington and the bedlam in Dallas, the National Football League went ahead with its full slate of Sunday games, including the Detroit Lions' contest at Minnesota. Commissioner Pete Rozelle later admitted the decision not to postpone play was the biggest mistake of his career. "On this somber, blackest of Sundays, when no heart could truly yearn for a game, the Lions gave momentary distraction," George Puscas wrote in the next day's *Free Press*, though it was the players who appeared most distracted. The teams lost ten fumbles between them as Minnesota squeaked out a 34–31 win. It was the first time the Vikings had ever beaten the Lions, but the cheers from Minnesota fans were muted. It was "neither a day for joy nor celebration," Puscas wrote. "The tragedy of Washington hung over the stadium as it hangs over the nation, and not even the galloping athletes could fully escape the heaviness of the death of President Kennedy." WJBK-TV in Detroit did not broadcast the game originally scheduled to air. There was no regular programming during the four days of assassination coverage, meaning Lions fans had to be content with watching an edited one-hour replay of the game, narrated by Van Patrick, two nights later.

That Sunday, the networks, which normally went off the air an hour or so after midnight, continued into the wee hours with a commercial-free mix of news updates, features, and live coverage of the public viewing. Classical music played. "All night long the

Tens of millions of television sets were turned to coverage of the president's funeral, including this one inside a Metro Detroit home. (Author's collection)

mourners are still visible, moving past the coffin under the great dome," *TV Guide* reported. "They are still coming at 9 that morning."

Monday, November 25, had been declared a national day of mourning. Schools and several major retailers, such as Hudson's and Winkelman's, closed for the day. Most other businesses, reluctant even during a time of national tragedy to lose an entire day of holiday sales—Thanksgiving was three days away and Christmas exactly a month off—shut down only for the hours of the state funeral. At auto plants, managers sent the day shift home at noon. Churches and synagogues were full. Ten thousand people overflowed the site of old City Hall—now Kennedy Square—for Detroit's official tribute. The weather was wet, cold, and blustery. Flags, which would remain at half-staff for an entire month, appeared starched against the gray sky. Most people spent the day in front of the television. They saw the most poignant image of the entire weekend: John-John, on his third birthday, saluting his father's flag-draped casket as pallbearers brought it down the steps of St. Matthew's Cathedral.

In a country of 180 million people, an estimated 41.6 million televisions were tuned to the funeral. One of them belonged to Dearborn attorney Vance Maliszewski. His daughter Alice remembers him setting up his 8-mm home-movie camera on a tripod in the den. "There were no VCRs back then," she says today, "so if you wanted to copy a program you had to actually film the TV screen." The footage that Maliszewski primitively lifted off his television some sixty years ago survives, a vaporous segment tucked in among snippets of carefree family life. No audio accompanies the fluttering frames, so the natural sounds of that day are missing: the bagpipes, hoof-clacks, and muffled drums as the miles-long cortege moved from the Capitol Rotunda to St. Matthew's for Mass, then on to Arlington Cemetery for interment. The reel's disjointed chronology is slightly jarring. Earlier is footage of a beaming seven-year-old Alice Maliszewski in her snow-white First Holy Communion dress. It's the spring of 1963, and the world around her is soaked in Kodachrome and sunshine.

At 3:08 p.m., Army trumpeter Sgt. Keith Clark sounded "Taps." The thirty-five-year-old Grand Rapids native had played flawlessly at hundreds of military funerals. For this most important of all performances, he had stood in the cold for hours and was momentarily deaf from the twenty-one-gun salute that had just been fired. On the sixth note, Clark briefly fluttered off-key. He was devastated, but the "broken note" seemed to capture the mood of a nation whose heart had been crushed. As William Manchester would later write in his best-seller, *The Death of a President,* Clark's flub had the effect of "a swiftly stifled sob." At 3:34 p.m., the president's casket was lowered into the ground, after which Jackie Kennedy lit the "eternal flame" at the gravesite. Moments later, the bands, military formations, and crowds of dignitaries began to slowly disperse. In Detroit, stores re-opened and autoworkers punched in for the afternoon shift. America's long vigil was over.

* * *

In the days and months that followed, Metro Detroiters joined people everywhere in trying to come to grips with the assassination. "I remember there were a lot of conspiracy theories—Cuba, the Soviet Union—and a lot of nervousness," says Don Kolke of Fraser. "You know: 'If they can kill our president, what else can they do?'

Things calmed down after the Warren Report came out." The seven-member Warren Commission, which included US Congressman (and future president) Gerald Ford of Grand Rapids, released the results of its probe in September 1964. It concluded that Oswald and Ruby both had acted alone, findings that have never been fully accepted by the public.

Memorials took various forms. Kolke, who hosted a children's program on CKLW called *Hercules* that networks preempted for assassination coverage, dedicated his first show back to the president. "It was live and all off the cuff," he says. "I talked to the kids about what a fine man the president had been, talked about his accomplishments. I wanted them to know that, hey, we're all going to get through this."

Candy Greer, a fifteen-year-old student at Grosse Pointe High, became a minor sensation when her poem, inspired by John-John's salute, was unexpectedly turned into an illustrated book. *Six White Horses* sold tens of thousands of copies, was read into the *Congressional Record*, and moved the president's widow to write the young author a personal note. Sculptor Marshall Fredericks, whose *Spirit of Detroit* monument was ringed by mourning wreaths, later spent two years working on a half-ton bust of the martyred president. It stands in the Mount Clemens plaza (now Kennedy Square) where JFK gave a speech during the 1960 campaign. Berry Gordy and his girlfriend, Margaret Norton, were expecting a baby at the time of the assassination; when the boy was born the following March, they named him Kennedy. (In the 1980s, Kennedy Gordy performed as R&B artist Rockwell.) "I was deeply saddened by the death of John Kennedy," Berry Gordy reflected in his autobiography. "I believed him to be an honest man and a good man. I believed him to be a great president who had embraced and created hope for Black people that had not been felt in modern times. A feeling of loss and shock hung over everything in those months of 1963 and early '64."

Until Dallas, the 1960s had been in many ways a continuation of the bland and orderly '50s. Kennedy's murder, however, abruptly changed the trajectory. Those four black days in November are now viewed as the gateway to that part of the '60s that history remembers best—a divisive period of war, protests, urban riots, psychedelia,

Marshall Fredericks at work on his bronze sculpture of the president. Commissioned by the JFK Macomb Memorial Committee for the County Building in Mount Clemens, the finished work was unveiled in 1970 near the site where Kennedy delivered a campaign speech in 1960. (Author's collection)

and more assassinations. By the end of the decade, the turmoil had many Americans fearing that the country would implode. "To me," says Nadine Scodellaro, "the assassination changed everything. How could something like that happen here? I adored Jackie and the kids and JFK. They were all so youthful. It had been a time of such hope, at least to an eleven-year-old. And I couldn't stomach having a geezer like LBJ as president after JFK." Lyndon Johnson had the presidential limousine painted black; he felt the public too closely associated its original midnight-blue color with the assassination. The Lincoln was retired in 1978 and donated to The Henry Ford in Dearborn, where today its presence continues to inspire strong emotional responses among museum visitors of a certain age.

"I'm a romantic," Vanda Skuras says. "I always felt that the entire Camelot image was so perfect and beautiful. President Kennedy's death kind of freezes him in time. We never had to see him grow old, or maybe go through a divorce, or watch him have to deal with all of the stories that came out afterward. In our minds, he'll always be this young and vigorous figure."

Jack Ruby's Detroit Connection

Soon after Jack Ruby fatally shot Lee Harvey Oswald, Detroiters learned of a local connection. Earl Ruby was a forty-eight-year-old Birmingham resident who owned Cobo Cleaners on Livernois, near the University of Detroit, and a fashionable second home in Boca Raton, Florida. He was the youngest of eight children of Joseph and Fannie Rubenstein, all of whom experienced a miserable upbringing in Chicago. Elegant, soft-spoken, and highly successful, Earl was a sharp contrast to his older brother Jack, a hot-headed blabbermouth who never repaid the thousands of dollars he had borrowed from Earl over the years. Nonetheless, when the assassin of the president's assassin went on trial, Earl was his staunchest supporter.

Why did Ruby shoot Oswald? The nightclub owner regularly associated with the police, gangsters, and lowlifes. But Earl always maintained Jack was not "mobbed up" or part of some grand conspiracy; he had simply used his connections to roam freely around the Dallas police station the weekend of JFK's murder. Earl believed that his brother, an ultra-patriotic type who had served honorably during World War II, was genuinely distraught and acted impulsively when the opportunity arose. In 1979, Earl testified before a Congressional subcommittee that Jack had told him that "when Oswald walked out of that doorway he had a silly smirk on his face, as though . . . he really felt good about it, and that is when Jack lost control of himself and shot him."

In March 1964, a Dallas jury convicted Jack Ruby of murder and sentenced him to the electric chair. The Texas Supreme Court overturned the verdict when it ruled that the defendant's request for a change of venue should have been granted. He was

Earl Ruby in 1990. (Peter Yates)

awaiting a new trial when he died of cancer on January 3, 1967. An autopsy revealed fifteen brain tumors, lending some substance to the defense's claim that Ruby, whose mother had spent a dozen years in a mental institution, was suffering from "episodic insanity" when he shot Oswald.

Following Ruby's death, there was a protracted legal battle over ownership of the murder weapon, a .38-caliber Colt Cobra, until a probate court finally ruled in Earl's favor. Earl sold the revolver at a 1991 auction for $220,000, most of which went to settling Jack's attorney fees and back taxes. On November 24, 1993, the thirtieth anniversary of Oswald's shooting, the gun's new owner had Earl fire 100 rounds from it into a steel drum painted ruby red; the bullets and casings were then sold to memorabilia collectors. Earl Ruby died in Florida in 2006, having contemplated the serendipitous nature of his brother's vigilantism. "If Jack had been 30 seconds later," he mused, "he would have missed Oswald."

17

Under a Paper Moon

Barn raisings, hayrides, logging camps, goat carts, and coal delivery wagons—real-photo postcards are treasured today for their glimpses of a vanished America.

Welcome to Tinderville, population 60,000—and growing by two or three every day.

Tinderville is the name an impressed visitor gives Dave Tinder's ever-expanding collection of photographic postcards, a community of cardboard rectangles crowded into vintage oak cabinet drawers inside his cramped Dearborn Heights apartment. Nearly all of the cards—commonly referred to as "real photo postcards," or RPPCs—are a century or more old. The quaint images represent a cross-section of Americana in the early 1900s: barn raisings, airships, paper moons, locomotives, trolley cars, vaudevillians, holiday parades, harvests, blacksmiths, Fourth of July parades, family gatherings, circuses, hay rides, saloons, train stations, logging camps, county fairs, Model T Fords, coal and ice delivery wagons, Main Street storefronts, and one-room schoolhouses.

The singularity of these black-and-white or sepia-toned photographic postcards distinguishes them from the glut of mass-produced colorized postcards that vendors sold to tourists and conventioneers—those oh-so-familiar views of Belle Isle, City Hall, and the floral clock at Waterworks Park. While many RPPCs were formal shots created by professional photographers, often inside studios or arcades, most were highly personal pictorial fare,

Ten-year-old Hazel Beach and three-year-old Violet Nash sit among the stars in this real-photo postcard created inside a Saginaw studio, circa 1909. (Author's collection)

so-called vernacular photography, the product of hobbyists and ordinary folks using a simple, inexpensive Kodak camera made specifically to create postcard-sized negatives.

"You'd send the film to Kodak and they'd make copies for a few pennies," says Tinder. Each came back with a printed backing. All someone needed to do at that point was add an address, a penny stamp, and maybe a message. Until the craze finally fizzled out around the time of World War I, untold millions of these one-of-a-kind images were mailed, with many more unposted cards tucked inside letters, scrapbooks, and family albums.

On his way to becoming a noted authority on early Michigan photography and assembling his impressive collection on a limited income, Tinder—who is fast approaching ninety—has had to make a few choices as to what's essential in his life and what's not. He doesn't have a stove, preferring to zap Vienna sausages inside a small microwave. The last television he owned was stolen sometime in the '70s. The battered orange futon dates back several presidential administrations. Light bulbs are regarded almost as luxury items. Often the only light inside the cramped apartment is the

History in his hands. Dave Tinder has collected more than 60,000 vintage photographic postcards from every corner of Michigan. (Michelle Gerard)

glow from the computer screen as he waits to bid in another online auction or continues work on his massive historical database of Michigan photographers.

"I'm a child of the Depression," says Tinder, an Ohio native who moved to Flint as a youngster in the 1930s. The retired product development engineer collects strictly Michigan-related RPPCs. He files them alphabetically by town, then arranges them within each town in a series of subsets: bird's-eye views, street views, industrial scenes, portraits, and so on. Like most collectors, Tinder has his favorites, such as obscure train depots, mail carriers, and railroad-related cards.

So-called disaster cards—cyclones, train wrecks, fires, spring floods—also are popular with collectors, including Tinder, who prefers his calamity laced with irony. He pulls out a series of cards depicting an ice warehouse hit by a blaze. The walls are burned down, revealing huge blocks of ice left intact. He rummages through another drawer and extracts a card showing Jack "The Human Fly" Williams scaling the side of the six-story Edwards & Chamberlain Hardware Building in Kalamazoo on October 4, 1916. Half the population of nearby Mendon turned out to watch the barefoot stuntman, unaware of a greater spectacle taking place back home.

"While they were gone, a fire broke out and most of Mendon burned down," says Tinder, producing several RPPCs of the town's charred ruins. "There wasn't anybody around to put out the flames."

Fellow collector Doug Aikenhead grew up on Detroit's west side and earned a master of fine arts degree in photography from Cranbrook Academy. He became attracted to photo postcards after buying a handful at a garage sale in 1977. "One was a downtown view of Calumet, Michigan, in winter," he says one afternoon inside his Ann Arbor home. "Three others showed a shipwreck in Keweenaw. That triggered something."

Photo postcards allowed Aikenhead to combine his two passions, photography and history. His hobby became a business after he left academia two decades ago. The best cards, he says, are those that combine "an arresting picture and historical relevance." He's

Jack "The Human Fly" Williams daringly scales the Edwards & Chamberlain Building in Kalamazoo on October 4, 1916. (Author's collection)

particularly fond of early Detroit photographer Louis Pesha, who was "one of the most prolific, most skilled postcard photographers of the period," he says. "The back porch of his studio faced the St. Clair River. He did these wonderful postcards of freighters." Pesha died in a 1912 auto accident, leaving his wife to carry on the business. "She ran it for about ten years," Aikenhead says. "The story is that she dumped thousands of negatives into the Detroit River. They've never been found."

Postcard shows, once supplemented by online auctions, are now slowly being supplanted by them, says Aikenhead. "The majority of them used to be sponsored by local postcard clubs, but those events are getting smaller and fewer." Most successful shows are now professionally managed, he says, with longtime shows in Kalamazoo and Lansing still popular draws.

Tinder generally pays between ten and forty dollars for a photo postcard, though if there's something that's especially appealing to him his wallet can open quite a bit wider. Aikenhead gets an aching head thinking about the number of times he has shelled out \$250 or \$300 for a card. However, as with any collectible, the right kind of card can fetch much more.

Recently a deep-pocketed collector outbid several others for a postcard featuring a constellation of head shots of the 1906 Detroit Tigers. Among those pictured on the card was a fresh-faced outfielder named Ty Cobb, a teenaged phenomenon then in his first full season as a Tiger. It was Cobb's earliest known appearance on a baseball RPPC. The card, which originally could be bought for a penny or two at any downtown drugstore or tobacco shop, wound up selling for a rousing \$2,121.

Aside from its aesthetic qualities, a photo postcard through its image and accompanying message can offer a one-of-a-kind slice of social history: a young man writing of life in a lumbering camp, for example, or a transplant to the city asking her farm family to make sure they take care of her pet duck. One card from a private collection, postmarked January 22, 1911, shows a young man studying a book inside his cramped but neat rented room. "This is my home in Detroit, a little room I have with a musician couple," the unnamed correspondent writes Jim in Kansas. "Say Jim, couldn't you make a trip to Mich.? Say that would be a fine time we would have." An even more plaintive card from the same collection shows a young boy and his new dog, posed in front of their Detroit home one snowy day in the 1920s. The dog apparently was a Christmas present. On the reverse is the inscription: "Scyba, nine months, Scotch Setter. Run over at Lakewood Theater Lakewood & Jeff[erson] Detroit Mich. Feb. 25, 1923. Had him 2 mos."

Academic institutions are showing growing acceptance of photographic postcards. According to art scholar Rosamond B. Vaule in her book, *As We Were: American Photographic Postcards, 1905–1930*:

> Photo cards are compelling because they are early examples of photography in mass culture, both in subject matter and usage, and because they occur at a remarkable time in American history. Their images present a broad spectrum of American life and occasionally reveal its darker side. It was Americans—urban, small-town, and rural—who bought, sent, or saved these postcards. They were made at a time of social, demographic, and technological change: when the nation was shifting from a rural to an urban society; when record numbers of immigrants were entering the country; when family members were leaving "home" to spread across the land; and when electricity, the telephone, radio, and automobile were entering mainstream culture.

Tinder has earmarked his cards for the William L. Clements Library at the University of Michigan. The library will add them to the sizable collection of nineteenth-century cabinet photos, stereoviews, and cartes de visite he had previously donated.

"Libraries and museums have a strong interest in photographic postcards, and they're contending with private collectors," Aikenhead says. "But while the pool of collectors grows, there's a finite supply of cards. That can drive up prices."

Unlike Aikenhead, who buys and sells cards at shows around the country, Tinder is strictly a buyer. On this day he is monitoring

Someone in this group of frolickers thought the first hayride in Cedar Springs, Michigan, was an occasion worth documenting with their Kodak camera and turning into a postcard. (Author's collection)

The subjects of this playful souvenir RPPC were photographed one day in 1910 on the beach at Saugatuck. (Author's collection)

Local girls pose next to the two locomotives that collided in Livingston County on November 21, 1908. Disaster cards, be they of cyclones, fires, floods, or train wrecks, were always in demand. (Author's collection)

This RPPC shows a group of men, most likely conventioneers, at Detroit's Palmer Park sometime around 1910. (Author's collection)

an online auction. The card is of a crowded car ferry dock at Mackinaw. There is no postmark, no accompanying message, but the clothes and cars suggest the image dates to sometime around 1920. One can only guess who these people were, what their lives were like, how they all wound up. The mystery is part of the allure. With just moments remaining in the auction, Tinder taps a couple of keys. His last-second "sniping" is successful. The winning bid of $73.77 was more than the mayor of Tinderville wanted to pay, but it simply was too nice an image to pass up. And thus his community continues to grow, one card at a time.

18

The Birdman Takes Flight

During the 1930s, aerial pioneer Clem Sohn drew gasps and headlines as he soared, swerved, and swooped across the sky with his homemade bat wings.

When Clem Sohn met his end at a Paris air show in 1937, flailing desperately as he plunged to earth with a pair of tangled parachutes, his death was considered tragic but hardly shocking. The winged daredevil, alternately known as "Bat-Man," "Michigan Icarus," and the "Human Bird," had been tempting fate for years, masking the danger with an air of nonchalance. "I feel as safe as you would in your grandmother's kitchen," he said before his final jump, which culminated with him hitting the ground at an estimated 100 miles per hour. It wasn't the sort of impact the twenty-six-year-old Sohn had hoped to leave on the world.

"Sohn's rise from the status of unknown parachute jumper . . . to international celebrity in his line amazed many persons," the *Battle Creek Enquirer* remarked upon his death. "The man may have anticipated his tragic end. But danger and, ultimately, failure do not cloud the ingenuity and persistence of a man who knew what the public wanted in entertainment and, at great risk to himself, gave it to them."

But Sohn was more than a nervy showboat. He was a dreamer who felt his homemade wings were advancing the science of aeronautics. His ultimate goal was to create a practical apparatus that would allow someone up in the clouds—a pilot in distress, say, or an ordinary joe on a lark—to glide to a landing instead of using a parachute. "Some day," he said, "I think that everyone may have my wings and be able to soar from the house tops." That has yet to happen, though today he is regarded in some circles as the unofficial godfather of wing-suit jumping, an extreme form of skydiving with military and sport applications. It's also been suggested that the creators of a new comic-book superhero had Sohn in mind when they were developing Batman in the late 1930s, though the character's rigid wings wound up being replaced by a cape.

Clements Augustine Sohn was born April 7, 1910, in Fowler, a farming community about a hundred miles northwest of Detroit. He was eight years old when his mother died, causing relatives in Clinton County to raise him and his older brother, Fran, separately. Clem often occupied his time on his uncle's farm by building wooden model airplanes that he could never quite get to fly. He preferred mechanics to sports, and later expressed an interest in studying aeronautical engineering.

The family reunited when Sohn's father, who had taken a job as a policeman in Lansing, remarried when Clem was fourteen. He attended Eastern High School, a personable but serious-minded teenager who enjoyed hanging around the local airfield. There he became acquainted with Art Davis, a renowned stunt pilot and speed racer who regularly won trophies at aviation meets around the country. His wife, Rhoda Davis, also was an accomplished pilot. Among Art Davis's protégés was Roger Rae, an accomplished jumper who had been a grade ahead of Sohn at Eastern High.

Davis literally took Sohn under his wing, teaching him to fly and incorporating the eager and fearless redhead into his parachute act. Sohn, who made his first jump in 1930, broke into print when the *Lansing State Journal* announced that the young unknown would be substituting for Rae at an aviation show at Lansing's Capital City Airport on Sunday, May 22, 1932. A week later, Sohn made the news again, this time for overcoming a stiff breeze to win the parachute jumping contest at a meet in Omaha, Nebraska.

Parachuting was still considered a stunt, not a sport. (The word "skydiving" wouldn't even enter the lexicon until 1955.) Davis would fly his two-seater plane "upstairs" to between 8,000 and 12,000 feet, at which point Sohn would hurl himself out into space. He'd pull his ripcord with thousands of feet to spare, then hope the wind wouldn't carry him too far past his targeted landing spot. While accurate landings would remain a challenge for even the most experienced parachutists, the drops themselves soon became "an old story" for Sohn, who was exploring new challenges. He experimented with delayed drops, waiting until the last possible moment to pull his ripcord. By 1933, they were a standard feature of Davis's air shows. To make such seemingly suicidal stunts even more compelling, sometimes two daredevils would bail out of separate planes at the same time, engaging in a game of "chicken" on the way down.

Detroiters' first look at Sohn was on Sunday, July 30, 1933, the daring finale to a three-day show at Wayne County Airport. Sohn and Detroiter Wayne "Mile High" Wagner, dubbed the "human comets" by the press, jumped out at 10,000 feet and were still hurtling as they got to within 800 feet of the ground. The two-mile plunge had spectators holding their breath. Then billowing chutes suddenly appeared like white brushstrokes against the sky, and the pair floated down to earth amid "a burst of relieved applause," reported the *Detroit Free Press*. "The suspense for the 20,000 spectators had been terrific."

In the spring of 1934, Jerry Wessling, a fellow "parachute jumping ace" from Lansing, was killed at an air meet in Brooklyn, New York, in which both men were performing. Just days after serving as a pallbearer at his friend's funeral, Sohn was back at it at the same airfield, setting a new world record for a delayed parachute jump by free-falling 18,500 feet—three and a half miles—before pulling his ripcord.

By now Sohn had some 200 jumps to his credit. But leaping out of an airplane was one thing, controlling what came after was quite another. Some early practitioners, like Sohn, were discovering that by making swimming motions in the air they could manage their descent, as well as make more accurate landings. "I found out that I could actually slow myself, go into a dive, and flatten out again, and

I wondered whether I could not do better with a set of canvas wings," Sohn explained. "And there you have the origin of my bat wings act. I found they actually did work."

Sohn had been studying birds, bats, and flying squirrels for years while working on an experimental set of wings. Davis assisted in its design and construction. Canadian correspondent Matthew Halton described the cumbersome contraption: "His wings are nine feet from tip to tip. They are made of metal struts covered with strong cloth, and they work on the umbrella idea. The wings are strapped to the waist, with a metal bar, and they have a handle on each tip, which he holds in his outstretched arms."

The metal bar at the waist relieved some of the strain. A triangle of sturdy cloth fastened between his waist and each ankle acted as a giant fin. With his wings and fin, he could steer himself as easily as he could a car, Sohn said. "It's fun, but it's awful hard work. Imagine holding those wings out, and keeping your legs wide apart so the fin will work! When I get to the ground I'm so tired I can hardly stand up." The main and emergency parachutes weighed a total of seventy-five pounds, quite a load for a 140-pound man.

Sohn unveiled his wings on February 27, 1935, in a 12,000-foot jump over the airport in Daytona Beach, Florida. Davis piloted the plane. While slowly counting to seventy five, the free-falling Sohn did several loops, sharp banks, and some gliding, before opening his chute at 2,000 feet. "Strictly speaking, his adventure was not so much a flight as a sustained fall," *Time* magazine noted. "Yet fly he did, on homemade wings, and landed on his feet to tell about it."

In subsequent jumps Sohn continued to improve the length and complexity of his aerial performance. His routine was to climb out on the wing and jump head-first, wings folded at his side, plummeting like a rock for a few seconds before opening his wings and leveling off. "When I first open them," he said, "there is a terrific pull on my body, but in five or six seconds I feel myself flying like a bird." Still no more than a speck in the sky, he would release a bag of flour or set off a smoke canister fastened between his legs, allowing spectators to follow his trajectory as he began his antics—looping, climbing, and gliding back and forth with the air currents. After

Clem Sohn soared into the headlines on homemade wings. (Author's collection)

several minutes of maneuvering across the sky, he'd finally pop his chute somewhere between 600 and 1,000 feet and flutter, like a dropped handkerchief, back to earth. It was the ultimate in performance art.

Sohn's "sky-skiing" was a hit at county fairs, carnivals, and air shows across the country. He was featured in such publications as *Modern Mechanix* and *Popular Science*. Businesses came calling, growing his fame and bank account. According to *Time*, he was asking $300 for "newsreel pictures of himself on the wing." Chevrolet hired him to publicize a plant opening and new model introductions, with "Two New Chevrolets" stenciled on his wings and tail fin. In 1936, Sohn traveled to London to put on a series of forty jumps for which the sponsoring newspaper was paying $1,000 apiece.

That promotion, tied to the opening of an airport, ended prematurely on his seventh jump. "At 800 feet, he pulled the ripcord of his main chute, and the chute became entangled with his wings," recalled Harold Tolles, a Clinton County native who was married to one of Sohn's cousins. At 200 feet, Sohn yanked the ripcord of the smaller emergency chute positioned between his legs. The deployed chute arrested just enough of his speed that he was able to survive crashing into the roof of a parked car. "The steel tubing of his wings broke his arm and dislocated his shoulder on impact," Tolles said. "That was as low as anyone had pulled a chute ripcord and lived to tell about it."

For all his fearlessness and attention to detail, Sohn seemed almost resigned to having the odds finally catch up with him one day. He matter-of-factly told a reporter in London that he didn't expect to live to see thirty. Such a grim prospect had already thrown a wrench into at least one promising relationship. Darwin Beaufore, then an impressionable boy of six or seven, remembered his "childhood hero" dating his teacher, Beatrice Motz, who boarded with the Beaufore family at their farm in Victor Township. "Beatrice stopped dating Clem because he would not give up his bat wings and parachute," he said. Instead she married a local farmer. Motz's decision seemed to be the right one: a few weeks before her wedding, a young pilot in homemade bat wings was killed in Flint emulating Sohn's stunt.

At times Sohn appeared conflicted about the intersection of science and entertainment he found himself at. He would make comments about cutting back on the derring-do that was bringing him fame and money, or even quitting his act altogether, while also describing efforts to design and test improved versions of his wings. According to Tolles, "Clem never considered himself a stunt man. He always thought of himself as an aviation pioneer, and that his skydiving was a first in the annals of aviation."

* * *

On April 7, 1937, Sohn boarded the French liner *Lafayette*, bound for Europe. He had agreed to stage several exhibitions in France, with the possibility of scheduling more events in Switzerland and other countries. Rhoda Davis came along to manage his appearances. His first performance would be headlining an air show in Vincennes, outside Paris. A like-minded predecessor had tested a similar device in Paris a quarter-century earlier—with catastrophic results. In 1912, Franz Reichelt leaped off the Eiffel Tower in a hand-tailored "parachute-suit" featuring folded silk wings. The wings never opened and the "flying tailor" left a six-inch-deep impression in the ground.

In England, prior to crossing the channel to France, Clem took in a performance by eighteen-year-old Margot Fonteyn, the future prima ballerina of the Royal Ballet Company. "After our ballet performance one Saturday matinee," the famous dancer related in her memoirs, "I received a little bunch of flowers with a note saying, 'I don't want to be a Birdman anymore; I wish I was a ballerina like you. Clem Sohn.' A week later he had flown to his death. I mourn him still and wish that I had had the chance to talk to him."

April 25, 1937, was a bright, breezy Sunday in Paris. Sohn was mobbed by reporters, photographers, and admirers as he appeared for the show's featured event. It was approaching four o'clock in the afternoon when *L'Homme-Oiseau* (The Bird-Man) clambered aboard the two-seater biplane that would carry him two miles up. The craft was at 10,000 feet when Sohn, goggles pulled down and wings tucked in, jumped out. After a brief plunge, he threw open his arms, slowing his air speed, and went on to swerve, loop, and bank for about two minutes, riding along with the gusty wind. Tens of thousands of mesmerized spectators watched and clapped. He was about 1,000 feet above the ground when he folded in his wings and pulled the ripcord of his main parachute.

According to one chronicler, the chute "started to open, then caught in the meshes of his wings. The spirited French crowd that had been loudly applauding, suddenly hushed. Through binoculars Sohn could be seen pulling the rings of his spare parachute. It, too, failed to open. Within a couple of seconds, while scores screamed, fainted—and many cried—his body thudded to the ground and buried itself near a grandstand." Davis, screaming hysterically, had to be restrained as spectators stampeded to the site of her friend's crumpled figure.

Newsreel cameras captured Sohn's fatal fall (and, like Reichelt's, it is viewable online). His death was page-one news on both sides of the Atlantic, but it was no surprise to Sohn's father. "I've been expecting it," he said.

L'Homme-Oiseau (The Bird-Man) poses in front of the poster advertising what would turn out to be his final appearance. (Bibliothèque Nationale de France)

The tragedy led to all sorts of conjecturing. The leading theories were that the wings, which were new, had malfunctioned, or that moisture had seeped into the parachutes during the stormy transatlantic crossing. Davis said Sohn's failure to repack the chutes may have resulted in the damp silk sticking together and not deploying properly.

Family brought Clem home and buried him at Holy Trinity cemetery in Fowler, with a pilot friend skywriting "SOHN" above the crowd of mourners. Like so many other headliners throughout history, his fame proved as vaporous as those puffy letters spelled out in the blue. Aside from the winged flying suit displayed at the Library of Michigan, the most tangible token of his brief time on earth—and above it—is a commemorative plaque in the lobby of Eastern High School. It reminds students that, many years ago, one of their own once soared high above the crowd: "There are some pioneer souls who blaze their paths where highways never ran."

19

Twist of Fate

It was Detroiter Hank Ballard, not Chubby Checker, who was the originator of the hit song and dance craze of the early 1960s.

Any discussion of "The Twist," one of the seminal songs in pop music history, threatens to throw an old rhythm and blues fan like Doc Lawrence slightly out of joint.

"It will always be Hank Ballard's song," insists Lawrence, who over the years saw the Detroit-born artist perform more times than he can remember. "Everybody else just stole it from him. Especially Chubby Checker."

To the masses, the zigzagging and perpetually beaming Chubby Checker is synonymous with the Twist, both the song and the worldwide dance craze it inspired. His chord-for-chord cover of Hank Ballard and the Midnighters' 1959 B-side single is still the only record of the rock-and-roll era to top the charts on two separate occasions: first in 1960, then again in 1962. A generation later, Chubby's collaboration with the Fat Boys on "The Twist (Yo, Twist!)" demonstrated the song's remarkable durability. In 2008, *Billboard* magazine named "The Twist" the biggest hit in the history of its Hot 100 charts.

Given such extraordinary success, the man promoted as "The High Priest of The Twist" understandably feels very proprietary about the song—which may be why Checker's camp ignored an interview request for this story. Like the pointy-toe shoes Chubby screwed into the floor in those low-budget "Twist-errific!" dance movies of the early 1960s, any reminder of the debt he owes Ballard probably rubs a sore spot.

It doesn't help matters that Ballard was an early inductee into the Rock and Roll Hall of Fame, later joined by the Midnighters (who in 2012 were elected as a group), while Chubby continues to wonder who he cheesed off on the selection committee. "If it wasn't for Hank Ballard, I wouldn't be here," he conceded in a 2010 interview in *Keep Rockin'* magazine. "But listen, you know, people always talk about Hank Ballard . . . It seems like people are angry at me because I recorded 'The Twist'."

Actually, the snub is not that surprising, says longtime Detroit music writer Susan Whitall. "Hank is seen, rightly so, as an R&B legend who wrote most of his own material, while Chubby was a manager-created phenomenon."

Ballard was born John Henry Kendricks in Detroit on November 18, 1927, though as a performer he routinely shaved nine years off his age by claiming a 1936 birthdate. His father, a truck driver, died when he was seven, after which he moved to Bessemer, Alabama, to live with relatives. It was a strict Baptist household, but as he grew older he became bolder, slipping out his bedroom window on occasion to compete in amateur blues shows in Birmingham.

He was fifteen when he returned to Detroit, having soaked up such disparate influences as church gospel music and Gene Autry, the singing cowboy. He was working on the Ford assembly line when he was invited to join a local doo-wop group, the Royals. When the Army drafted the lead singer in 1951, Ballard became the main man. Gone were the romantic harmonies. "I had them change to a more driving, up-tempo thing," he recalled. "You know, let's get funky!"

Ballard wrote and sang lead on the Royals' breakout hit, "Work with Me, Annie." The lyrics ("Annie, please don't cheat / Give me all my meat / Oooo-weee") were raunchy enough to cause the Federal Communications Commission to ban the song from the airwaves. Nonetheless, it was a jukebox favorite and the top-rated R&B song of 1954. To avoid confusion with another group, the Five Royales, the

Hank Ballard in a promotional photo taken sometime in the mid-1950s. (Ace Records UK)

Royals renamed themselves the Midnighters. In the studio the ensemble recorded a string of blues-based hits with infectious gospel-style harmonies, while on stage they cranked up crowds with their full-bore, joyously risqué song-and-dance performances. Over the span of a decade the Royals/Midnighters would place twenty songs on the pop or R&B charts.

"The Twist" was first recorded as a demo in Miami in early 1958, remembers Norman Thrasher, a still-active Detroit vocalist who joined the Midnighters that year. "Cal Green, our guitarist, worked with Hank on it," he says, though Ballard claimed sole ownership of its composition.

The group recorded a polished master at King Records' Cincinnati studios on November 11, 1958. Ballard thought it had hit potential, but instead the label released it as the "B" side to the Midnighters' "Teardrops on Your Letter."

The dance slowly caught on when the Midnighters took their act on the road, though Thrasher grew exasperated by the group's total disdain for rehearsal of any kind. "We're not twisting," he told them at one point. "We're wiggling."

Whatever one called it, by 1960 teenagers in Baltimore were swiveling to the rhythm on a local television dance show. Its popularity drew the attention of Dick Clark, the producer and host of Philadelphia-based *American Bandstand*. The program aired live on the ABC network every weekday afternoon, reaching an audience of 20 million.

Clark's baby-face wholesomeness masked a savvy and not always ethical business sense. He recognized the song's huge potential and wanted to release it on Parkway Records, a label co-owned by his wife. Clark worked out a deal with Sid Nathan, the cigar-chomping president of King Records, who never liked "The Twist." In exchange for granting Parkway the rights to record its version, Nathan got a cut of the profits and Clark's promise to showcase other Midnighters songs on his nationally broadcast show. These turned out to be "Finger Poppin' Time" and "Let's Go, Let's Go, Let's Go," a couple of hip-shakers whose sales benefited greatly from their exposure on *American Bandstand*.

Clark never considered having the streetwise Ballard as the "face" of the Twist. He was thirty-two years old, had dark skin and processed hair, smoked dope, and had a name that in R&B circles was synonymous with censorship. In Clark's view, Hank Ballard was not the right kind of Black man to be invited into America's living rooms.

However, a sunshiny, light-skinned eighteen-year-old named Ernest "Chubby" Evans was. Evans, a South Carolina transplant who worked at a local poultry shop, already had recorded a couple of singles with Parkway. One was a mildly successful parody in which Evans mimicked the voices of various singers. He sounded almost exactly like Ballard. Clark's wife, playing off the name of crossover R&B artist Fats Domino, suggested Chubby Evans call himself Chubby Checker.

In the late summer of 1960, the Midnighters' reissued version of "The Twist" was moving steadily up the charts when Chubby's version, heavily promoted on *American Bandstand,* shot past it, on its way to earning a gold record as a certified million-seller.

"Man, when we first heard it, we all thought we were listening to our own song," Thrasher recalls. "Chubby copied it, note for note."

Checker not only appropriated the Midnighters' song and borrowed Ballard's voice, Thrasher says, he also took their dance moves. "He came up to us at the Uptown Theater in Philadelphia—this was in 1961—and asked us to help him out." Everybody ignored him except Thrasher, who soon had Chubby's choreography looking correct.

It's hard to overstate the impact "The Twist" had on the music industry and on pop culture. Priests, PTA boards, police officials, and stodgy dance instructors were predictably outraged. One self-appointed guardian of public morality, James I. Flanigan, declared the dance was "of evil origin" and was "used by Satan in inducing thousands of teenagers in a type of hypnotic ecstasy."

Few paid any attention. Doing the Twist was fun. Even highbrow dance master Arthur Murray came on board, his national chain of studios offering flat-footed fuddy-duddies "six easy lessons" for twenty-five dollars. For the first time ever, moms and dads were joining the kids on the dance floor, all grinding away like the agitator in the family washing machine.

They had plenty to dance to, as record companies scrambled to capitalize on "Twistmania." The outpouring included Sam Cooke's "Twistin' the Night Away," Joey Dee and the Starliters' "Peppermint Twist," and the Isley Brothers' "Twist and Shout" (later a hit for the Beatles). Motown's Berry Gordy released *Twistin' the World Around,* a forgettable album by the Twistin' Kings (who actually were the house band later known as the Funk Brothers). Gordy also rushed the Marvelettes into the studio to record "Twistin' Postman," the follow-up to the teenage group's "Please Mr. Postman," Motown's first number-one pop single. "Twistin' Postman" was just one of twenty Twist singles to make Billboard's Top 40 between 1960 and 1962.

Ernest "Chubby" Evans covered Ballard's song and, as the newly minted Chubby Checker, twisted all the way to the bank. (Author's collection)

Nobody cashed in like Checker, whose output featured the Grammy-winning "Let's Twist Again" as well as several novelty dance songs: "The Fly," "The Hucklebuck," "Pony Time," and "Limbo Rock." At one time he had six of the ten top-selling albums in the country, something no other recording artist has ever done. In January 1962, seventeen months after his version of "The Twist" reached number one on the pop charts, a reissue again reached the top spot. Chubby was ubiquitous, rich, and famous. To top it all off, the one-time chicken-plucker from Philadelphia's projects dated (and later married) Miss World of 1962.

In November 1961, about the time Motown's Twist platters dropped, Ballard appeared on the popular television game show, *To Tell the Truth*. As he and two impostors were introduced to the show's audience, the voiceover declared: "I am the composer, author, and originator of 'The Twist.'"

Sleek, dapper, and effortlessly cool, softly moving his hips and lips as the panelists fired questions, Ballard stood out from the bland pretenders. However, when asked to choose between him, an erudite psychologist, and a bulky end for the New York Giants, only one of the four panelists could correctly identify "the real Hank Ballard." The performer left with $750, a carton of Salems, and a reaffirmation that, when it came to the song and dance that were sweeping the planet, there was Chubby Checker, and then there was everybody else.

Not that anybody was complaining, Thrasher says. "It didn't take anything from us. We were working every night, and Hank was cashing those songwriting checks, so nobody cared."

The Midnighters were playing three hundred gigs a year, including a booking at Florida State University. Doc Lawrence was part of the student entertainment committee that convinced school officials to invite Ballard to campus. "They asked me, 'Do you think he's appropriate for homecoming?'" Lawrence, now a producer and writer in Atlanta, recalls with a chuckle. "I said, 'Oh yeah, he's a perfect choice.' Hank came in and put on the most stimulating, daring, raunchy performance. 'Work with Me, Annie,' all those great songs. Flawless. Nobody was in his league."

Ballard, who like most artists of his era justifiably complained of being exploited by agents, producers, and publishers, was not above taking advantage of others himself. He didn't share writing credits on "The Twist" and other songs, and as the group's front man he became more demanding.

"Hank wanted all the money," Thrasher says. Ballard and the Midnighters went their separate ways around 1964, "and Hank never did have another hit record after that."

Ballard blamed the breakup on several members becoming Black Muslims and refusing to perform before White audiences. "It was tough on me because they were the act, they're the ones that did everything on stage," he said years later. "Me, I just sang."

He eventually gained legal rights to the group's name and toured with a new set of Midnighters. But like most acts of his era, the

Concert posters, such as this one from 1963, typically advertised Hank Ballard as the creator of "The Twist." (Author's collection)

musical revolution of the 1960s turned him into an anachronism. He had a short-lived fling on soul singer James Brown's label and resisted the oldies circuit for as long as he could. A self-described drifter, he moved around the country, including stops in New York and Nashville.

In 1975, desperate for cash, Ballard sold his composing rights to "The Twist" for a mere $5,000, but he later regained them thanks to a favorable untangling of the song's copyrights. "I made a lot of money on that song," he told music writer Bruce Pollock in 1979, by which time he was living in a small Miami apartment with his second wife. "Of course it was just a drop in the bucket to what Chubby made."

Ballard, whose Cadillac bore the vanity plate TWSTER, always maintained that he bore no animosity towards the man who overshadowed him, though he once had his lawyers challenge Checker's claim in a TV spot that he was the "creator of the Twist." The commercial was for Oreo cookies, a rather unflattering irony that apparently was lost on Chubby and the advertising agency that hired him.

Ballard was enjoying a resurgence of recognition when he was inducted into the Rock and Roll Hall of Fame in 1990. He recorded in England, contributed to soundtracks, and otherwise kept professionally busy. But within a few more years his distinctive, driving voice was stilled by throat cancer. He was seventy-five when he died in Los Angeles on March 2, 2003.

Today, Checker continues to profitably churn his geriatric hips at nightclubs and private parties. Norman Thrasher recently was in New Orleans at a benefit for Fats Domino. Chubby was there, and so was Little Richard, who called the old Midnighter up on stage. Thrasher, approaching eighty, responded by giving the crowd a taste of the Twist.

"Oh yeah," he says. "You're never too old to twist."

From left: Bob Troy, Donie Bush, and Fred House at spring training, 1913. (Bain Collection/ Library of Congress)

20

Digging Up Bob Troy

Whether on a pitching mound or in the trenches, Robert "Red" Troy was an imposing figure. This is the story of the only Detroit major leaguer ever to die in combat, and his belated return home from France.

The only surviving photograph of Bob Troy as a major leaguer is a gimmicky grouping of three Detroit Tigers taken by the Bain News Service during spring training in March 1913. In it, low-slung shortstop Donie Bush is positioned between Troy and another towering pitching prospect, Fred House. While Bush and House stare soberly at the box camera, Troy is gazing off into the distance, a wry expression on his face.

A few days later, the team assigned Troy to Chattanooga of the Southern Association. He was clearly frustrated about being farmed out for "seasoning" yet again, but he maintained his dry wit. "By the time I'm forty," he said, "I ought to make good."

This is the story of Robert "Red" Troy, who was born in Germany in 1888 and died in France thirty years later—killed in a monumental clash between the armies of his adopted homeland and the country of his birth. For several summers in-between, the rangy redhead managed to scratch out a living playing America's national game, most notably in Adrian, where for two seasons he was the workhorse of the Southern Michigan League.

Troy made only a single big-league appearance, but his "cup of coffee" was an experience many fans, then and now, would swap all they owned for: a pitching duel with the great Walter Johnson at Detroit's spanking-new Navin Field, on a diamond sprinkled with future Hall of Famers and before a crowd of thousands cheering him on. The result that Sunday afternoon wasn't what Troy had hoped for, and most certainly neither was the mortal wound he suffered on the Western Front a few years later. But overall it was an adventurous if truncated life for the obscure German immigrant, who during the 1910s wore the uniforms most remindful of that gingery era: the jerseys of a traipsing ballplayer and the tunic of a crusading doughboy.

* * *

When the S. S. *Russia* steamed into Baltimore's harbor in October 1891, there was no shimmering Statue of Liberty to command one's gaze and lift one's soul, just squawking gulls and the dizzying commotion of the country's busiest port outside of New York City. The immigrant ship had left Hamburg two and a half weeks earlier. Among the nearly two hundred "alien" passengers disembarking the steamer that day were four members of the Treu family.

August Treu was a strapping twenty-nine-year-old Prussian with an eighth-grade education. He hailed from Drenow, a small rural community in the free state of Prussia. Like all males looking to emigrate, he had to provide authorities with documented proof that he'd fulfilled his compulsory military service before they allowed him to leave Germany. His wife, Bertha Arndt Treu, was a sturdy, unschooled country woman who turned twenty-seven the day before the *Russia* docked in Baltimore. Their first child, Robert Gustave Treu—the future ballplayer—had been born on August 27, 1888, in Wurzach, southern Germany, a few weeks after Wilhelm II assumed the crown as the last Kaiser. Two years later, Bertha gave birth to a second son, who was given the emperor's name.

There were roughly 3 million German-born immigrants living in the United States on the day three-year-old Robert Treu arrived. Half of them had come during the previous decade, including August Treu's twin sister, Augusta, who had settled in McDonald, a small community about twenty miles southwest of Pittsburgh. Following Augusta's lead, August Treu and his young family also put down roots in McDonald.

August's prospects seemed bright in western Pennsylvania, where men were starting to take coal and oil out of the ground in earnest. At the time, the McDonald oil field was producing greater yields than anywhere in the world. Looking to assimilate, August anglicized the family's surname to Troy, but they continued to speak German at home.

The 1900 census shows August Troy as a coal miner living on Coal Street. That year he, Bertha, and their sons became naturalized citizens. Bob was still in grammar school, but that would soon change. He was a big, strong kid, so there was no sense in wasting several prime physical years inside a classroom. As the oldest of eight siblings—by 1906 his mother had given birth to six more children, all girls—the family expected him to contribute to their income. Many boys, including Bob and his brother, worked the bituminous coal seams of various Allegheny County mines. Later, as a young pitcher, Bob would occasionally experience back problems—a byproduct, perhaps, of heavy manual labor underground.

McDonald offered plenty of opportunities to work off energy in pick-up games and organized leagues. At some point Bob picked up a baseball and threw it—*hard.* Ultimately the blue-eyed boy was striking out older men on ragged diamonds in the rolling hills around Allegheny and Washington counties. He would mature into an imposing physical specimen for the era: six-foot-four, two hundred pounds, with long arms and big feet.

Troy broke into professional baseball in 1909 with a local independent team. Word of his prowess got around. As *Sporting Life* described it, Philadelphia Phillies scout Frank Haller "dug up" Troy, who at season's end worked out with the National League club and received an offer for a contract.

In early 1910, the twenty-one-year-old prospect reported to the Phillies' training camp. For a short while that spring Troy was teammates with Eddie Grant, the club's regular third baseman. Grant, a

Harvard graduate and a practicing attorney in the offseason, was a solid fielder and dependable batsman during his eight-year big-league career with Philadelphia, Cincinnati, and New York Giants. The extent of Troy's interaction with the erudite, pipe-smoking veteran on and off the field is unknown. "Colts" and regulars didn't always mix much. However tenuous their connection as teammates in 1910, Troy and "Harvard Eddie" would later share a tragic destiny as infantrymen in the Argonne Forest.

Organized minor leagues were classified from Class D, the lowest, to Double-A (established in 1912), with the competition growing keener as a player moved up the ladder. Philadelphia sent Troy to Worcester in the New England League, a Class B circuit, for seasoning. But he failed to impress and Worcester soon released him. The Phillies next sent him to Johnstown of the Tri-State League, another Class B circuit, but the team let him go after just one disastrous start. "He had the speed and curves," *Sporting Life* noted, "but lacked control and acted too much like an amateur on the ball field." That ended the Phillies' flirtation. Troy spent that summer and the next playing for a series of flailing clubs in Pennsylvania and Ohio.

The spring of 1912 found Troy working out with the Saginaw Trailers of the Southern Michigan League, a Class D operation. Before the start of the season, he was traded to the Adrian Lions for veteran catcher George Dworski. "He looks a big, husky man . . . with a world of speed," observed the *Adrian Daily Telegram*, reporting on Troy's arrival at Adrian's Franklin Park on April 24. The newcomer was on the mound for the season opener on May 9 at Jackson. It was a German-speaking battery, as his catcher was future major leaguer Emil Huhn, a quiet, brawny twenty-year-old whose parents had emigrated about the same time as Troy's. Despite a shaky ninth inning that saw him get pulled for a reliever, Troy got credit for the 7–5 win.

It took some time for Troy, who lost six of his next nine decisions, to gain his stride and the favor of the fans. Once he did, he became the catalyst of Adrian's unexpected climb out of the basement to the top of the standings. The club's pennant run was a much-needed boost to local morale. In June, the factory of the Lion Motor Car Company—one of Adrian's biggest employers, as well as the source of the team's nickname—burned to the ground. A collapsing wall killed one fireman, injured another, and threw three hundred workers suddenly out of a job. The community recovered; the company never did.

Adrian, seventy miles southwest of Detroit, was the smallest city in the eight-team loop, which that season also included such colorfully named clubs as the Battle Creek Crickets, Jackson Convicts, Lansing Senators, Bay City Billikens, Flint Vehicles, and Kalamazoo Celery Pickers. The Lions had the lowest payroll in the league. However, the team claimed a rabid fan base, one that wasn't always quite sure how to view "Big Bob."

"Troy is a player of peculiar disposition, and one little understood by fans who do not know him well," an Adrian sportswriter observed. "When he is slow to make himself a 'good fellow' among men he does not know, they think he is 'chesty.' As a matter of fact, he is diffident, almost to the point of bashfulness. He hardly ever expresses himself seriously, and is delighted to exchange wit with any member of the [Adrian team] or visiting teams who happen around. Troy is one of those dry humorists which keep one puzzled whether to laugh with him or at him. His funny remarks are often sarcastic, and spoken as if in good faith."

According to standard baseball reference works, Troy was nicknamed "Bun." Its origin remains unknown, and its use was generally limited to Pennsylvania papers. Perhaps it reflected an unusual craving for the tasty "sticky buns" (*schnecken*) popularized by German-Americans. (One of Troy's six sisters worked in a local bakery.) Adrian and Detroit sportswriters usually called him "Red," probably a reference to his chestnut-colored hair or inspired by the fair-skinned pitcher's flushed face.

Although Adrian was unaffiliated with any major-league team, the Detroit organization kept close tabs on the club, and the league as a whole. Tigers owner Frank Navin hailed from Adrian. He had previously purchased players off Southern Michigan League rosters and was pleased with the results. Now his scouts were eyeing

Troy, and they had company. By mid-July, Troy had rebounded to win eight straight games and scouts from four big-league clubs were in the stands. On July 15, Adrian president Will King accepted Navin's $2,000 offer for Troy. Navin allowed Adrian to keep him through the end of the season. Soon fans were talking about holding a "Troy Day," an idea the *Adrian Daily Telegram* heartily endorsed: "This would give the fans an opportunity to show just how much they think of the big pitcher whose ability to win ball games has had a great deal to do with Adrian's standing in the league race, and also brought a neat sum of money to the Adrian coffers from the Detroit club for his services."

On August 18, Troy started and won both games of a Sunday doubleheader against Kalamazoo, the defending league champs. Two weeks later, Adrian edged Battle Creek for the pennant on the last day of the season, despite Troy losing twice in the four-game showdown with the Crickets. Troy, who still wound up with 23 victories and a league-high 268 strikeouts, "was almost heart-broken, yet was ready to go back in and pitch Sunday's game, if needed," observed a local scribe. "His arm thrown out by constant work, he couldn't show his best in the game he wanted most to win."

Troy reported to Detroit immediately after Adrian's season ended. Tigers manager Hughie Jennings chose to give the newcomer a few days to rest his tired right arm. The Tigers were mired in sixth place. It had been an eventful season, nonetheless, with the grand opening of Navin's new concrete-and-steel ballpark, a July 4 no-hitter by George Mullin, and the suspension of Ty Cobb for climbing into the stands in New York to beat up a disabled heckler and the ensuing players' strike by protesting teammates.

Finally, Jennings told Troy he would start on September 15, a Sunday contest against Washington at Navin Field. The second-place Nationals were futilely chasing the Boston Red Sox, who would win the American League pennant and the World Series in 1912. To make his big-league debut even more daunting, Troy would be going head-to-head with the storied Walter Johnson, the lanky, modest speed-baller who'd recently had a record sixteen-game winning streak snapped. "As Little Walter generally holds the Tigers

A postcard view of Navin Field in 1912. (Author's collection)

to three or four hits and a couple or no runs, all Robert has to do is likewise for the Nationals," suggested the *Detroit News-Tribune*. "The theory of this stunt is that if Troy stands this he will stand anything."

The game started at three o'clock. Due to a hard morning rain, the outfield grass was slick, and there were small puddles around first and third base. It was overcast all afternoon, with the sky growing darker as the game wore on. Official attendance at Navin Field was 7,535, meaning the 23,000-seat park was about one-third full. "A large delegation of Adrian fans will be on hand to assist in making the 'coming out' party a success," the *Free Press* noted. There were smaller groups representing other Southern Michigan League towns and some friends and family members made the train trip from Pennsylvania.

It was an odd afternoon, in many respects. Washington lost three players during the course of the game; two were injured and the third was ejected. The Tigers also had a man tossed for arguing a call. In addition, both managers, Jennings and Clark Griffith, were missing from the bench because each was serving a suspension. Most bizarre was Troy's first big-league inning, when the Nationals collected two hits, a walk, and two stolen bases off the twenty-four-year-old rookie—but still failed to score.

Troy walked the first man he faced, Dan Moeller, who promptly stole second base. The next batter, Eddie Foster, tapped the ball to third baseman "Red" Corriden, who bluffed a throw to first and instead picked Moeller off second. As fielders hung Moeller up between second and third, Foster strayed too far off first, and after Moeller was tagged out, a snap throw caught him too. Clyde Milan followed this unusual double play with a single. He stole second and tried scoring when the cleanup hitter, Chick Gandil, singled to left. However, a strong throw nailed Milan at the plate.

Troy was regularly in trouble through the first six frames, but continued poor base-running by Washington allowed him to escape unscathed. "Until the seventh," Eddie Batchelor wrote, "the Nationals could not rock Troy's confidence though they whacked him vehemently at times." Meanwhile, the Tigers were able to scrounge out three runs against Johnson.

The score stood at 3–0 through six innings. George McBride started off the top of the seventh by laying down a bunt, but Corriden pounced on the ball and threw him out. Troy was now just eight outs away from achieving the impossible: blanking the second-place Nationals and out-dueling "The Big Train" in his major-league debut. He was "being wildly applauded by the hopeful fans," reported the *Washington Post*'s Joe S. Jackson, with the Adrian fans, in particular, whooping it up. But the bunching clouds were portentous. In the words of Eddie Batchelor, the "coming-out party became a knock-out party."

Next up was "Rip" Williams. The Washington catcher sent a bouncing grounder off Corriden's glove and narrowly beat the throw to first for a scratch hit.

That brought Walter Johnson to the plate, who sliced one of Troy's offerings to right field. By the time "Wahoo Sam" Crawford chased the ball down, Williams was about to score and Johnson was on his way to third. However, Crawford's throw hit umpire Bob Hart, and the rulebook stipulated that Johnson had to return to second base. Although the Nationals had finally broken through with their first run, Troy's luck seemed to be holding.

With the score now 3–1, Moeller singled to center, Johnson stopping at third. This put the tying runs on with one out. With Ray Morgan at bat, Moeller stole second base. Morgan then tapped the ball to Corriden, who threw home to retire Johnson at the plate. Once again the tying runs were on the corners, this time with two outs.

Into the batter's box stepped Milan, who slapped a single to center field. As Moeller crossed the plate for Washington's second run, Cobb fumbled the ball, then heaved it wildly into the Detroit dugout. Cobb's two errors on the play brought Morgan in with the tying run and put Milan on third base with the go-ahead run.

Cobb's misplays also put Troy out of the game. Big Bob dejectedly left the mound, having seen a three-run lead evaporate like a puff of smoke. Edgar Willett took over, and he promptly gave up a base hit that gave Washington the lead for the first time. Willett surrendered two more hits before settling down to get the last two outs. In a matter of minutes, Washington had exploded for six runs to seize a 6–3 lead.

As the sky grew darker, Johnson's heater became practically invisible. He set down the Tigers in order in the seventh and the eighth. With the clock approaching five o'clock and the Nationals needing to catch a train to St. Louis, home plate umpire Tom Connolly called the game after eight innings. The final line on Troy read: nine hits, three walks, one strikeout, one hit batsman, and four earned runs in six and one-third innings. Scorers charged him with the loss. The pitcher reportedly was so "furious" over the horrible support given him by Detroit fielders that he "jumped" the team, vowing never to play for them again.

If the rookie felt any embarrassment over his performance, he shouldn't have. As the *Detroit News-Tribune* pointed out in its recap, "They could not send him against a tougher proposition in the baseball world" than Johnson. The *Adrian Daily Telegram* opined: "Troy made a good impression. . . . He showed nerve in the pinches, and by the way the Washington team kept hitting Willett, they were there with their hitting clothes." However, he was roundly criticized for allowing runners to get a flying start; the Nationals stole six bases on him. Jennings's plans did not call for any more outings by Troy in 1912. But his audition had gone well enough for him to be invited to camp the following spring.

The Tigers were in bad shape when they opened training in Gulfport, Mississippi, in February 1913. Cobb was holding out and the pitching staff was turning Jennings's hair gray. The manager said that every one of the pitching recruits in camp would be given at least one start on the big-league schedule to see what he could do. But in late March, after getting knocked around in a start against the Montgomery Rebels of the Class A Southern Association, Troy was the first pitcher Jennings farmed out. "The fact that he was hit hard did not make so much difference, but he gave evidence of having so much to learn about all branches of the pitching art that Jennings had no hesitation in dismissing him from consideration as a big leaguer," Eddie Batchelor wrote. In addition to his flawed mechanics in fielding and holding runners on base, Troy's speedball lacked "jump" and the break on his curve was ordinary. "By working hard, he may come back to the big show some day prepared to hold a job."

So it was on to Chattanooga, a Southern Association club managed by Norman "Kid" Elberfeld. The abrasive ex-Tigers shortstop was unconvinced of Troy's potential. One wonders how well Troy took to instruction and criticism. Was he too "chesty" and uncompromising? His chronic cynicism couldn't have helped. He wrote a friend upon being farmed out: "Detroit has kept lots poorer pitchers than I am, and the worst of it is, I know it." The ace of the Lookouts' staff was Harry Coveleski, another one-time coal miner from Pennsylvania, who would claim a permanent spot in the Tigers' rotation the following season.

In mid-May, the Lookouts unconditionally released Troy and Navin put him up for sale. The Fort Wayne club in the Central League offered $500 but Navin, apparently looking to do Adrian's fans a good turn, instead loaned him to Adrian for $300. However, the Detroit owner kept a "string" on the pitcher's services, retaining the option to recall Troy later in the year for reassignment.

The Adrian club was now nicknamed the "Champs" in recognition of its 1912 pennant that Troy had been instrumental in winning. However, the Champs failed to repeat in 1913. Troy, rejuvenated by familiar surroundings, won a league-leading twenty-three games. With a composite record of 46–30 in two stints with Adrian, he was at the apex of his career. During that stretch he was the workhorse of the Southern Michigan League, pitching more games and innings and posting more victories and strikeouts than any other hurler. His friends knew him as "an ambitious player who thought well of his own ability, as he had a right to, and was ready to work as hard as might be to make good up in the big leagues."

Troy moved up a couple notches in 1914, to the Pittsfield Electrics of the Class B Eastern Association. The Massachusetts club was owned and managed by Jack Zeller, who had a working arrangement with Detroit. Troy was the ace of the Pittsfield staff in 1914, notching nineteen victories with a league-high 212 strikeouts. Zeller signed Troy for 1915, but legal issues caused organizers to cancel the season. In July, Pittsfield joined the Western Massachusetts League, a newly organized independent circuit that was a bust at the gate. Troy moved on to the Troy Trojans in the New York State League, yet another team on the verge of collapse.

By then the Tigers had given up on their prospect. After several years of stalled development, and likely sporting a burned-out arm, he was on the downslope of his diamond career. The following summer the itinerant twirler turned twenty-eight, with faint hopes of grabbing a roster spot in the low minors, much less a return trip to the majors. Scattered references in the press during this period had him playing for semipro teams close to home. By the spring of 1917, with war contracts transforming Pittsburgh industry into "the arsenal of the Allies," he was using his pitching hand to punch the clock at the Allegheny Forging Company in McDonald.

* * *

On April 6, 1917, the United States finally entered the great European war it had been awkwardly dodging for nearly three years. Troy was still a bachelor living at home with his sisters. Although he was the family's main support, he was one of the first members of the 80th Infantry Division when it formed. The Army inducted him at Bridgeville, Pennsylvania, on September 18, 1917, and within three weeks promoted him to corporal. About this time, his father found work in a wire mill and moved the family to Monessen, about thirty miles from McDonald.

Troy donned khaki in a climate of heightened anti-German sentiment, where critics derided those of German stock as "hyphenated Americans." In this toxic environment, sauerkraut became "Liberty cabbage," dachshunds were renamed "Liberty dogs," schools banned German-language instruction, hundreds of German newspapers folded, and critics questioned the loyalty of even the most industrious and civic-minded German-Americans and threatened their livelihoods. Many kept a low profile or changed their names. Troy's former battery mate, Emil Huhn, insisted people pronounce his name "Hoon" instead of "Hun." Meanwhile, the citizens of Berlin, Michigan, successfully agitated for the community to be renamed Marne. Troy knew enough about his ancestry not to paint all citizens of Deutschland as rapacious Huns. But, as the saying went, "Love of one's mother does not detract from love of one's bride." In going "Over There," many German-Americans were demonstrating to xenophobes that they were willing to do their part to "save the world for democracy." More than a few, including perhaps Troy, were motivated as much by adventure as patriotism.

The 80th ("Blue Ridge") Division comprised 23,000 conscripts and volunteers from western Pennsylvania, Maryland, Virginia, and West Virginia. Recruits assembled at Camp Lee in Virginia for several months of training. "Dear bunch," Troy scrawled on a postcard to his family after his first week in uniform, "got here safe some camp down here." Troy was given Army Serial No. 1826927 and assigned to Company G, 2nd Battalion, 319th Regiment, one of the four regiments that made up the 80th Division. An avid outdoorsman, and with Prussian blood flowing in his veins, Troy was in some respects a natural fit for the military. Because of his age, commanding size, and comparative worldliness, he was treated with

Bob Troy as a doughboy in 1917. (Author's collection)

some deference by his fellow citizen soldiers. In the parlance of the barracks, he "knew the score."

Throughout the spring of 1918 recruits mastered the manual of arms, suffered through grueling marches, and tried out their pitching arms in the hand-grenade pit. In late May, the 80th Division steamed across the Atlantic in convoy, part of the American Expeditionary Force that would eventually number more than 2 million troops in France. Corporal Troy "was cheerful on the day of his departure," a local journalist noted, "and sought to enliven those of his comrades who were oppressed by the sense of what was before them." That summer, battle-hardened British instructors trained Troy's regiment in trench warfare; the regiment guarded prisoners and took its first casualties. "All the men were full of confidence," recalled an officer in the 319th, "and anxious to get the Hun out in the open and show him that the American doughboy had faith in his bayonet."

On August 7, 1918, Troy was promoted to sergeant. As a noncommissioned officer, his responsibilities on the battlefield were far weightier than they ever were on the mound—a matter of life and death, not mere wins and losses. Troy evaluated his chances on the Western Front with characteristic irony. "I'm so tall," he said, "the enemy will find me an easy mark."

Troy's last known letter home was written six weeks before his death. "Dear Mother and Father," he wrote, "just a few lines to let you know that I am still well. . . ." He mentioned his outfit had spent ten days in the trenches and the last day and a half on a train. Although none of the Yanks were aware of it, they were being moved into position for the greatest American undertaking of the war: the Meuse-Argonne offensive.

Meuse-Argonne remains the deadliest battle in US military history. More than 1.2 million Americans took part in the savagely fought offensive, which commanders launched September 26, 1918, and which continued right up to the armistice seven weeks later. By then, 10 percent of the American force was dead, wounded, gassed, captured, or missing—an average of 2,597 casualties per day, or one doughboy every thirty-three seconds.

Several days into this "hellish tournament" fought over hills, swamps, and woods, Troy became a statistic. On the evening of October 4, his battalion moved into action north of the pulverized village of Nantillois. They advanced on the Bois d'Ogons, a woods bristling with machine-gun nests, trench mortars, artillery, and snipers. Commanders launched a division-wide assault on the heavily fortified woods on the moonless night of October 5. It was costly and confusing, with many Americans becoming lost as they blundered about

An American attack in the Argonne. The Meuse-Argonne offensive in the fall of 1918 was the deadliest battle in US history. (Author's collection)

the splintered trees, gas-filled shell craters, tangled barbed wire, and treacherous undergrowth. By the morning of the sixth, several depleted companies, including Troy's, had passed through the woods, regrouped, and formed a defensive line along its northern edge. They remained there throughout the day, raked by the incessantly chattering Maxims, strafed from above by Fokkers, and pummeled by the high-velocity artillery shells dubbed "whizz-bangs."

Sometime during the fighting of October 5–6, Troy suffered a "GSW—Chest," army shorthand for a gunshot wound to the chest. He was struck by one or more bullets, undoubtedly a victim of the powerful Maxim machine guns that could fire 600 rounds per minute and accounted for the vast majority of gunshot wounds.

How long Troy waited for help after being wounded is not known, but it wasn't long enough for him to bleed out. He may have found his way back to an aid station, a few hundred yards to the rear, on his own or with the help of a buddy. (The latter was discouraged, as it took a healthy combatant out of the fight.) A roving member of the battalion's medical detachment might have found him and treated him on the spot, then assisted him to the aid station. If too seriously wounded, then litter carriers, whose perilous job was to comb the battlefield for fallen men, would have transported the fallen sergeant.

Once there, medics would have given Troy first aid, kept him warm to prevent shock, and brought his hemorrhaging under control. Medics would have given him morphine and antitetanic serum, marking a "T" being on his forehead with an indelible pencil. After that, medics would have moved him to an ambulance dressing station, where medical staff evaluated and stabilized casualties as best as possible. Medical personnel loaded transportable casualties into four-litter ambulances for the harrowing ride along jammed roads to nearby evacuation hospitals, a linen tag detailing each patient's diagnosis and treatment tied in a buttonhole of their tunic.

Troy was taken to Evacuation Hospital No. 8 at Petit Maujouy, a complex of large tents and roughly carpentered one-story buildings near Verdun. There were other evacuation hospitals handling the flood of casualties from the Argonne, but medical command sent the most seriously wounded, including all sucking chest wounds, to the one at Petit Maujouy.

During the Meuse-Argonne campaign, it took an average of ten to twelve hours to move a casualty from the battlefield to an ambulance dressing station. By the time a wounded man was transferred to an evacuation hospital, he was often on the cusp of death. The greatest danger was slipping into shock. In a postwar memoir, hospital orderly Frederick Pottle described the shock ward at Petit Maujouy: "Here, usually in their clothes just as they came from the ambulance, lie these poor fellows, with surgeons and nurses expending all their efforts to recall their vitality sufficiently to make an operation possible. They wrap them warmly in blankets, warm them further by small oil stoves placed under the cots, and give them stimulants, injections of saline solution, and blood transfusions. The shock ward is a sad and discouraging place, for the heat and rest which the patients must have furnish exactly the condition most favorable for the rapid development of infections. The air is heavy with the odor of decay, which we mask somewhat by sprinkling carbolic acid on the gravel floor. Many of these poor fellows die here without rallying at all. If they are operated on, their chances for life are slight."

Chest and head wounds always received top priority. It's unknown what, if any, surgical procedures were performed in an attempt to save Troy's life. Although the National Archives houses the records of all army hospitals, it does not have custody of patient records. Individual medical reports are part of a soldier's Official Military Personnel File. Unfortunately, a devastating fire at the National Personnel Records Center in St. Louis in 1973 destroyed Troy's file, like those of most of the enlisted men who served in the army during the war. His Form 52, which would have recorded his date of admittance, detailed the extent of his wounds, and described the nature of his treatment, was among the documents lost.

The groggy, overworked medical staff at Petit Maujouy doggedly did its best to keep every last man alive, though many were beyond repair. Evacuation hospitals were the intermediate stop for wounded soldiers. From there, medical personnel moved transportable patients by train to base hospitals in the rear. If they made it that far, their prospects for survival were good.

Troy was not one of them.

A century later, one wonders how he died. Did he breathe his last shortly after the jarring ambulance ride from the front, or did he succumb to shock in a room that smelled like rotting cabbage? Did he give out on one of the white enameled operating tables, or did he slip away in the recovery ward, mumbling deliriously to the end? Did he call out for his mother, as so many soldiers did? If so, were his cries in English—or German?

In the end, of course, it doesn't really matter. At some point on Monday, October 7, 1918, Sergeant Bob Troy officially "died of wounds received in action." He became one of the 26,277 Americans that history records as having died during the Meuse-Argonne offensive. His body was taken to the morgue tent on the edge of the nearby woods. There was no embalming. Attendants wiped him down, then wrapped his long frame in a wool blanket. For a shroud, they placed a gunny sack over his head and a second sack over his feet. Later, workers loaded him and the rest of the day's dead into the back of a truck and drove them down the broad road toward Senoncourt, where a small hillside cemetery, dotted with apple trees and slippery with mud, sat on the outskirts of the village. Each grave was marked by a rough wooden cross with an identification tag bearing the soldier's name and serial number nailed to it. Troy was placed in Grave No. 90.

The steady flow of blanketed, plank-like bodies that October grew as monotonous as the rain. A staffer at Petit Maujouy described a burial party leaning impatiently on their shovels, their thoughts straying as the chaplain droned on: "I am the Resurrection and the Life. . . . I go to prepare a place for you. . . . Then shall the body return to the earth . . . ashes to ashes, dust to dust." American Cemetery No. 607 outside Senoncourt was just one of some 2,400 makeshift burial grounds scattered across Europe, all filled with slumbering doughboys.

The War Department notified Troy's parents in a telegram. On November 11, 1918, exactly five weeks after his death, an armistice went into effect. The shooting stopped all along the Western Front. A few months later, negotiators hammered out a peace treaty in Paris, officially assigning blame for the war to Germany. Many called the Meuse-Argonne offensive the war's turning point. Believing this provided some solace to families of the fallen. All of the killing had to have served some higher purpose. Wasn't this the war that would end all wars?

* * *

The grass is waking in the ground,
Soon it will rise and blow in waves—
How can it have the heart to sway
Over the graves,
New graves?

—Sara Teasdale, "Spring in War-Time" (1915)

The war produced some 17 million military and civilian deaths, including 116,516 Americans. Eight former big leaguers died, six of them swept away by accidents or disease. Troy and his erstwhile spring-training mate, Eddie Grant, were the only ones killed by hostile fire, dying within a couple of days and a few miles of each other. Grant had by far the most accomplished career and the greatest name recognition; thus, his death has always dominated any conversation of ballplayers who "gave their all" in the Great War.

On October 5, 1918, two days before Troy's death, Captain Eddie Grant, a company commander in the 307th Infantry Regiment, became "Baseball's First Gold Star." He was on a mission to rescue the storied "Lost Battalion," several hundred men cut off by German fire in the trackless Argonne, when shrapnel from an overhead shell burst killed him instantly. He was thirty-five years old.

Grant's death was front-page news on both sides of the Atlantic, with many periodicals publishing tributes. Baseball officials, Harvard alumni, and Grant's family immediately sought ways to keep his memory alive. Soon there was a subscription to erect a memorial and plans to name a major highway after him. Meanwhile, Troy's death drew scant notice outside his hometown. In fact, in the official history of the 319th Infantry published in the spring of 1919, editors unaccountably left Troy's name out of the appendix listing the unit's "Honored Dead."

Officials had earlier decided that American war dead would not be sent home until after the fighting had stopped. In 1919, the Graves Registration Service contacted next-of-kin, asking families to decide on the final disposition of their sons, fathers, husbands, and brothers. The Graves Registration Service gave families the option of having a body returned to the States, at government expense, for burial in either a national or private cemetery, or of having the deceased permanently laid to rest in France at one of the elaborate military cemeteries then being planned. About two-thirds of the respondents wanted the body brought home. By the end of 1922, the Graves Registration Service had repatriated 45,488 Americans at an average cost to taxpayers of $396 per body.

Digging up tens of thousands of American soldiers and arranging for their final disposition was an enormous and sensitive task,

A temporary American cemetery in the Argonne. (Author's collection)

one complicated by displaced populations, troop movements, political squabbling, and the utter devastation of northern France, particularly its ruined infrastructure. Like countless other parents, Bertha and August Troy anxiously awaited the return of their son. Bertha belonged to the Mothers of Democracy, a Pittsburgh group formed to assist the families of fallen soldiers. A member of the organization likely composed the several letters that the Troys sent to Washington under their quivery signatures, asking for updates. "I have been patiently waiting for some information," Bertha wrote the secretary of war in one such letter. "Can you not tell me when the boys will be brought home."

By now, officials were forwarding all such letters to the Quartermaster General, whose Cemeterial Division was in charge of repatriating remains. Two years after the war, there finally was a breakthrough, as described in a letter dated December 9, 1920, from the office of the division's chief to Mrs. Troy:

> *In reply to your letter of November 30th . . . you are advised that the American Cemetery at Senoncourt, Department of*

> *Meuse, wherein the remains of your son, the late Sergeant Robert Troy . . . are interred, lies within the "Zone of the Armies" where operations incident to the removal of the soldier dead could not be commenced prior to September 15, 1920. While the work in this Zone is being expedited as much as possible, the magnitude of the task must be realized as well as the many transportation and labor problems and unforeseen difficulties to be overcome in this area. It is, therefore, impossible to state at this time when this particular case will be reached. You are assured, however, that the work is being prosecuted as vigorously as conditions and the accurate and reverent handling of our soldier dead will permit.*

On April 18, 1921, just as a new major-league season was underway, a work party began the grim job of disinterring Bob Troy and others buried at American Cemetery No. 607. A dozen years before, an impressed Phillies scout had "dug up" the young ballplayer on some scruffy diamond in coal country. Now local laborers, working under the direction of a government-contracted undertaker named Tomlinson, pulled the remains of his once sinewy body from the pungent French soil. Worms, bugs, enzymes, and bacteria had done their usual work, leaving behind "Things without shape, at which mothers would collapse," as novelist Owen Wister had written three days earlier in the *New York Times*.

There initially was some hesitation as to whether the body in Grave No. 90 was actually Troy. The aluminum ID tag that should have been attached to the blanket, matching a similar tag on the cross, was not found. Other means of positive identification were problematic. In his report of the exhumation, Tomlinson noted that the body was "too badly decomposed to estimate height or weight" and that it was "impractical to take tooth chart without mutilation."

Ultimately Tomlinson decided that it was indeed Troy. Workers removed the remains and took them to a processing area. There they were spread out, sprayed with disinfectant, and wrapped in a new blanket. Workers then placed the remains, arranged so as to "appear in the most presentable condition," inside a lined, leakproof metal casket. They used excelsior casket pads ("wood wool") to support the remains and prevent them from shifting about during transportation. In keeping with army policy, the cross that had marked Troy's grave was burned instead of salvaged. Caskets were stored in a tightly guarded, flag-bedecked port warehouse before being packed in individual wooden shipping containers for transport across the Atlantic.

On Memorial Day 1921, as Troy's remains awaited shipment home, officials unveiled a five-foot monument dedicated to Captain Eddie Grant in the deep reaches of center field at New York's Polo Grounds. The wreath-laying ceremony would be repeated every Memorial Day until the ballpark closed after the 1957 season. Some fans thought the player actually was buried there. In fact, Grant's family chose to have him interred at the Meuse-Argonne American Cemetery in France.

Hoboken, New Jersey, was the receiving port and distribution hub for all repatriated doughboys. On August 5, 1921, a uniformed escort brought Troy home. Two days later the family buried him with full military honors at the gently rolling grounds of Robinson Run Cemetery, outside McDonald. First Presbyterian Church, the one he had attended as a boy, was jammed with one thousand mourners. The many floral arrangements included one from Frank Navin. It was a soggy Sunday, just as it had been nine years earlier when Bob Troy took the mound in Detroit and, for one glorious hour or so, battled the great Walter Johnson to a standstill.

21

Why Not the Indians?

Detroit's hopes of reentering the National Football League hinged on an audition pitting a semipro club against Bronko Nagurski and the mighty Monsters of the Midway.

If the National Football League and Madison Avenue are to be believed, every season's Super Bowl is the "Game of the Year." Early on in its history, it was breathlessly promoted as "the ultimate game," causing one thoughtful player to ask, "If it's the ultimate game, why are they playing it again next year?"

Facetiousness aside, it's a fact that no other American sporting event attracts more eyeballs or generates as much revenue. But as we prepare to gird ourselves for several hours of sensory overload on this most super of Sundays, let's lower the trumpets for a moment, call a time-out on the hype, and turn the game clock back to 1933—back before the Super Bowl, television, or even the Detroit Lions existed—to a long-forgotten moment when Detroit hosted its own ballyhooed game of the year.

In that throwback season, the NFL was still a regional league struggling for survival. Membership was open to just about any organized team in the East or Midwest that could demonstrate a certain level of financing, enterprise, and fan support. Finding an individual or a company to bankroll a franchise remained the biggest challenge. But from a purely competitive standpoint, the problem was that most semipro clubs of the era fielded players, both local and imported, who loved the game but fell short on talent.

Today, the notion of such a team "auditioning" for a spot in the NFL is beyond ludicrous. Yet on a Wednesday night in the middle of the Great Depression, an overmatched squad of scrappy semipros known as the Detroit Indians squared off against George Halas's powerful Chicago Bears, defending NFL champions. At stake was the Indians' membership in the country's top pro circuit.

"If the caliber of the Indians' play and the attendance warrant it," stated the *Detroit Free Press*, "the Indians will be offered a franchise in the league for next season."

What transpired is one of the most intriguing events in the long history of Detroit sports.

The date was November 1, 1933. The place was Dinan Field, home grounds of the University of Detroit at Six Mile Road and Livernois. Erected in 1925, the stadium was torn down in 1971. Today the site is a tract of synthetic turf at what is now the University of Detroit-Mercy.

The game was broadcast on WJBK radio and attracted between 7,500 and 10,000 spectators (reports vary), among the largest football crowds yet assembled in Detroit. NFL commissioner Joe Carr was among those present, ready to pass judgment on the Indians' application.

Both teams were undefeated through six games. Halas, owner and coach of the Bears, had a roster loaded with future Hall of Famers, including such famous names as halfback Red Grange and fullback Bronko Nagurski. Rookie guard George Musso reportedly was the largest player in pro football, weighing 262 pounds. End Bill "Stinky" Hewitt, a Bay City native who had played at the University of Michigan, was noted for using his freakishly long arms to block kicks. Leather helmets had become the norm in football at all levels, but Musso and Hewitt preferred to play without headgear, making them even more intimidating.

Meanwhile, "Detroit's Own Undefeated Warriors" had held their opponents to a mere nine points in six games. Among their victims were the defending state champion Flint Yellow Jackets, who could muster just 10 yards of total offense and a single first down. The Indians benefited from home cooking as they played all the games at city-owned Chandler Park, south of City Airport. Roosevelt Post No. 130 of the American Legion sponsored the team. Tickets ranged from fifty cents to a dollar, with the bulk of the proceeds going to welfare programs. An American Legion band and glee club performed at every game.

Newspapers rated the Detroit squad as among the strongest independent teams in the country, though they may have been less influenced by the string of victories than by the boasts and public relations efforts of Don Ridler. The Indians' gregarious twenty-eight-year-old tackle and head coach was a creative promoter who would go on to become the longtime athletic director at Lawrence Tech and one of Detroit's leading sports figures. His flair for publicity was such that, upon his death in 1963, the Detroit Autorama—just one of the many organizations or events he later shilled for—named one of the show-car world's highest honors after him.

Ridler was a husky Detroit prep star who had captained the Michigan State squad in 1930. He played briefly with the Cleveland Indians in 1931, the club's only season in the NFL, and was the last man cut during a tryout with the Portsmouth Spartans in 1932. He spent that autumn coaching the Detroit Red Devils, one of the top semipro teams in Michigan. His success with the Red Devils led to his being named Indians head coach in 1933.

According to the *Free Press,* the Indians team Ridler helped to assemble consisted of "former college stars and the pick of Detroit's sandlot," including more than a few former Red Devils. Halfbacks Harry Koss and Peter "Red" Shepherd sparkled on offense and defense and accounted for most of the Indians' touchdowns. Unlike their pro counterparts, who typically were paid between fifty and one hundred dollars a game, the Detroit gridders depended on a share of ticket sales for their meager football wages. Most held regular jobs. They practiced after work and played at night and on weekends. Felix Fabro, for instance, drove a laundry truck when he wasn't lined up at right end.

Cash-strapped NFL clubs routinely filled in their calendar with exhibitions. It didn't matter if the opponent was the caliber of the Grand Rapids Polish Athletic Club. At a time when the average

As captain, coach, and starting tackle for the Detroit Indians, Don Ridler (*top*) tried without success to corral the famous Bronko Nagurski. (Author's collection)

laborer made twenty dollars a week, when he worked, a buck was a buck. So when Ridler approached Halas with the right numbers to travel to Detroit and suit up against the Indians, "Papa Bear" probably didn't hesitate long before saying yes.

Newspaper ads, radio spots, and press releases touted the upcoming match as "The Game of the Year," which it may have been, but only in Detroit. The country's fourth most populous city had been home to a succession of NFL flops during the 1920s—the Heralds, the Tigers, and the Panthers—but failures were common throughout the early years of the NFL. Most franchises started off as struggling semipro teams. Because of its market size, Detroit remained ripe territory for a pro football franchise. Some asked, "Why not the Indians?" They would soon find out.

* * *

In anticipation of drawing a larger crowd than Chandler Park could handle, the Indians rented Dinan Field for the game. Kickoff was scheduled for 8:15 p.m. Dinan Field had no covered grandstand, just two giant banks of bleachers open to the elements. Both teams agreed that if rain was falling at 7:30 p.m., the game would be rescheduled for the following evening. Because it was a night game, officials would use a white painted ball to assist visibility on the floodlit gridiron.

The game started on time. The Bears took the opening kickoff and moved smartly down the field, the Chicago offensive line opening giant holes in the Indians' defense. Nagurski scored the first touchdown of the evening, taking a lateral and racing in from five yards out to cap a 65-yard drive. Grange missed the extra point, but the Bears were still up, 6–0, before many fans had a chance to enjoy their first hot dog.

Chicago quickly struck again. According to the *Free Press*, "Grange alone was responsible for the next touchdown. 'Red' intercepted Wurster's pass and was downed on the Detroit 23-yard line. On the first play he sifted through tackle, cut back and sidestepped his way across the goal line." This time Nagurski missed the point-after, making it 12–0, Bears.

A Bears scoring pass in the second quarter, followed by Jack Manders's extra point, made it 19–0 at the half.

Because of limited substitution rules, regulars played both offense and defense, with some never leaving the field. This was smash-mouth football, with the "Monsters of the Midway" outweighing the Detroiters by an average of twenty-five pounds per man. The Indians gradually wore down, though they threatened to score on three separate second-half drives, once reaching the Bears' one-foot line. But with their main backfield threats of Koss, Shepherd, and Frank De Ronge continually bottled up, they couldn't dent the end zone.

In the third quarter, the Indians were driving when Nagurski picked off a De Ronge pass and ran it back 90 yards for his second touchdown of the evening. Ridler snuffed Grange's extra-point try, keeping the score 25–0. The Bears kicked off. A minute or so later, Hewitt blocked De Ronge's punt at the Detroit 25, picked up the loose ball, and fled into the end zone for yet another Chicago touchdown.

The fourth quarter was scoreless, as the Bears eased their paws off the pedal and fans headed for the exits. The final score was

The Detroit Indians and Chicago Bears faced off before a packed house at the University of Detroit's Dinan Field. (Author's collection)

The program from the Bears-Indians clash breathlessly advertised "The Largest Aggregation of Football Stars ever assembled in one Stadium." (Author's collection)

Chicago 32, Detroit 0, but most observers agreed it could have been worse. The *Windsor Star* declared the game "a one-ring circus."

The battered Indians could barely get out of bed the following morning. One player, substitute quarterback Jack Steck, spent a week in the hospital with a concussion. Four others, all former University of Detroit players who may have been especially embarrassed by the Indians' performance on the old school grounds, quit the team. Several injured regulars, including Ridler, were unable to suit up for their next game, a 6–0 upset loss to the South Bend Shamrocks, and the casualty list caused organizers to cancel another contest. Oddly, the rout of the Indians also appeared to take something out of the Bears, who would go winless in their next three league games before rebounding to capture their second straight NFL title.

The Indians had a chance to redeem themselves. In November, they regrouped and traveled west to play the St. Louis Gunners, another independent club angling for the pros. The Gunners shelled Ridler's "heavily advertised" squad, 41–0, and the NFL admitted them the following year as a late-season replacement for the financially troubled Cincinnati team. Ridler, undeterred by the beatdown, immediately went to work on another promotion, this time scheduling a Thanksgiving Day game where the Indians would play four teams, facing a different squad each quarter.

Such gimmicks came to an end in 1934, when the Indians failed to field a team. But things worked out football-wise in Detroit after all. That fall, fans welcomed the city's newest NFL franchise. Local radio magnate George A. Richards had purchased the Portsmouth Spartans, moved them from Ohio to Detroit, and christened them the Lions. The Lions would play their first several seasons at Dinan Field, winning the 1935 championship on the same ground where the Detroit Indians, full of hype and hope, had so spectacularly flunked their NFL audition.

22

The Old Shipbuilder

Inside his home in landlocked Lincoln Park, a maritime historian is preserving Downriver's rich shipbuilding past, one carefully crafted replica at a time.

On November 7, 1959, an era rich in local tradition was already drawing to a close when the freighter *Arthur B. Homer* was launched from the Great Lakes Engineering Works. It turned out to be the final splash for Downriver's last remaining shipyard, a storied builder best known by its acronym, GLEW.

"Two years later, GLEW was dissolved and sold," says Keith M. Steffke. "That was it." At one time, Detroit and Downriver builders were responsible for half the tonnage on the Great Lakes, including such famous vessels as the *Edmund Fitzgerald* and the Bob-lo steamer *Columbia.* But they couldn't compete with low-cost foreign firms. After nearly one hundred forty years of commercial shipbuilding along the Detroit River, economic forces stilled forever the once-familiar sound of rattling riveting guns in River Rouge, Ecorse, and Wyandotte.

Steffke, whose Prussian ancestors came to the Wyandotte area (then known as Ford City) before 1870, has several generations of Great Lakes maritime lore in his blood. He also has it stuffed into nearly every available space of the unassuming 1920s Lincoln Park bungalow he shares with his wife and two college-age children. Boiler gauges, engineer plates, and life preservers hang on the walls. Boxes of blueprints, charts, records, ledgers, and photographs overflow his book-lined second-floor study. More books are stacked on the

Keith Steffke and his model of the steamship *Frank E. Kirby*, an excursion vessel built by the Detroit Dry Dock Company in Wyandotte and launched in 1890. The maritime historian and model maker meticulously creates replica ships in his basement workshop. "I thrive on the obscure," he says. (Michelle Gerard)

steps of the narrow stairwell leading up to it. He has fashioned the handrail out of an oar from the passenger steamer *Tashmoo*.

"You see these?" he says, pointing out several cracks in the living room ceiling. "That's from the weight of all the stuff I have upstairs."

If the groaning floorboards overhead were to suddenly give way and bury Steffke in a pile of plaster, lathe, bookcases, filing cabinets, storage boxes, and vintage nautical equipment, the bow-tied eccentric could report to The Great Lighthouse Keeper in the Sky that he had done more than just about anybody to carry on Downriver's once-thriving shipbuilding industry, albeit on a teensy scale. For not only is Steffke one of the country's leading maritime experts—the kind of voluble brainiac that curators, historians, preservationists, appraisers, authors, and documentary filmmakers crave—he's also an accomplished model-maker, one who can accurately recreate a three-dimensional miniaturized replica of just about any vessel that ever plied the Detroit River.

"I thrive on the obscure," he says. "I won't do any World War II ships. I'll tell someone who asks, 'You can get a kit at the store. Why do you need me?' I do the ships that were historically important, the ones that represent the technological transition from wood to iron and then steel."

Steffke has branded himself "The Old Shipbuilder." His models typically command between $1,500 and $6,500 each, the price tag determined upfront by the number of hours he figures he'll need to research and build it. He pieces each together with meticulous attention to detail.

It's painstaking work. In his crowded basement workshop, where a score of vessels are in various stages of completion, Steffke points to the work-in-progress currently on his finishing table, the *Pretoria*. The 338-foot schooner-barge was one of the largest wooden ships ever built when it was launched in what was then called West Bay City in 1900. It sank in a storm five years later. Steffke is reproducing the ship in one-eighth-inch scale, meaning each of its twenty-two foot lifeboats will measure a mere 2¾ inches. There are 147 pieces in the Lilliputian lifeboat he just completed. "That alone probably took me over a week," he says.

Steffke, a bouncy, fast-talking, self-confident fellow in his fifties, is eager to share the wealth of maritime minutiae he has at his fingertips. "I have the employee records of the Detroit Dry Dock Company," he says. "Henry Ford worked for them. I can tell you the dates he worked and how much he was paid." He fires off figures and anecdotes, names and dates, fueled by his admittedly abnormal intake of black coffee and Coke Zero. "If you're an insomniac, a caffeine addict, and a type-AA personality, you can really get things done," he says.

What he has done to date is remarkable. Over the course of three decades, starting with a shirt box of photographs he inherited from his grandfather, he has amassed a private collection that rivals the holdings of many institutions. In addition to boxes of blueprints, personal diaries, logbooks, seasonal timetables, advertising brochures, and other ephemera, he has more than sixty thousand photographs, including a very rare 1843 daguerreotype of the famous USS *Michigan*, the Navy's first iron-hull warship, which has never been published. He has about three thousand reference books and journals, including a complete set of the *Annual Report of the Lake Carriers' Association*, published between 1902 and 1999. He has compiled some two thousand comprehensive subject files ranging from such utterly forgotten firms as the Davis Boat & Oar Works to such famous figures as Frank E. Kirby, whom he regards as the greatest naval architect. Although he is more interested in documents than artifacts, along the way Steffke has acquired such prize items as the ship's bell from the 1890 lighthouse tender *Marigold* and a silver tea set presented to the captain of the *Columbia* in 1902.

To grow his collection, he has rummaged through attics, basements, and dumpsters, snooped around yard sales, sniped on eBay, and approached the families of prominent figures to see if they would be willing to donate or sell a decedent's personal papers. He's paid as much as $5,000 for a document. "I'm most interested in builders and shipyards, but I collect anything related to the river and the Great Lakes," he says. "People, animals, fisheries, shipwrecks, steamship companies, the lifesaving service."

He puts the material to use when researching his models, especially those early nineteenth-century ships for which little information may exist.

Steffke admits it helps to have an understanding and supportive spouse. He met Angela Gorman, a schoolteacher whose ancestors came over on the *Mayflower*, while both worked as historical interpreters at Greenfield Village. They were engaged on the *Columbia*, where Steffke once worked as a deckhand. Today, they share a ship captain's bed that Steffke built in the alcove of a room off his study. To a landlubber's novice eye, the unusual sleeping arrangement seems tight and claustrophobic, with a slanted wood ceiling that could scramble one's brains if not careful, but Steffke insists, "You get used to it." A vintage harpsichord is incongruously parked in the middle of the cramped bedroom, presumably because there's no other place to put it. "I also play the piano and tuba," he says, plinking a key.

Steffke has always waltzed to his own music. He grew up in Wyandotte. A thin and sickly child, he "aspired to be a 98-pound weakling," he jokes. He shunned sports and poured himself into natural science. His mother, an artist, encouraged the boy to "Always be unique" even as he filled the freezer with dead mammals and his bedroom with stuffed birds, animal skins, rare eggs, and rocks. By the time he was a teenager, he was giving classroom lectures and operating "The Steffke Collection of Natural History" out of his finished attic. He startled neighbors by walking around with a convalescing great horned owl named Archimedes perched on his shoulder.

His absorbing interest in natural science competed with another developing passion: the history of shipbuilding on the Detroit River, particularly as it applied to his own family. His great-great-great-grandfather was an ironworker at the Wyandotte Iron Shipbuilding Company, co-founded by Captain Eber Brock Ward, Detroit's first millionaire. Five of Steffke's ancestors worked at the Detroit Dry Dock Company. Other branches of his family have been involved in one activity or another along the Detroit River for the last two hundred years. Some were marine engineers or commercial fishermen, others were lighthouse keepers or ordinary seamen.

Steffke wanted to be an ornithologist or a history teacher, but he never completed his undergrad studies at Wayne State University. He held various positions in mortgage banking and real estate before turning to model making full-time when he was about forty. "Up to then, it had been a hobby," he says. He was eight years old when he built his first vessel, the Confederate ironclad *Monitor*, out of a rat trap and a broom handle. His stepfather, a cabinet maker who operates a shop in Romulus, taught him how to work with wood.

Steffke builds his ships in a variety of sizes. The most popular is what is known as American Museum Scale; that is, where 1/8 inch on the model equals one foot on the actual ship. Thus a 375-foot vessel would measure just under four feet long when completed. Anything larger, such as an ore freighter, is typically built at 1/16 inch = 1 foot scale so that it can still fit on a fireplace mantel or desktop. There is also the Builder Scale of 1/4 inch = 1 foot. "This makes for a larger, dramatic model," he says. "This is perfect for vessels less than one hundred feet in length, like lightships, tugboats, and rowing barges and shells."

He makes most models by using the builder's original drawings and various photos or engravings. The real challenge is recreating a ship for which there is scant documentation. He combs his archives to find something—perhaps little more than a description in a diary, newspaper, or journal—to guide him. He'll use the ship's known length, beam, and depth of hull, and his own deep knowledge of shipbuilding technology, to create a conjectural drawing. There's room for interpretation. "I approach it as an artist, not an engineer," he says.

Steffke habitually makes two of each ship he's commissioned—one for the customer and the other for a possible future "off-the-shelf" sale. Overall, he has built about 250 models, though the time involved in each varies widely. He's always taking on new commissions, but he asks clients to accept a flexible deadline.

His customers fall into one of three groups. "You have buyers who have an emotional connection to a certain boat, such as the passenger steamer *Tashmoo,* but really don't care about every last detail. Then there are the interior decorators who appreciate it as a design element and don't mind paying more. And then there's the intense maritime history buff or a museum that wants a top-quality piece."

Steffke has lived his entire life Downriver. "I know some people don't like Downriver," he says. "But I can't imagine living anyplace else." That said, he regrets not having dropped anchor in his hometown, close to the river that's played such a central role in his and his ancestors' lives. As a young newlywed, he explains with a sigh,

Downriver shipyards once were among the country's busiest. Here workers launch the Great Lakes freighter *William G. Mather* at the Ecorse yard of the Great Lakes Engineering Works in 1905. (Library of Congress)

he got a good deal on a starter home. "When I bought this house, I said, 'Okay, we'll stay here five years and then we'll move.' It's been twenty-five years now. I'm going to die in this house."

Resigned to his fate in land-locked Lincoln Park, Steffke doubled down, buying the house next door as a kind of annex for his ever-expanding archives. He assumes that the Steffke Memorial Maritime Collection eventually will wind up in the Michigan Historical Museum in Lansing, though he refuses to give up on his dream of one day opening a Downriver Maritime Museum in Wyandotte to house it. Either way, Steffke's private archives, which he only occasionally opens up to carefully vetted researchers, merit a public space, says Joel Stone, senior curator at the Dossin Great Lakes Museum.

"It's an incredible collection," Stone says. "He knows more about a wide range of subjects than anyone I know. It's his lifework. Now, if you're talking about a museum, you have the issue of financing, as well as competition, to consider." In addition to the Dossin, there's the National Museum of the Great Lakes in Toledo. Among the Ohio museum's exhibits are two life rafts recovered from the *Edmund Fitzgerald* when the storied freighter went down in a storm on November 10, 1975. That's impressive, but Steffke has a few unique pieces of the vessel's history himself, including heavy steel test plates from the hull. "They were reference plates for each batch of steel as it was being built," he explains. He also has GLEW's corporate records.

"Do you want to know the exact cost of building the *Edmund Fitzgerald*?" he asks. "I don't know if that's ever been published before."

He scrounges around for a ledger book from 1958 and flips through the pages. He runs his finger across a few columns of neatly written figures before settling on a number. "Here it is. The total cost was $3,966,086."

The Old Shipbuilder flashes a satisfied smile. "Who else would have this stuff? When you understand what it is, it's priceless."

23

A Blast from the Past

Bomb shelters, both public and private, were a ubiquitous feature of the atomic-age landscape as fears of the Russians dropping "The Big One" took hold.

During the height of the Cold War era, Patty (Chevalier) OHara never found "a Red under the bed," as the anti-Communist hysteria of the day put it. But she did come home from grade school one day in 1963 to discover a crane in the backyard, which was an only slightly less curious sight.

"I thought, 'Well, that's strange,'" says OHara, one of five Chevalier kids who grew up in the snug bungalow on Cornell Street in Dearborn. "That was our first clue that a bomb shelter was being built."

Larry Chevalier, a lumber salesman and former GI who'd made it through the Battle of the Bulge, was determined to have his young family survive nuclear Armageddon. OHara, today a retired chemical engineer living in California, recalls the finished product. "It was a very high-end design," she says, unlike the "buried tin cans" many contractors offered. "I'm sure Dad paid dearly for that shelter."

Contractors constructed the ten-by-ten-foot underground chamber like a small separate basement. It had three-foot-thick walls made of reinforced concrete and connected to the house via a six-foot-long tunnel. "So to get to the shelter from the house, you went down to the basement bedroom, through a steel door to the tunnel, and then through another door into the shelter room itself." The shelter room featured a hand-cranked ventilator, shelves stocked with canned food, a drum of drinking water, and two sets of triple bunk beds. A ceiling hatch opened to the outside; when closed, it was just part of a cement patio.

"We had the only bomb shelter in the neighborhood," OHara says. "When we mentioned it at school, some kids would laugh. Others would say, 'What's that?'"

The Chevaliers' cement sanctuary, like countless others carved out of basements and backyards across the country, was one of the cultural by-products of the heated geopolitical and technological rivalry between the United States and the Soviet Union in the years following World War II. It was a nerve-wracking era. As the two superpowers jockeyed for dominance, developing ever-more powerful bombs and the means to deliver them, millions of baby boomers practiced "duck and cover" drills in the classroom and key industrial targets like Metro Detroit bristled with anti-aircraft missiles.

What was it like for an atomic-age family to live cheek by jowl in a confined space for several days? In the fall of 1960, Huntington

Larry Chevalier and his atomic-age family in the spring of 1961, two years before he built a bomb shelter in the backyard of their Dearborn home. Patty (Chevalier) OHara is at bottom right. (Patty OHara)

Woods optometrist Harold Roland and his family volunteered for a one-week stay inside an above-ground shelter at Northland Mall in Southfield. It was a tight squeeze—Dad, Mom, and two pre-teens crammed into a space fourteen feet long and 5½ feet wide—but the seventy-seven square feet they bumped around in actually was considered spacious by Civil Defense standards, which held that ten square feet of space per person was adequate for shelter occupants. "Sometimes I think I don't give my family enough time," Roland said. "This ought to be enough togetherness to last us all for awhile."

The experiment literally provided a view of ordinary human behavior under abnormal conditions. A large soundproof window took up one wall, allowing curious passersby to observe the Rolands as if they were oversized hamsters. The family could draw curtains when needed. Otherwise, Northland shoppers saw the occupants reading books and magazines, playing board games, and practicing the cha-cha. Minor mishaps helped alleviate the crushing boredom. The fridge broke down, one of the kids threw up, and somebody sat on a favorite Frank Sinatra record. Seven days later, the Rolands emerged triumphant, gratefully gulping fresh air and flashing a sign that said, "We Made It!" They received $500 for their efforts.

Harold Roland was asked for survival tips. "There has to be some kind of discipline," he said, "since you're getting in each other's way. I guess the most important thing is a sense of humor."

Nobody was laughing in October 1961, when the Soviets detonated the largest thermonuclear weapon ever created, a terrifying warhead with the explosive power of 50,000 kilotons of TNT. The bomb, subsequently dubbed the *Tsar Bomba*, was three times more powerful than anything the United States ever tested and 2,500 times more powerful than the atomic bombs dropped on Hiroshima and Nagasaki. The fireball was seen 600 miles away and the mushroom cloud was forty-two miles high. All these decades later, this off-the-charts demonstration of Soviet might remains the most powerful man-made explosion in history.

The *Tsar Bomba* was an impractical, one-off nuclear device. But its shock waves cracked windows 500 miles away and figuratively

A 1960s brochure offered this cutaway view of a backyard shelter doubling as a recreation room. (Author's collection)

rattled the White House, which was already ratcheting up Civil Defense preparations to unprecedented levels. In addition to films and pamphlets educating citizens about how to best survive an atomic blast, officials created hundreds of thousands of public fallout shelters across the country and stocked them with essentials. At its peak, Michigan had more than 20,000 designated shelters in schools, banks, factories, libraries, office buildings, gymnasiums, mines, and other locations. Detroit's Wayne State University alone had thirty-one fallout shelters scattered around its campus. A distinctive sign colored in flat black and reflective yellow identified all locations. The federal government issued supplies for each shelter, the volume of water, medicine, and foodstuffs based on its capacity. The fully stocked government shelter contained the following items, all of which citizens could also purchase to stock their own home shelters.

- Medical kits that included basic supplies (bandages, aspirin, eye drops, scissors, forceps) and such medicines as penicillin, phenobarbital, and sulfadiazine. Unfortunately, within a few years the medicines expired and the alcohol evaporated. Each kit was stamped: "This box contains no narcotics."

- Steel barrels of water, double-lined with plastic. Bottled water as we know it today wasn't around then. Each 17½-gallon drum was intended to supply five people with one quart each per day—enough water for 14 days.
- Sanitation kits that included toilet paper, sanitary napkins, plastic gloves, liner bags, and packets of toilet chemicals. The kits came inside a cardboard drum that, when fitted with the enclosed plastic toilet seat, served as a temporary toilet until shelter occupants could employ emptied metal water barrels for that purpose.
- Tins of cereal-based foodstuffs, principally crackers, biscuits, and wafers, along with nugget-size pieces of hard candy that actually were carbohydrate supplements. Shelter occupants were expected to follow a chart that limited each person to 700 calories a day.

In this climate of theoretical annihilation, there also was a fair amount of apathy. Some openly disdained the notion of Russian no-good-niks forcing red-blooded Americans to flee underground. Dr. Lawrence Richard, for one, erected a large wooden sign in the yard of his Oakland County home. The Richards signed it with their own name and addressed it to "K," Soviet leader Nikita Khrushchev: "No bomb shelter here. K—We aren't rats like you. We live above ground." A Muskegon paper quoted another commentator as being "fed up with negative piddling about bomb shelters and other disgraceful evidences of a gutless generation."

Such bravado would have vanished in a nanosecond had the Soviets ever decided to drop "The Big One." In 1962, the *Detroit Free Press* described what would happen if a five-megaton nuclear bomb fell on the intersection of 12 Mile and Ryan roads in Warren. "A red ball of fire, hotter than the center of the sun, erupts with a roar and boils outward in all directions, spreading death," Neal Shine wrote. "In a three-mile radius from ground zero, there is total destruction. The neat rows of brick homes in the quiet subdivisions in the western part of the suburb of Warren disappear." The blast, equal to 5 million tons of TNT (one-tenth as powerful as the *Tsar Bomba*), would leave a crater a half-mile wide and 200 feet deep. It would level parts of Warren, Hazel Park, Royal Oak, and Sterling Heights, and instantly kill 40 percent of all people within five miles of the explosion. Those not vaporized by the blast or the heat would have to contend with lethal radioactive particles falling like dandruff from the sky.

In addition to the installation of hundreds of thousands of public Civil Defense fallout shelters, the Kennedy Administration vigorously promoted private bomb shelters, with agencies offering building plans and financing to interested homeowners. There are no precise numbers, but it's thought that several thousand private shelters were built in Michigan during the Cold War. How many survive today as a workshop, spare bedroom, recording studio, home gym, man cave, or storage space is anyone's guess. Most were built between 1957 and 1963, with any spikes in "bomb-shelter-itis" linked to such geopolitical flash-points as the building of the Berlin Wall, atmospheric nuclear tests, and the Cuban Missile Crisis.

For Earl Reichert, the impetus apparently was the Soviets' 1957 launching of Sputnik, the world's first artificial satellite. Reichert, owner of a steel company in western Michigan, had the resources to construct one of the state's largest and best equipped private shelters. The forty-foot-long shelter, built in 1958 on a lot adjacent to Reichert's home on Graves Avenue in Battle Creek, was protected by a twenty-one-inch steel-beam roof covered by five feet of earth. It could survive a twenty-kiloton atomic bomb—the size of the one that flattened Hiroshima in 1945—dropped up to a third of a mile away. It was tastefully painted, decorated with rugs and overstuffed furniture, and could comfortably accommodate all seventeen members of his extended family. The entrance was protected by a blockhouse with a gun slot. The shelter's price tag was reportedly as high as $80,000, a figure approaching a cool million in today's dollars. That didn't include the cost of the 2½-ton armored vehicle the industrialist had specially built to round up family members once word came that Soviet bombers were headed for Battle Creek.

The majority of private shelters were built in metropolitan areas, with Wayne County granting the most building permits of any county in the state. Nearly all were the size of a small bedroom, no matter how large the family. The cheapest and most basic enclosures were basement shelters, which pushed out from the existing cinder-block foundation walls. The surrounding earth provided protection on two sides while solid masonry walls were built on the other two sides. Builders installed a thick masonry ceiling under the main-story floorboards. The cost for a do-it-yourself homeowner typically was $125 to $200 in materials. Larger, more elaborate sanctuaries usually were detached from the main dwelling. Their cost ran into the thousands of dollars. Whether located in the cellar or the backyard, a home shelter became a popular selling point for builders and real estate agents, who touted its dual-purpose use as a recreation room. In 1962, the Marx Toy Company included a bomb shelter in one of its line of metal dollhouses.

The shelter industry had little government oversight. Fast-talking, fear-mongering salesmen went door to door, selling installations. Shoddy workmanship led to consumer complaints. Of the first eighteen shelters built by one leading Detroit-area outfit in 1961, all but one of them sprang leaks, including the company owner's. "The makeshift, improperly designed, and poorly equipped basement shelters being prepared by many householders might well prove death traps instead of life-saving shelters," warned Muskegon columnist Vera Ridoutt. Even properly built shelters were a housekeeping headache. Homeowners needed to periodically check and replace canned goods, dry cell batteries, and stored water; fans, radio, flashlights, and other equipment had to be regularly tested; and bedding, blankets, and clothing required an occasional airing out.

Peter Bahl, a forty-two-year-old technician living in Walled Lake, thirty miles outside Detroit, knew firsthand the vital importance of a well-built, well-designed shelter. As a German paratrooper recuperating from his wounds in 1945, he had more than survived the Russian artillery and American bombers that had pulverized

Peter and Nora Bahl and daughter Barbara pose inside their bomb shelter in Walled Lake, thirty miles outside Detroit. A substantial library and a six-month supply of foodstuffs competed for shelf space. (Author's collection)

his native Berlin—he had turned himself into a civil defense expert specializing in bomb shelters. He brought the hard lessons he learned to the United States when given his "second chance" after the war, wrote the *Detroit News*' Jim Lycett, who toured Bahl's private shelter in late 1961: "that concussion kills as surely as shrapnel; that bomb shelters must be deep, with adequate air and water supplies; that small shelter doors are safer than big ones. . . . Looking back on his own terrifying experience and remembering the thousands of unprepared civilians who died in bombing attacks, Bahl takes a realistic approach to survival."

Most basement shelters were useless, Bahl told Lycett. "A hole in the ground is a death trap unless it is engineered properly." To that end, Bahl built his concrete-block shelter five feet deep into the thick clay surrounding his lakefront home. The two-room sanctuary was wired for electricity (with back-up twelve-volt batteries) and featured a water pump system and a ventilation system run by a gas generator. One room housed a shower, escape hatch, and stocks of canned food while the larger chamber contained a kitchen, bathroom, and sleeping quarters. There were large bunk beds, games, a substantial library, and enough food and water for Bahl, his wife Nora, and their daughter Barbara to last 200 days. "A shelter is not as temporary as some people think," Bahl explained. "You must be prepared to live in one for some time in case your house has been destroyed, or the radiation count is too dangerous to go outside."

At the same time Bahl was putting the finishing touches on his bunker, forty-nine families in Laketon Township, near Muskegon, were pooling their resources to construct one of the country's first privately built community shelters. The cost exceeded $10,000, with participants buying shares in the nonprofit corporation set up to finance it. The labor was donated, as was the land it was built on. The property owner was local dentist Joe Verschueren, who in a 1972 interview expressed no regrets over the large investment made in a shelter that within a decade had become a crumbling relic used to store off-season snowmobiles. "We figured it served its purpose. If we needed it, good. If we didn't, real good."

The cement shelter was covered by three feet of dirt. In the event of a nuclear attack, it could house and feed 297 designated people. All others would be turned away—the gun turret mounted on the roof would see to that. "People said they'd get in when the time came," Verschueren said. "In case they tried to get us out with bulldozers, we had a case of armor-piercing ammunition and two BARs [Browning Automatic Rifles]. I also had shotguns. It was to keep our thing private. With fallout, people knew they'd die and they'd go wild and try to get us out and ruin our thing."

The prospect of such cold-blooded calculus came to trouble Larry Chevalier, whose next-door neighbor was his sister and her seven children. "At some point," Patty OHara says, "my dad realized that if a bomb was dropped, my aunt and cousins would come

A community bomb shelter goes up outside Muskegon in the fall of 1961. Access was limited to shareholders and controlled by a rooftop machine gun. (Author's collection)

knocking on the door, and he'd have to say, 'No, you can't come in.' That's when he regretted building it."

Most people, no matter which side of a locked door they might find themselves, were fatalistic about the aftermath of a nuclear strike. What kind of world did survivors expect to find when they emerged from their cement matchbox with a bellyful of All-Purpose Survival Biscuits and a wildly beeping Geiger counter?

OHara admits to having had doomsday fears as a child.

"That's why I studied nuclear engineering in college," she says. "The way you quell your fears is by understanding them. And I came to understand that our shelter would've done no good whatsoever. We'd either have been incinerated instantly or slowly died of radiation fallout."

The Berlin Wall fell in 1989 and the Soviet Union officially dissolved two years later, but thanks to various bilateral treaties and a Washington-Moscow hotline, nuclear tensions had already eased considerably over the years. In the mid-1970s, the federal government quit stocking public shelters, Civil Defense signs started to come down, and warehouses of government-issue crackers were donated to livestock feeders and Third World relief agencies. With long-range bombers no longer a threat—intercontinental ballistic missiles had replaced them—the military decommissioned the anti-aircraft missile sites ringing Metro Detroit since the mid-1950s. Anxiety gave way to apathy. Inside the shelter on Cornell Street, the Chevalier kids practiced their instruments and hosted the occasional sleepover, while their father found a quiet refuge where he could enjoy an undisturbed nap.

"Our bomb shelter served a lot of purposes," OHara says. "It just didn't serve the purpose of a bomb shelter."

A bloodied and bandaged Leon Czolgosz, severely beaten by outraged bystanders after shooting President McKinley, peers out from his cell. This photo appeared on the cover of the September 9, 1901, issue of *Leslie's Weekly*. (Library of Congress)

24

The Nobody Who Murdered McKinley

In gunning down the twenty-fifth president of the United States, radicalized Detroit native Leon Czolgosz believed he was striking a blow for the exploited workers of the world.

"Great God! He's shot. They've shot him!"

The radical working-class movement in the late 19th and early 20th centuries was rife with anarchists and assassins, fanatics who viewed stabbings, bombings, and gunfire as legitimate responses to the abuses brought on by capitalism, imperialism, and racism. Their ranks included an incipient revolutionary named Leon Czolgosz, a native Detroiter who spent the first sixteen years of his truncated life in Michigan.

Czolgosz (pronounced CHO-gus) had grown to hate all people of wealth and position. He claimed their power came at the expense of mistreated workers, millions of whom shared his family's impoverished immigrant roots. Consumed by hate and inflamed by a radical ideology that he only superficially understood, he decided to strike a symbolic blow for the have-nots. "I didn't believe one man should have so much service," he would say later, "and another man should have none."

On the afternoon of Friday, September 6, 1901, the twenty-seven-year-old Czolgosz stood in line inside the Temple of Music exhibition hall at the Pan-American Exposition in Buffalo, New York, waiting to shake the hand of President William McKinley. A handkerchief draped over his right hand concealed a .32-caliber revolver.

The line of well-wishers moved briskly. At 4:07 p.m., as McKinley moved to take Czolgosz's extended left hand, the assassin pressed his weapon against the president's vest.

C. J. Emmons, general foreman of the Detroit House of Correction, was among the thousands of Detroiters taking advantage of discounted railway and steamship fares to visit the exposition. He was standing ten feet from McKinley when he heard two muffled pops. It took a few seconds for the crowd to process what had just happened—and then all hell turned loose, said Emmons. "Women screamed and the men were shouting and cursing. I never saw such punching and screaming in my life." The mob nearly beat Czolgosz to death before police pushed through and hustled the badly battered and bloodied shootist away.

McKinley was shot at point-blank range. One bullet grazed a button and deflected from the breastbone, the other entered his abdomen about five inches below his left nipple. He underwent emergency surgery to repair the stomach wound and, for a while, it appeared he would recover. But infection set in and he died eight days later, on September 14. On the day of his funeral, Detroit churches were full, saloons were closed, and effigies of Czolgosz were strung up and burned. By then Vice President Theodore Roosevelt had been sworn in as chief executive, and all the world knew of the assassin's Michigan ties.

Those ties remain a bit murky to this day. There are no known birth, baptismal, or school records for Czolgosz. When arrested, he named Detroit as his birthplace, though some genealogists today believe he may have been born upstate, in Alpena. Lloyd Vernon Briggs, a Boston psychiatrist compiling case studies for a book he was writing about murderers, remains perhaps the best source. Within months of the assassination, he visited Detroit and Cleveland, using interpreters to interview clannish neighbors and family members.

According to Briggs, Czolgosz's father left German-occupied Poland for Detroit sometime in the early 1870s. Paul Czolgosz was a sober, hard-working laborer who would outlive two wives and several of his twelve children during his one hundred years on earth.

Like many male immigrants, he concentrated on finding work and housing before sending for his wife and children. Within a few years the family was renting the first floor of a brick house at 141 Benton, in the Polish neighborhood springing up around St. Albertus Catholic church.

Leon Frank Czolgosz, the future assassin, was born May 5, 1873, presumably at home. (Some sources have him born in 1874.) By the time of Briggs's visit, the Mincel Coal Company shared the site. Today, all of it lies under the Chrysler Freeway. The landlady's daughter, Margaret Mincel, who lived above the Czolgoszes, described them as "a law-abiding family." Paul Czolgosz worked in the city sewers while his wife took in washing. A neighbor recalled Leon's being baptized under the name Czolcholski. By the time the boy was six, he was selling newspapers and shining shoes on Detroit's streets. Around this time the family moved north, the 1880 census showing the growing Czolgosz brood in Alpena. The itinerant family continued to move around northeastern Michigan, to such predominantly Polish communities as Posen, Krakow, and Rogers City.

The youngster's irregular schooling lasted six years. He was handy with tools, an expert small-game hunter, and fond of reading. He rarely got excited and never swore. He was close to his mother, a steadying influence who thought him the most promising of all her children. He was ten years old when she died after giving birth to her eighth and final child. His father remarried and sired four more children. Leon detested his stepmother.

Leon grew into a quiet, pleasant-looking young man of medium build, with pale blue eyes, tousled light chestnut hair, and a dimpled chin. He was always clean and neatly dressed. Possibly influenced by an older brother, he took to the woods. Like many before him, Leon saw northern Michigan's pine forests as an escape, somewhere he could test his manhood while finding some adventure. He traveled to the wide-open Upper Peninsula town of Seney, infamous for its saloons, brothels, and gambling dens (and best remembered today for Ernest Hemingway's short story, "Big Two-Hearted River"). In 1952, *Detroit Free Press* reporter Riley Murray visited the now faded community. He learned from old-timers that Seney, "even in its dying lumbering days, was too tough for Leon. He steered clear of brawls; he wasn't much of a drinker; poker held no fascination for him." Instead of handling a crosscut saw out in the woods, Czolgosz received an assignment to work on a railroad section gang.

When Leon was a teenager, the family left Michigan for Pennsylvania—where he worked in a bottle factory—before finally settling in Ohio. In 1893, he lost his job at a Cleveland wire factory, the result of his participation in a strike. He managed to get rehired by using a pseudonym: Fred Nieman. Fred was his nickname while the Polish-German surname translates to "nobody," a reflection of his growing disenchantment with industrial society and his place in it.

At twenty-four, Czolgosz quit working. There are indications he suffered a breakdown of some sort. He became a hypochondriac, convinced he was dying of some undiagnosed ailment. He was especially fearful of the horrors that accompanied venereal disease, which disfigured and killed many in these pre-penicillin days. Once an observant Catholic, he now disowned the church, believing priests were only interested in parishioners with money. He lazed about the farm his father had bought outside Cleveland, joined a moderate socialist group called the Sila Club, and immersed himself in radical literature. The pamphlets Leon read and the lectures he attended described a system of unfettered capitalism, where the workers who were responsible for creating great wealth for the Carnegies and Rockefellers of the world were exploited with impunity. He began to form anti-imperialist views, influenced in part by the return home of a traumatized brother who had fought in the Philippines as the United States under McKinley flexed its expansionistic muscles.

The country—the entire world—needed to dramatically change, Czolgosz decided. But how best to effect such change? The most extreme activists, in America and Europe, endorsed a theory known as "propaganda of the deed," which held that bombings and assassinations were the best ways to draw attention and arouse the masses. The slaying of King Umberto I of Italy in July 1900 particularly intrigued Czolgosz, who kept a scrapbook of clippings about the murder. He fixated on reports that the assassin, an Italian-American from New Jersey named Gaetano Bresci, had acted entirely alone. In May 1901, Bresci committed suicide in prison, elevating him to martyr status in the eyes of many, including Czolgosz.

Czolgosz desired to emulate Bresci, but he came across as an unformed crank. As he tramped around the industrial heartland, known radicals that he approached, bluntly seeking their advice and encouragement, found him so naive that they figured he must be a spy. In fact, a notice went out in the September 1, 1901, issue of *Free Society*, a radical Chicago-based newspaper that Czolgosz read, warning about the awkward, unnamed young man and providing a description. There is some speculation that this may have prompted Czolgosz to immediately act, as if he was determined to demonstrate his radical bona fides.

Newspapers announced President McKinley would be spending three days in Buffalo, where the modern, electrified city was hosting the Pan-American Exposition. The exposition was a showcase of new technologies and a celebration of prosperity, ultimately drawing 8 million visitors. Czolgosz beat the president there. He rented a two-dollar-a-day room over a saloon, paid $4.50 for a revolver at a hardware store, and plotted his next move.

McKinley, fifty-eight years old and serving his second term in the White House, arrived at the exposition on Wednesday, September 4. Czolgosz edged nearer McKinley as the president got off the train and an entourage greeted him, but he decided his target was too tightly guarded for an accurate shot. The next day, Czolgosz was among the throngs who turned out to hear McKinley give an address at the fairgrounds, but the jostling crowd kept him from getting close to the podium. He decided to return the following day, when the president would be receiving the public inside the Temple of Music.

Anarchists were very much on the minds of McKinley's staff throughout the stay in Buffalo. The president's personal secretary pleaded for him to cancel Friday's public reception. "Why should I?" McKinley argued. "No one would wish to hurt me."

None but Czolgosz. That afternoon he inauspiciously joined the serpentine queue of people eagerly waiting for the once-in-a-lifetime opportunity to shake hands—albeit briefly—with the president. McKinley's style was to seize an out-thrust hand, squeeze the fingers, then crisply send the well-wisher on their way before turning to the next, a technique that allowed him to exchange handshakes with up to fifty people a minute. Normally in such situations, security details instructed people to approach the president with both hands open and empty, but this time the security measure was overlooked. It was a stifling hot day in an era before air conditioning, and many people were mopping their brows with handkerchiefs or fanning themselves. Moreover, the scores of Buffalo detectives, soldiers, and Secret Service agents in the immediate vicinity, coupled with citizens shuffling rapidly along in fairly tight quarters, combined to obstruct some guards' vision. Thus Czolgosz was able to proceed without interference.

In line were Charles Gardner and his wife. "There were two people in front of us," the Detroit plumber recalled. "One had what seemed to be a bandaged hand and the other was a big guy. The bandage was holding a gun and when he shot, the big guy knocked him down." Gardner joined in with the infuriated mob that attacked Czolgosz. "I got in two good kicks, one right in the face, before police pulled me away," he said. McKinley, staggered by the shots, saw the men beating Czolgosz. "Go easy on him, boys," he said.

Another Michiganian visiting the Expo that day was B. R. Alward, part of a group from Hillsdale County. Alward didn't witness the actual shooting, but his views were unique, as he caught a glimpse of the assassin both coming and going.

"We were standing near the Temple of Music," Alward related, "when a man with his hand and arm bandaged and in a sling passed us on his way to the building. A short time after that, we saw crowds going that way. An officer in uniform told us there was a rumor that the president had been shot. My brother and I rushed to one entrance. A two-horse, closed cab with two men on top, rolled up. The crowd was shouting, 'Lynch him!' The Marines who had been guarding the president that day brought out Leon Czolgosz,

A McKinley mourning pin. "No one would wish to hurt me," the president told a worried aide shortly before his assassination. (Author's collection)

passing right next to us. The crowd pressed in upon the cab. The driver dropped his whip. I passed it up to him. Men grabbed the four wheels by the spokes trying to prevent its driving off. Czolgosz was lodged in the county jail. Crowds lined the streets that night. All lights in the jail were off. The National Guard was called out. These guards were stationed every few yards along the curb. The streets were dark."

Authorities moved Czolgosz to the state prison in Auburn, New York. He readily confessed to his crime.

> I made my plans 3 or 4 days ago to shoot the President. When I shot him I intended to kill him and the reason for

> my intention in killing was because I did not believe in presidents over us. I was willing to sacrifice myself & the president for the benefit of the Country. I felt I had more courage than the average man in killing president and was willing to put my own life at stake in order to do it.

Czolgosz was examined and found sane. There was no established history of mental illness in his family. Later, an autopsy of his brain would reveal no obvious defects. It was hard to argue that he didn't know precisely what he was doing. Indeed, Leon wanted full credit for his act. He rebuffed repeated attempts by investigators to have him implicate the notorious "Queen Anarchist," Emma Goldman, whom authorities briefly jailed as a possible co-conspirator and were desperate to put away for good.

The defendant utterly refused to cooperate with his court-appointed defense lawyers, resulting in a trial that lasted just eight and a half hours over two days, September 23–24. The jury deliberated a mere thirty-four minutes before finding him guilty of first-degree murder.

Czolgosz, sentenced to death, had no interest in filing appeals. On the eve of his execution, a couple of persistent Catholic priests visited him, against his will, pleading for the condemned to repent and instead getting a profane tongue-lashing for their effort. Czolgosz also met with a brother and a brother-in-law.

"Who got you into this scrape?" his brother asked.

"No one," Leon said. "Nobody had anything to do with it but me."

Paul Czolgosz did not leave his Ohio farm but instead sent his son a letter, wishing him luck and saying he had to "pay the price" for his actions.

Czolgosz went to the electric chair on the morning of October 29, 1901, fifty-three days after shooting McKinley. He was unrepentant to the end. His last words were: "I killed the president because he was the enemy of the good people—the good working people. I am not sorry for my crime. I am sorry I could not see my father." Instead of hailing Czolgosz as a martyr, most radicals disavowed the assassination, believing it hurt the movement.

Ghoulish promoters, looking to cash in on the assassination, didn't care one way or the other about the movement. The warden, wary of someone carrying off a gruesome relic to be sold for big money, refused to release the body to the family. Instead, following an autopsy, Czolgosz was buried in an unmarked grave on prison grounds. Workers poured sulfuric acid into his coffin to quickly dissolve the corpse, then burned his clothing and other belongings. It wasn't a proper Christian burial, but then Leon was adamant that he didn't want one. "Don't you have any praying over me when I am dead," he had told his brother. "I don't want it. I don't want any of their damned religion." It's thought that, some time later, whatever was left was quietly removed to a mass grave at Soule Cemetery, near Auburn, joining the reinterred remains of hundreds of unclaimed prisoners and mental patients originally buried at Fort Hill Cemetery. Today a stone marks the spot: FORT HILL REMAINS.

Throughout this national ordeal, there was widespread criticism of McKinley's inexpert security. Remarkably, he was the third US president in thirty-six years to be gunned down in public, joining Abraham Lincoln and James Garfield, who were assassinated in 1865 and 1881, respectively. Czolgosz should have immediately attracted suspicion, Detroit detective Pat O'Neil said at the time. "Experienced detectives doing duty as a bodyguard always watch hands in such gatherings."

In response to the criticism, the Secret Service, a unit of the Treasury Department whose main task was busting counterfeiters, beefed up its professionalism. In 1906, per an act of Congress, it officially assumed around-the-clock protective duties. In the century and a quarter since McKinley was killed, only one president, John F. Kennedy, has been assassinated, though there have been a few near-misses. This was an unintended and often overlooked consequence of Leon Czolgosz's nefarious deed. The nobody from Michigan made it more difficult—but still far from impossible—for future fanatics to successfully act on their murderous impulses. "The wild beast slumbers in us all," warned the doctor who examined Czolgosz's brain. "It is not always necessary to invoke insanity to explain its awakening."

Higher education: A young reader uses a footstool to search the shelves inside the Detroit Public Library's children's reading room, circa 1910. (Author's collection)

FOR FURTHER READING

The following mix of general and academic works is for readers wishing to learn more about some of the people and topics featured in *Welcome to Detroitland*, as well as its predecessor, *Detroitland* (2011). For a comprehensive Detroit-centric bibliography that roughly corresponds with the time period covered in both *Detroitland* books, see Thomas A. Klug's *Bibliography of Detroit History, Politics, and Culture: Late-Nineteenth Century to the Present* (https://detroitartsculture.wixsite.com/detroitstudies/detroit-bibliography).

Anderson, Carlotta R. *All-American Anarchist: Joseph A. Labadie and the Labor Movement.* Detroit: Wayne State University Press, 1998.

Bennett, Harry. *We Never Called Him Henry.* New York: Fawcett, 1951.

Berg, A. Scott. *Lindbergh.* New York: G. P. Putnam's Sons, 1998.

Bingay, Malcolm W. *Detroit Is My Own Home Town.* Indianapolis: Bobbs-Merrill, 1946.

Bishop, Thomas. *Every Home a Fortress: Cold War Fatherhood and the Family Fallout Shelter.* Amherst: University of Massachusetts Press, 2020.

Bradley, James (with Ron Powers). *Flags of Our Fathers.* New York: Bantam, 2000.

Brinkley, Douglas. *Wheels for the World: Henry Ford, His Company, and a Century of Progress, 1903–2003.* New York: Viking, 2003.

Brumm, Leonard "Oakie." *We Only Played Home Games.* Racine, WI: Brumm Enterprises, 2002.

Bryson, Bill. *One Summer: America, 1927.* New York: Doubleday, 2013.

Chapman, Mike. *The Tom Tyler Story.* Newton, IA: Culture House, 2005.

Clinansmith, Michael S. "The Black Legion: Hooded Americanism in Michigan." *Michigan History* 55 (Fall 1971): 243–62.

Clive, Alan. *State of War: Michigan in World War II.* Ann Arbor: University of Michigan Press, 1979.

Conot, Robert E. *American Odyssey.* New York: William Morrow, 1974.

Cooper, Patricia Ann. *Once a Cigar Maker: Men, Women, and Work Culture in American Cigar Factories, 1900–1919.* Urbana: University of Illinois Press, 1987.

Crathern, Alice Tarbell. *In Detroit Courage Was the Fashion: The Contribution of Women to the Development of Detroit from 1701 to 1951.* Detroit: Wayne University Press, 1953.

Dallam, Marie W. *Daddy Grace: A Celebrity Preacher and His House of Prayer.* Syracuse: New York University Press, 2007.

Dancy, John C. *Sand Against the Wind: The Memoirs of John C. Dancy.* Detroit: Wayne State University Press, 1966.

Davidson, Shayne. *Queen of the Burglars: The Scandalous Life of Sophie Lyons.* Jefferson, NC: Exposit, 2021.

Dawson, Jim. *The Twist: The Story of the Song and Dance That Changed the World.* Winchester, MA: Faber and Faber, 1995.

De Grave, Kathleen. *Swindler, Spy, Rebel: The Confidence Woman in Nineteenth-Century America.* Columbia: University of Missouri Press, 1995.

Dominguez, Henry L. *Edsel: The Story of Henry Ford's Forgotten Son.* Warrendale, PA: Society of Automotive Engineers, 2019.

Engelmann, Larry. *Intemperance: The Lost War Against Liquor.* New York: Free Press, 1979.

Ferry, W. Hawkins. *The Legacy of Albert Kahn.* Detroit: Wayne State University Press, 1970.

Fine, Sidney. *Violence in the Model City: The Cavanagh Administration, Race Relations, and the Detroit Riot of 1967.* East Lansing: Michigan State University Press, 2007.

Fine, Sidney. *Frank Murphy: The Detroit Years.* Ann Arbor: University of Michigan Press, 1975.

Gavrilovich, Peter, and Bill McGraw. *The Detroit Almanac.* 3rd ed. Detroit: Detroit Free Press, 2006.

Gordy, Berry. *To Be Loved: The Music, the Magic, the Memories of Motown.* New York: Grand Central Publishing, 1994.

Halliday, E. M. *The Ignorant Armies.* New York: Harper & Row, 1958.

Hamer, Alvin C. (editor). *Detroit Murders.* New York: Duell, Sloan and Pearce, 1948.

Harwell, Ernie. *Tuned to Baseball.* South Bend, IN: Diamond Communications, 1985.

Hersey, John. *The Algiers Motel Incident.* Baltimore: Johns Hopkins University Press, 1998.

Holli, Melvin G. *Reform in Detroit: Hazen S. Pingree and Urban Politics.* New York: Oxford University Press, 1969.

Holli, Melvin G. (editor). *Detroit* [Documentary History of American Cities]. New York: New Viewpoints, 1976.

Holway, John. *Blackball Stars: Negro League Pioneers.* New York: Carroll & Graf, 1992.

Katzman, David M. *Before the Ghetto: Black Detroit in the Nineteenth Century.* Urbana: University of Illinois Press, 1973.

Lewis, David L. *The Public Image of Henry Ford: An American Folk Hero and His Company.* Detroit: Wayne State University Press, 1976.

Lieb, Frederick G. *The Detroit Tigers.* New York: G. P. Putnam's Sons, 1946.

Lochbiler, Don. *Detroit's Coming of Age, 1873–1973.* Detroit: Savoyard, 1973.

Lodge, John C. *I Remember Detroit.* Detroit: Wayne University Press, 1949.

Lord, Walter. *A Night to Remember.* New York: Holt, 1955.

Louis, Joe (with Edna Rust and Art Rust Jr.). *Joe Louis: My Life.* New York: Harcourt Brace Jovanovich, 1978.

Lynch, Don. *Titanic: An Illustrated History.* New York: Hyperion, 1995.

Lyons, Sophie. *Why Crime Does Not Pay.* New York: J. S. Ogilvie, 1913. https://www.gutenberg.org/ebooks/59621.

Manchester, William. *The Death of a President: November 1963.* New York: Harper & Row, 1967.

Maraniss, David. *Once in a Great City: A Detroit Story.* New York: Simon & Schuster, 2015.

Miller, Scott. *The President and the Assassin: McKinley, Terror, and Empire at the Dawn of the American Century.* New York: Random House, 2011.

Morris, George. *The Black Legion Rides.* New York: Workers Library, 1936. https://dp.la/item/49ed1fe64a430f6c68a70822cd86769c.

Nachman, Gerald. *Raised on Radio.* Berkeley: University of California Press, 1998.

Nelson, James Carl. *The Polar Bear Expedition: The Heroes of America's Forgotten Invasion of Russia, 1918–1919.* New York: William Morrow, 2019.

Pollock, Bruce. *When Rock Was Young: A Nostalgic Review of the Top 40 Era.* New York: Holt, Rinehart & Winston, 1981.

Retzloff, Tim. "'Seer or Queer?' Postwar Fascination with Detroit's Prophet Jones." *GLQ: A Journal of Lesbian and Gay Studies* 8, no. 3 (2002): 271–96.

Ritter, Lawrence. *The Glory of Their Times: The Story of the Early Days of Baseball Told by the Men Who Played It.* New York: Macmillan, 1966.

Roberts, Randy. *Joe Louis: Hard Times Man.* New Haven, CT: Yale University Press, 2010.

Robertson, Breanne, Charles Neimeyer, and Douglas Nash. *Investigating Iwo: The Flag Raisings in Myth, Memory & Esprit de Corps.* Quantico, VA: US Marine Corps History Division, 2019.

Rockaway, Robert A. "The Notorious Purple Gang: Detroit's All-Jewish Prohibition Era Mob." *Shofar: An Interdisciplinary Journal of Jewish Studies* 20, no. 1 (2001): 113–30.

Salomonson, Terry, and Martin Grams, Jr. *The Lone Ranger: The Early Years, 1933–1937.* Whiteford, MD: OTR Publishing, 2021.

Salvatore, Nick. *Singing in a Strange Land: C. L. Franklin, the Black Church, and the Transformation of America.* New York: Little, Brown, 2005.

Smith, Suzanne E. *Dancing in the Street: Motown and the Cultural Politics of Detroit.* Cambridge, MA: Harvard University Press, 1999.

Stone, Joel (editor). *Detroit 1967: Origins, Impacts, Legacies.* Detroit: Wayne State University Press, 2017.

Sugrue, Thomas J. *The Origins of the Urban Crisis: Race and Inequality in Postwar Detroit.* Princeton, NJ: Princeton University Press, 2005.

Symon, Charles A. *We Can Do It! A History of the CCC in Michigan, 1933–42.* Gladstone, MI: C. A. Symon, 1983.

Thompson, Mark. *Steamboats and Sailors of the Great Lakes.* Detroit: Wayne State University Press, 1991.

Vaule, Rosamond B. *As We Were: American Photographic Postcards, 1905–1930.* Boston: David R. Godine, 2004.

Woodford, Frank B., and Arthur M. Woodford. *All Our Yesterdays: A Brief History of Detroit.* Detroit: Wayne State University Press, 1969.

Young, Bryan C. *Runaway: The Del Shannon Story.* Bloomington, IN: Xlibris US, 2023.

Young, Coleman, and Lonnie Wheeler. *Hard Stuff: The Autobiography of Mayor Coleman Young.* New York: Viking, 1994.

Zunz, Olivier. *The Changing Face of Inequality: Urbanization, Industrial Development, and Immigrants in Detroit, 1880–1920.* Chicago: University of Chicago Press, 1982.

Oral History Collections

"Ford Reminiscences," Benson Ford Research Center, Dearborn, Michigan. These oral histories were part of the Ford Motor Company's golden anniversary commemoration. Of the more than 300 interviews of Ford associates recorded between 1951 and 1956, 238 have been transcribed, indexed, and digitized for online access. https://cdm15889.contentdm.oclc.org/digital/collection/p15889coll2.

Oral and Written History Archive, Detroit Historical Society. This ongoing online collection of first-person experiences of ordinary Detroiters welcomes both researchers and contributors. The transcribed reminiscences are organized into such categories as neighborhoods, Black entrepreneurship, Covid-19, and the 1967 riot. https://www.detroithistorical.org/projects/oral-and-written-history-archive.

INDEX

DISCOVER THESE OTHER TITLES

FROM RICHARD BAK

Detroitland
A Collection of Movers, Shakers, Lost Souls, and History Makers from Detroit's Past

Compelling historical snapshots of figures and episodes in Detroit history, from the familiar to the obscure.

ISBN 9780814334997, $26.99 paperback

When Lions Were Kings
The Detroit Lions and the Fabulous Fifties

An in-depth look at one of the most storied dynasties in Detroit sports history.

ISBN 9780814350997, $29.99 paperback

A Place for Summer
A Narrative History of Tiger Stadium

A narrative and photographic history that captures the spirit of 140 years of baseball in Detroit.

ISBN 9780814325124, $39.99 hardcover

Turkey Stearnes and the Detroit Stars
The Negro Leagues in Detroit, 1919–1933

The extraordinary history of Detroit's first and foremost black professional baseball team.

ISBN 9780814325827, $25.99 paperback

Cobb Would Have Caught It
The Golden Age of Baseball in Detroit

A peek into the mind and soul of professional baseball as it was played in a dynamic city from the end of World War I through the early 1950s.

ISBN 9780814323564, $26.99 paperback

FOR MORE INFORMATION VISIT WSUPRESS.WAYNE.EDU
AVAILABLE WHEREVER BOOKS ARE SOLD